A DOOR LEFT OPEN

RICHARD CRAIG ANDERSON

HELLGATE PRESS   ASHLAND, OREGON

A DOOR LEFT OPEN

Published by Hellgate Press

(An imprint of L&R Publishing, LLC)

Hellgate Press

PO Box 3531

Ashland, OR 97520

email: info@hellgatepress.com

Interior & Cover Design: L. Redding

"The Unbeliever's Prayer" from *Death Be Not Proud* by John J. Gunther. Copyright (c) 1949 by John Gunther. Copyright renewed 1976 by Jane Perry Gunther. Used by permission of HarperCollins Publishers.

Excerpt from "The Hollow Men" from COLLECTED POEMS 1909-1962 by T.S. Eliot. Copyright© 1925 by Houghton Mifflin Harcourt Publishing Company, renewed 1953 by Thomas Stearns Eliot. Reprinted by permission of Houghton Mifflin Harcourt Publishing Company. All rights reserved.

ISBN: 978-1-55571-979-1

Printed and bound in the United States of America

First edition 10 9 8 7 6 5 4 3 2 1

This is for the Matthews of this world,
and for Pat and George—"Georgie" to his family

What Others Are Saying About *A Door Left Open*

"Rick Anderson is a true warrior and the finest operator; I trusted him with my life while serving in the Federal Air Marshal Service. His extensive experience and implementation of security for El Al, resulted in Miami International Airport (MIA) becoming an undesirable target after 911."

—*Bruno Tom, M.A., Former NCIS Special Agent and Retired Federal Air Marshal*

"Anderson courageously speaks the truth about the conflicts within one's self in the career of a first-responder, especially law enforcement. Those that have been there will relate to his words and those that haven't will find them remarkable. Either way, you'll want to read this adventure tale of a small warrior with a big heart."

—*Jim "Hondo" Halvorsen, Lieutenant, New York State Police, Retired*

"Richard Craig Anderson's new book, *A Door Left Open*, is a tremendous work. He clearly brings back the tumultuous period of the Anne Arundel County Fire Department's transition from volunteers to a career force, including its sharp growing pains. You are right there with the author as he brings real life insight into auto accidents, bloody medical calls and most sadly remembered, a tragic fire on Riverview Road that killed two firefighters. Incredible story—a real page turner."

—*Joseph B. Ross Jr., Retired Division Chief,*
Anne Arundel County Fire Dept., and Author of Arundel Burning

"Richard Craig Anderson starts and ends this remarkable memoir with an image of a doorway, inviting us in not only to his life, but to the magic of what a life well-lived can signify. From America's East Coast to its West, and out into the Pacific islands of Micronesia, Anderson's adventures give us insight into how love and loss, illness and grace can shape who we think we are, what we notice, and how we believe. Lives can be messy and Anderson's is no exception, yet his sometimes missed opportunities and ill-timed choices are easily outmatched by the joy and friendship he finds in people and four-legged creatures along the way. And when he leaves us at the end with a moment of connection, we realize that lives often come full circle and that what we are seeking might be right in front of us, if only we have the courage to walk through the open doors."

—*Teresa Cutler-Broyles, Professor, University of New Mexico*
at Albuquerque, and Perugia, Italy

"Rocky nails it again. I couldn't put this book down. He and I worked together as state troopers, and Rocky was always on top of things. *A Door Left Open* is entertaining, admirably frank, and deeply moving."

—*Sheriff Mike Lewis, Wicomico County Sheriff's Office*

A Door Left Open is a gripping adventure story that I could not put down until I reached its emotionally rewarding end."

—*Dr. Scott Simon Fehr, Psychologist, Professor and Best-selling Author*

Contents

*Some names and details have been changed to protect identities.

Books By Richard Craig Anderson

Light...Precious Light (University Editions)

Rivers of Belief (Georgetown Press)

The Levi Hart Thriller Series (Hellgate Press):
Cobra Clearance
Follow Apollo
Mark Air

A Door Left Open (Hellgate Press)

Prologue

A DOOR LEFT open. A boy walking by. Sixteen. Rebellious. Curious. He glances over his shoulder. Stops. Scowls.

In time he peers past the door, for inside are the dreams, and some of the dreams are his. The boy draws a deep breath, steps through the portal, and emerges a man.

I'VE MADE A lot of mistakes in life, and done some things I'm not proud of. But I also learned a lesson or two. These days some might call me an old man, although I still see a teen in the mirror. Perhaps this is why friends now say, "Rick, you should write down what happened, so others can see what you've discovered." What they mean is that I should show how I converted pain and setbacks into happiness.

For although it's true that I did find happiness, and that I can laugh fluently in seventeen languages, I must also add a caveat, and it is this: while contentment can indeed be pursued and even acquired, it can never be purchased for the simple reason that money and power are fleeting. Another thing: we don't have to be alone, not when we venture out to see what's there, because that's when we discover so many fascinating people. Anyway, even if much of what happened didn't make sense at the time, here's what that boy saw through a door left open.

PART ONE

Alone

A DOOR LEFT OPEN

CHAPTER ONE

Dealing with Death

August 1971 – A Quiet Sunday in Glen Burnie, Maryland

WITH ONE HAND on the door and the other on the mic, I keyed the transmit button and said beneath the siren's howl, "Ambulance thirty-three's on location." As we drew closer to the accident site, I assessed the dark blue Buick sedan. It's crumpled and jammed against a tractor-trailer's rear bumper, and white steam from its ruptured radiator hisses into a crisp blue sky.

Bob finally stomped on the brakes. I jabbed the seat belt release and hopped out. A wall of summer-infused humidity hit me. Then my nostrils protested the stench of spilled anti-freeze and burned rubber. I grabbed the trauma kit and took off running, my shoes slapping against the pavement, and creating an eerie contrast to the radiator's dying moan as I hustled toward the car.

"Fire department," I barked at a crowd gathered around the car. "Move aside."

✗ I'm only sixteen, but my volunteer firefighter uniform has clout and the crowd parted without protest. But by doing so they reveal a young woman behind the steering wheel. The impact apparently

✗ 1971 - 16 = born in 1955

1

drove the hood through the windshield, and its leading edge all but cleaved her head from her body, leaving her eyes bulging as if she'd entered a room where her family and friends jumped from hiding places to yell, "Surprise!" Then there was the bright red blood that had spilled from her severed arteries.

I touched my index finger to her carotid artery, turned to Bob, and was shaking my head when I heard a sob. Only, she wasn't the one who sobbed. It came from behind her.

Sprinting to the other side of the car, I found a young boy trapped in the rear seat. He couldn't have been more than five, and the Buick had folded itself firmly around him. Even worse, a chunk of drive shaft had torn through the floorboard and jammed itself against his gut. The force of the collision had also twisted him around so that he faced the rear. It had to be painful, but at least this twist of fate spared him from seeing his blood-drenched mother.

There were no portable radios back then. The only radios were the ones mounted inside each emergency vehicle. I caught Bob's eye and said, "Call for a rescue unit and a helicopter." He acknowledged me just as an unseen siren's yelp announced the arrival of a county police cruiser. I recognized the sound because the county cops used electronic sirens, and the state troopers had mechanical contraptions. As the cop's footsteps grew louder I shouted, "We have one up front and this one here." I purposely avoided adding that the driver was dead, since the boy would've heard.

Then I got busy with the kid. He wasn't bleeding and there were no marks on him but he was done for, his situation no different from that of a railroad worker pinned between two train couplings. Everything's okay so long as the body remains pinched together; the victim talks and might even say he feels fine. However, pull those couplings apart, and the victim does a nosedive over that bottomless cliff.

What's taking the rescue unit so long?

As the boy's sobs turned to a wail, I tried to squeeze into the passenger compartment to be next to him. After all, I was definitely on the skinny side. But when all I could do was brush his outstretched fingers, I pushed farther and grimaced when a glass shard sliced into my knee. It paid off, though—our fingers finally interlocked just as a stream of tears flowed down his cheeks.

For several seconds that's all there was, until all at once he shouted, "Mommy, mommy, mommy! Where's my mommy?"

I knew abandonment, and sweat streamed down my face as I looked into his eyes and quietly said, "Your mommy hasn't left you. She's in the front seat. But she can't talk to you right now. So you know what? I'm gonna stay here with you."

He stopped his terrified wailing, and after hitching and snuffling he grew quiet and stared at me with a sense of awareness beyond his years. Then as his eyes held mine in an unwavering gaze, he asked in a tiny voice, "Am I going to die?"

I didn't want to tell him what I suspected, but was damned if I would lie. That would be even more obscene than the carnage that had torn his world apart. So I looked directly at him and said simply, "I'm right here, you're not alone, and I'm not gonna leave you."

All this time the sun had been jack hammering the car and turning it into an oven. My clothes clung to me and breathing became a struggle, although of course my discomfort was nothing when compared to the boy's injuries. "What's your name?" I asked.

He responded automatically in a singsong voice with information that his mom must have drilled into him: "My name is Matthew Billings, and I live at 102 Montrose Avenue."

I tightened my hold on his fingers. "Hi, Matthew. My name's Rick, and I'm gonna take care of you. Is that okay?"

He nodded, but his eyelids fluttered. Then while sirens and air horns filled the air around us, I said, "Hold on, Matthew. For God's sake, hold on." Then, quietly and for his ears alone, I sang a few stanzas of Simon and Garfunkel's *Bridge Over Troubled Water*.

Matthew watched me in silence the entire time, his face composed yet solemn. Then as if someone had thrown a switch, he said in a weak voice, "I'm...afraid."

I squeezed his hand and whispered. "Of course you are. Even big boys would be scared. You know what, though? You're brave—even braver than many grown men are. Did you know that?"

"Really?" He seemed to be trying that one on for size. Then he opened his mouth to speak, but his voice trailed into nothingness.

"Matthew," I began. "Stay with me. Stay—" I was trying to say more when the diesel roar and the chuff of air brakes of an arriving rescue unit nixed that idea—and that was just for starters. Now the rhythmic *whump whump whump* of a state police medevac helicopter drowned all other sounds as it circled overhead prior to landing.

Maybe it was the noise, because Matthew abruptly cried out, "Mommy! Where's my mommy? Where's my—" Then his eyes rolled wildly as he blurted, "I'll be a good boy! Yes, I will! Mommy will come back if I'm good. She will." His voice began to fade. "Yes she will."

"I'm sure of it," I whispered back.

Although it seemed an eternity, no more than three minutes passed until his eyes closed. His head fell to one side a few seconds later, and then his body went limp. But I couldn't let go. I couldn't. He deserved dignity in death, and there was more—I didn't want his soul to be alone. So I held his hand even as firefighters worked around me to free him. I held it and felt the warmth desert him, first from his fingers, then from his palm and finally from his arm. I held his hand, unable to let go, until the firefighters got him out and the medical examiner took him away.

Matthew's mommy never came back.

Mine never did, either. At least not in spirit. Not after she and my old man split up and she all but tossed me aside, leaving me feeling alone, abandoned and angry.

EARLIER THAT DAY I'd walked out of my house and climbed into the emerald-green '67 Cougar XR-7 that I bought by working small jobs. But when friends and I weren't cruising for girls, I'd spin the wheel and set a new course for the Glen Burnie fire station.

A lot of kids dream of being a firefighter. Some pursue those dreams. Sure, there were altruistic reasons for wanting to safeguard the community. But whether you look at it inside-in or outside-out, the reality is simple—it's downright exciting. After all, where else can a sixteen-year-old kid hang onto the back of a speeding fire engine with the wind in his face while sirens and air horns blare, only to dash inside burning buildings moments later?

And make no mistake about it teens as young as sixteen were the bulwark of volunteer departments for decades, and my parents never gave a second thought to the idea that I would don an air mask, man a hose line and charge inside the aforementioned fiery structures.

This way of thinking was due in part to the men who built and honed the fire service. They were men of an old breed, with names that harkened back to an earlier time. There were Melvins and Calvins and Clydes (*oh my*). Other first names included a Forrest here and a Buck there, along with an assortment of Mikes and Ikes. If they liked you, they guided you. If not, they'd snarl and shout, "Get outta my way."

Or they might be gruff for a totally different reason—as one of the old breed was when I first stepped foot inside the station with my long hair. "Get a friggin' haircut," he shouted. "Then we might think about letting you join." I tossed my head, and as hair strands carelessly caressed the back of my neck, I nodded.

Training consisted of older hands—perhaps one as old as nineteen—showing rookies the ropes. "This goes here, an' that goes there," they intoned. I got it. Sure. Everything was straightforward and purpose-designed. Even the shape of a fire helmet had a function: the long extension at the rear of the helmet, the duckbill, kept hot water and cinders from dropping down your neck. If you had to advance on a flaming automobile, you turned the helmet around and wore it backward to let the duckbill deflect heat from your face.

Since what would develop into the Day of Matthew involved going to the firehouse, I parked in front and went inside the ultra-modern building. The county called it "Company 33," and the station housed a mix of volunteer and career firefighters. We called the career people paid men. They referred to us as vollies.

There had always been at least one paid driver on duty in every firehouse, men who worked a rotating schedule of twenty-four hours on, and forty-eight off. These drivers were called enginemen, a term that harkens back to the days when pumpers were powered by steam engines that were pulled by horses (the term also came about long before women were hired as firefighters). Even today, a pumper is an engine, the crew assigned to it is an engine company, and a hook & ladder is always called a ladder truck—or more simply, a truck.

Enginemen drive the apparatus, operate the pumps, and remain with the unit in case firefighters need an extra attack line or a change in water pressure. Ladder trucks are different. The enginemen who drive them do enter burning buildings to perform rescues, raise ladders, ventilate the smoke and heat, and assist in extinguishing the blaze.

But when the number of vollies diminished along with the demise of Small Town America, the county hired more and more paid men. Unfortunately, all growth creates friction and the fire service was not exempt. So while the old guard sought to hold onto their traditions, the county pointed to the realities of growth and the need for consistent fire protection. It sounds logical, but try selling it to diehard volunteers.

As a measure of progress, the county had recently placed a tractor-trailer style ladder truck at Company 33. The spanking-new Seagrave required two drivers, which by default meant two additional paid men per shift. Next, the county assigned career firefighters to 33 after fewer and fewer volunteers were on hand to answer calls at the busiest station around.

The station itself housed two engines. There was a 1965 Ward LaFrance with an open cab and a jump seat equipped with two self-contained breathing devices. Known simply as air masks, firefighters could don them while en route to an emergency. Those who weren't fast enough to claim a jump seat stood on the tailboard and held on tight while speeds approached eighty miles per hour. Today it's considered unsafe to ride on a tailboard at any speed. At the time though, we saw it as the norm. The other engine, a 1962 GMC, lacked a jump seat. Finally, an ambulance, a brush truck and a foam unit occupied the remaining floor space.

I walked in that day to find the units in their assigned bays, fueled and ready to respond. After greeting Clyde, the tall rawboned engineman, I stood under an open overhead door to embrace the lazy summer afternoon and watch the world go by. In my case however, seeing others moving on with their lives served as a blunt reminder that my world had already taken a pass on me, making me just another lost kid wondering where fate would push him next.

I was lost in just such a reverie when the station's hot line rang.

The county fire department's central alarm facility dispatched fire apparatus by radio. But ambulance calls required a direct phone call, since dispatchers never knew if volunteers were present to respond. So they used the hot lines—red phones that when they rang, sounded like a school bell. The career guys answered them, and if there were no volunteers in the station, the paid men called their homes in search of a crew to man the ambulance.

But on this sweltering day—long before the advent of emergency medical technicians or paramedics—when training consisted solely of Red Cross and CPR training—we had a crew on hand: me and Bob.

So when the hot line rang, I watched Clyde from the corners of my eyes as he grabbed the handset and listened briefly, hung up, and then shuffled drowsily toward us while speaking in his gravelly voice. "Auto accident. Dorsey Road at the overpass. Car hit the back of a truck."

A DOOR LEFT OPEN

CHAPTER TWO

Margins

I N HER LIFE, my mother made a lot of mistakes. Outsiders might have accused her of harboring malice, but they would have been resoundingly wrong. However, even early on there were indisputable indicators that she suffered from a steadily worsening mental illness. Yet no matter how bizarrely she might act, she at least meant well.

As for my father, he never shied away from hard work or demanding challenges. And while it's true that he did trip over himself quite often, he took ownership of his mistakes later in life and did his *mea culpas*. Unfortunately, Dad never reconciled himself with certain realities.

The greatest reality is that he never should have married Mom. As a son of impoverished Irish Catholics from the wrong side of Washington, D.C.'s Depression-era tracks, Dad shoved bits of newspaper inside his shoes to cover the holes that peppered them. When his sign painting father experienced set-backs and could barely put food on the table, my fifteen-year old father asked his parents to lie about his age so he could enlist in the Marines. The year was 1939 and the old breed Marines didn't suffer fools. But he got three squares a day and shoes without holes, not to mention war in the Pacific two years later.

On the flip side, Mom's parents emigrated from Europe to the United States around 1906 and settled in the nation's capital. One of her father's brothers was Dr. Mario Mollari, and when Uncle Mario wasn't working alongside Dr. Albert Schweitzer, he served as head of the department of microbiology and tropical medicines at Georgetown University.

As for her father, he held a Ph.D. in philosophy from Salzburg, was fluent in seven languages, and could read and write twenty-one others. In the aftermath of WWII, he directed a project that translated captured Japanese records of the gruesome medical experiments that they conducted on Allied POWs. For example, how long does it take to kill a man by boiling him in oil? Or, what if we remove a man's right arm and reattach it to the left side? Will it still work? Hmm. Let's find out.

My maternal grandfather also befriended a hereditary Russian nobleman who fled Russia in the wake of Tsar Nicholas II's assassination. That nobleman was Dr. Basil Peter Toutorsky, and after he opened Washington's prestigious Toutorsky Academy of Music, he taught the piano to my mother. For her debut recital, she played Rachmaninoff on a piano once owned by Franz Liszt while Sergei Rachmaninoff himself sat in the audience, along with celebrated actress Helen Hayes.

While Mom played, Dad marched to the beat of an infantry drummer and ate whatever the Marine mess felt like serving. The reality was that my mother required a mature husband, while he needed a stronger woman for a wife. But it was wartime and he cut a dashing figure in his Marine uniform. She fell in love with him, gave up the piano, and got married.

Enter five kids.

WE GREW UP along a variety of margins. Jim was ten years old, Janice eight, and Bob five by the time I was born in an Army hospital in April of 1955. My younger brother Tom entered the world some two years later. This was in Laurel, Maryland, where we lived in a shoebox home on a dead end street that was separated from a rambling tuberculosis sanatorium by nothing more than an abrupt road barrier.

Before that however, in 1949 the Army lured Dad away from his beloved Marines by offering to make him an officer and a gentleman. This was heady stuff for an Irish kid from an impoverished childhood, and he seized the opportunity and accepted the commission, only to end up in Korea when hostilities erupted a year later.

He returned with a Bronze Star with a "V" device for valor, and three Purple Hearts. Years later when the Korean war-inspired movie *M*A*S*H* hit the theaters, Dad barely cracked a smile even when the audience was roaring with laughter. He explained on the way home. "The movie was total reality." He paused. "MASH surgeons saved my life that time." He grew quiet, further explanation unnecessary. We all knew. *That* time was when a bullet pierced one side of his neck and made an abrupt exit out the other side. I also understood his appreciation of the movie's arguably awkward chaplain, "Dago Red," because a similar chaplain gave Dad the last rites *that* time.

Aside from his physical injuries, eighteen months of Korean combat also left him shell shocked. We call it PTSD these days, and while shell shock can lead to psychological deficits, it also causes physical harm. This is mostly the result of repeated concussions from incoming artillery, which rattle the brain. Johns Hopkins University found that the brain tissue of combat veterans exhibit a pattern of injury in areas responsible for decision-making, memory and reasoning. In some cases, veterans of long-ago combat can experience mood changes brought on by something as simple as weather-related changes in air pressure.

So when he returned from the war with fresh memories of the suffering he'd seen among so many helpless children, he was ready to be a father—a real father as opposed to the distant figure he had been to my older siblings. My mother on the other hand told him that she'd had enough children. But he wanted a child, and nine months later he rushed Mom to the military hospital when I started banging for escape.

I apparently started out being contrary by not being in the correct position in the birth canal, and the doctor had to grip my head with forceps to get me squared away. Years later, I opined that the forceps were what created my sharp wit; my sister laughingly countered that they merely left a dull impression on my mind.

Whether dull or sharp, impressions do vary. But nobody could deny that Dad now had a miniature version of himself. Even as a newborn my resemblance to him was clear, and in his zeal for absolute self-replication, he told the doctor not to circumcise me. But the unkindest cut was compulsory in military hospitals, so when the doc denied the request, my father had a word with the hospital's commanding officer, who happened to be an old crony. And so it goes.

Then something even stranger happened: Dad became a dad. He changed my diapers, which he'd been loath to do for the others. He showered me with affection. Wait, what am I saying? He deluged me; he polished that apple of his eye, and on the seventh day he saw what he'd created and called it good.

That hadn't been the case with my siblings. His attitude toward them ranged from indifference to blatant nastiness. But since it was clear that he loved me unconditionally, this led to the hope that his newfound feelings might dampen his previously mean behavior. It was not to be, however. Wartime memories still plagued him, and too many people at the time had no clue of what combat can do to a person.

That could be why my mother didn't seek the counseling that might have helped her understand Dad's problems. Instead, she would take his aberrant behavior personally, then grow sullen before picking one of two possible paths: to withdraw, or to come out swinging. Since none of us kids could predict which road she might take, we learned to duck and cover when her bitter epithets led to Dad's clenched fists. But by the next morning they would have already made up and I would think, Okay, *cue the cartoons, 'cause it's time to escape to another kind of craziness.*

When I was four, the Army sent Dad to Kaiserslautern, in what was then West Germany. We lived on-base in an apartment situated on another dead end street, and my playground bordered a massive bomb-crater, courtesy of the Army Air Corps. While we were there, I saw castles on the Rhine and walked across nearby farmlands. Now and then, I also climbed into the station wagon with Mom and my brothers and sister for an abrupt road trip to Luxembourg. These were not pleasure excursions, though. The quick-trips were Army-mandated drills in case the Soviets decided to move on the West, the idea being that the Allies, including our father, would hold them at bay while the civilians escaped.

Each Saturday my father took me to the railroad yards and gave cigarettes to the German workmen. Lucky Strikes. With the bold red center. Unfiltered. Of course. The same as he smoked, usually a pack a day, lighting each one with the Zippo he carried in WWII and Korea. The men tied bandannas around their necks to absorb the dripping sweat, they wore rough shoes and had even rougher hands, and some of those hands might have held rifles they used to shoot at G.I.'s during the war. As my father handed out the Luckies, I watched the men. They took them wordlessly, but showed their gratitude with a dignified nod of the head. This was my first lesson in compassion and he would teach me other lessons through the years, for despite his faults—and they were many—he readily related to the poor and the dispossessed.

Later, after I turned seven and with my sister Janice's help, I hosted a neighborhood carnival to help raise money for muscular dystrophy research—M. D., they called it—and seeing kids my own age relegated to a life in a wheelchair struck me deep inside. So when the hosts of children's TV shows began to tout the carnivals, I wondered, *why not?*

We raised a grand total of fourteen bucks and some change with that carnival. It doesn't seem a lot, but it wasn't all that shabby in

1962 dollars. Over the course of the next few years, I organized three more Muscular Dystrophy Carnivals. Why? Because it seemed the natural thing to do—natural, because I'd seen my father doing things for others.

That was my dad all right, always gregarious, whereas Mom had difficulty making friends. Fortunately, I must have inherited his nature, because I found that showing soft eyes and a bright smile went a long way toward establishing long-lasting friendships—and I had to rely upon friends years later when I faced troubles of my own.

Back to Europe. While living there I assimilated bits of their values and cultures, and at the end of Dad's tour we flew home on a USAF Super Constellation. This beautiful airplane was the last of the propeller-driven airliners, sleek and fast with a dolphin-like fuselage and triple tail. To this day I can vividly recall landing in the Azores to refuel in order to reach New Jersey's McGill Air Force Base. It was during this blessedly long trip that I fell in love with flying, and vowed to one day become a pilot.

We finally reached "the Land of Round Door Knobs" and briefly settled back into the Laurel homestead before moving up the street into a four-bedroom Cape Cod. America back then was still a land of screen doors and one TV per household. Cars had three-on-the-tree manual transmissions, and don't even think about being able to afford a car with a/c and FM radio. Kids wore hand-me-downs, mothers patched torn trouser knees, and on Friday nights our family huddled around a bowl of popcorn and two 6.5 ounce bottles of Coke.

My father meanwhile took to huddling around bottles of a different sort, and to bringing me along when he visited his favorite watering hole. Denny McCahill's Town Tavern was a long narrow wooden building that sat precipitously atop a hill alongside a small river. The customers were mostly working men who came there to either forget or to vent or do both. Some—Dad included—could end up stoking the boiler and building dangerous levels of steam. This usually led to further episodes of parental battling and bickering.

As if the home battles weren't enough, I was a second-grader at

St. Mary's Catholic School when the Cuban Missile Crisis erupted. Nuclear war seemed inevitable, with predictable and completely understandable levels of panic in some households—although most Americans remained calm, this despite the fact that we lived only twenty miles from the nation's capital.

Because my brother Jim had enlisted in the Navy the year before, he was on the cruiser U.S.S. *Canberra* as part of the Cuban Blockade. While Jim was doing his part, my friends and I still walked two miles to school each day, with instructions to duck and cover if we saw a bright light in the sky. Yeah, things were so much simpler in those days.

Meanwhile, the nuns told us to bring two week's worth of food and other provisions to school. I relayed this to my parents. Dad had recently retired, and was awaiting a call-up of the reserves. That left Mom to listen when I mentioned the required supplies, and in response she gave me two cans of Chef Boy-R-Dee spaghetti. When the nuns saw my "provisions," they ranked me out in front of the class but never bothered following up by calling my folks—the concept of PTA talks having not yet taken root within the parochial school system. Although I felt diminished, some primal part of my brain had registered the notion that a nuclear exchange would doom all of us anyway. So I thought to myself, *Why get bent? They're cans of cheap spaghetti. What did it matter?*

When my classmates and I were not practicing our duck-and-cover drills twice daily, we formed lines and practiced dashing into the basement fallout shelter—just in case. The nuns also kept portable radios going inside the classrooms, albeit at a low volume, and took us to church each morning for mass. Parishioners were packing the place, and the grownups were so awfully serious that during the priest's Latin blessing, my irreverent friends and I would whisper: *Dom-in-aay Nabisco, after this we play bingo.*

Years later, we learned that our close proximity to D.C. guaranteed our immolation, with multiple thermonuclear devices turning back-yard fallout shelters into Dutch ovens. In any event, the days passed in benign ignorance until the other fellow blinked. Once reassured that there would be no bombs bursting in air, national tension waned and we emerged unscathed.

Unfortunately, the end of that crisis did not signal an end to, or even a thawing of, the cold war at home. If anything, things grew more heated. Since I knew how much my father loved me, I came to him to ask, "Why?" Sadly, he was incapable of displaying public affection and he would lapse into silence instead.

Meanwhile, my mother lashed out at husband and children alike, telling us she wished none of us had ever been born, yadda yadda. I knew even then that I didn't want her approval. Not really. So I'd blow air from my cheeks and mutter, "Here we go again." But a moment or an hour or a day later, she would abruptly shift gears and become an endearing mother.

Then the piano lessons began. She had taught the piano to my sister, but my two older brothers scoffed at the idea of learning to play. So there I was, six years old, and perhaps she saw in me her final chance at the musical career she never had by living it vicariously through me. In any event she force-fed so many piano lessons into me that at age six I could proficiently play portions of Grieg's *In the Hall of the Mountain King*. But as any boy would, I resented her teaching methods and refused to take any further lessons. Today I can barely play *Chopsticks*.

At the opposite end of the spectrum, Dad would drop me off at the Ft. Meade horse stables while he went to the Officers' Club for a quickie, and I quickly evolved into an accomplished horseman. Sometimes my older brother Bob would ride with me, or else my sister Janice might take me riding along with her friends.

Dad would also deposit me at the base swimming pool for lessons, and I took to water like the proverbial fish. But in the lessons' wake when all the other students and the instructors were gone, hours would pass before Dad remembered to pick me up. Still, I was learning things that would help me walk through doors left open later in life.

I was eight when a lone-wolf loser killed JFK, and during the next four days my friends and I were riveted to the TVs. We saw Ruby shoot Oswald in real-time. Then the following day, when I saw John Junior's famous salute to his father's passing casket, I made a solemn vow to do the same for my dad. Wow, the things that can go through a youngster's head.

The assassination could have helped my mother put things into perspective by yanking her from the micro-world of kids to care for and a husband to deal with, and shaking her into understanding that there are ways to deal with problems. Instead, it appeared to leave her further unhinged. Two months later she filed for divorce and dragged her kids to an apartment on the other side of town. Although I missed my father, I understood that it would be better for the folks to go to their separate corners for awhile—at least until the bell rang anew. As for me, visitation rights had to suffice.

What troubled me further was that my friends were just far enough away, that seeing them was not an option. I had a bike and I could have ridden the four miles, but that still wasn't going to cut it. So I made new friends—and with this fourth move by the eighth year of my life, the motions of making new friends were becoming routine.

Our mother also began neglecting us. Oh, I don't mean that she didn't feed or otherwise care for us. Nor did she stop tucking my younger brother and me into bed and sing lullabies, or drill us in proper manners—and mine were such that even as a child I could have conducted myself properly at a White House dinner (although on the flip-side, Dad showed me how to fit in while eating among stevedores). I also respected my elders, opened doors for ladies and got next to ladies on sidewalks to shield them, in case cars running through puddles sent up geysers of water. No, Mom abandoned her children in other ways.

In truth, even when they were together, neither of my parents monitored our activities; never hovered nearby to ensure completion of homework assignments, nor groomed any of us for our inevitable transitions to adulthood. Nor did they have sit-downs with any of us to discuss college or a career.

No, the folks left us to fend for ourselves, and I ran wild as a result. Going shirtless and shoeless in summer seemed only natural, so that's what I did. Remember, this was back in the days when flip-flops were not yet en vogue, and those that were available were the thin shower shoes that people only used in locker rooms. So I ran barefoot five months out of the year, every year. Or to borrow from Mark Twain's description of Huck Finn—whose life by the way I had readily identified with while reading the book—I was always the first among my friends to shed shoes in the spring, and the last to resume leather in the fall—a lifestyle that endured well into my late teens.

And so it was that at age five I would finish breakfast, tell my mother, "Bye," and troop off on my own to make the rounds of friends' homes. Upon gathering a large enough cohort, we then roamed through fields and woods and shopping centers totally un-supervised until noon, when I came home to eat only to disappear again until the street lights snapped on, when I would show up with dirty and often bee-stung feet with only one thing in mind: "What's for dinner?" In many ways it's why I feel rooted to the earth even today.

But this lack of supervision also meant that I didn't see the need for daily showers or a daily change of clothes. I never developed a sense of grooming either, and didn't learn that brown belts don't go with black shoes. But I did learn to read, and I found refuge in worlds of exploration and adventure. I read a children's version of *Robinson Crusoe*, and while watching the movie *Old Yeller*, I thought it was normal that fourteen-year-old Travis would trap wild pigs and hunt deer to put food on the table while his father was away on a cattle drive—just as my dad was away. As a fifth-grader, when I read Neville Shute's *On The Beach*, I vowed to accomplish two goals: to visit Australia and to become an author.

Watching movies and TV also sparked daydreams of adventure. Like all kids, I wanted to be a firefighter and a cop and a cowboy. But television and movies of that era performed another service in an age when latchkey kids were emerging from society's fabric: whether it was *The Munsters* or *Father Knows Best* or even *Flipper*, each of these shows and most movies included a morality tale. They also stressed that parents and adults were in charge, and teens did not show contempt for grownups, because guess what? Teens still had more learning and growing up to do.

But despite the solace of books, television and movies, resentment festered deep inside. I began to rail against what was quickly turning into an annual ritual of moving to another city, attending yet another school, and being torn away from close friends again. I also grew to resent getting the brush-off from an overwhelmed mother who had no time for a nine-year-old boy's need for even a few moments of affection, and I grew to hate the manifestation of her devolution, when she would verbally lash out at her children for the slightest offenses.

The offenses included ripping a shirtsleeve while climbing a barbed-wire fence, an act that would result in a seemingly ceaseless tongue-lashing. A dirty collar from too much play also risked her rage. The list of high crimes and misdemeanors ran long and erratic.

Despite her behavior, I didn't acquire a sense of animosity. In the final analysis, I realized even then that she was ill. And so it was that by age ten I hung around my friends' homes until it grew dark—or until their parents diplomatically invited me to leave in an age when the term "street kids" was not yet used. Yet that is what I'd become, for I would rather walk aimlessly through town than return home. At least my sister made the great escape when she got married during the summer of '67.

IN 1968 I turned thirteen, and on carefree barefoot summer evenings I'd casually tell my mom, "I'm gonna sleep at a friend's tonight." This turned into a three-times a week ritual, and she invariably nodded without bothering to call the other parents. Then I'd walk to a girl-friend's house and tap on her bedroom window until she quietly eased it open. And just like that, two naked teens with raging hormones were twisting and squirming while trying to keep the noises under control—usually by letting the Beatles and Simon & Garfunkel throb in the background, while we throbbed between the sheets.

Once school was back in session, some of us brought girls to an isolated storage room to pass the lunchtime with a form of playtime not envisioned by the principal. What can I say? We were randier than three-balled tomcats, and long before condoms in schools became an issue, we managed to soldier-on—especially since kids couldn't buy condoms. They were kept inside drug store pharmacist counters, the idea of displaying them for shoppers to pick and choose still light years away.

So we did without, and while the temptation to tsk-tsk us for having sex at such a tender age is there, it doesn't change the facts. Nor does it challenge the fact that there were no pregnancies, at least none that I knew of. Besides, for us the idea of getting-it-on usually had its basis in friendships—although I'd be lying if I didn't admit that some of it also amounted to a search for the affection that I wasn't getting at home.

In my self-serving defense, I'll also point out that it was 1968. Free love and Woodstock were in the air, the girls were eager and willing, and the following year Sly and the Family Stone released *Hot Fun in the Summertime*. To this day I can't help but smile whenever I pull out an old 45-rpm version of *Hot Fun* to listen to its upbeat lyrics and buoyant rhythms.

It was also the year that friends and I stood along the railroad tracks to watch the train carrying Bobby Kennedy's body pass by.

In time, my mother returned to my father, which led to three moves within two years until we finally settled into a house in Glen Burnie, a few miles south of Baltimore. Although this marked my eighth move and sixth school by age fourteen, things were looking good and I thought, *Yes, now she'll have time for me.* She didn't, though. Not even when it came to discussing death.

CHAPTER THREE

Smoke Eater

SIX WEEKS HAD passed since the day of young Matthew's violent death from that auto accident. Strangely, I didn't dwell upon his fate. After all, hadn't I already learned Life 101 by diving into adventure stories and tales in which death loomed as a constant presence? In addition, living through the Cuban Missile Crisis and JFK's murder sharpened my appreciation of life. Anyway, I'd done my best with Matthew, while also learning that the mere act of doing *something* is key to dealing with big world problems. Yep, I had it pegged; I was on top of things. At least that's what I thought. However, I was about to learn another hard lesson.

It was a warm September evening. A little past seven. Still plenty of daylight left. Marvin Gaye's *What's Going On?* played on the radio while I drove to the fire station. Once there, I joined Tim, Russ and Bryan on the front ramp. Russ Hewitt was my age. Tim Doegen and Bryan were three years older, and we were talking about sex and drugs and rock an' roll when the radio speakers erupted.

"Alert! Box nine-one! Engines 18, 33, 34 and Truck-33 respond to a dwelling fire, First Avenue and Hilltop. Be advised that we have multiple reports of a man trapped inside."

We pulled on turnout coats and stepped into boots. Tim headed for the ladder truck. Russ and I climbed into the Ward La France's jump seats. Bryan settled into the officer's position up front. Four others got on the tailboard and gripped the handholds.

Clyde was the engineman, and he usually moved with the blinding speed of a sloth on Librium. Not this time. He leaped into the engine, hit the starter button, and took off like a striped-ass ape. As we turned onto Central Avenue, I glanced to the rear. The ladder truck's normally laid-back driver also had the accelerator to the floor, and was right on our tail.

Bryan made the siren scream while Clyde laid into the air horns. Russ and I cinched air bottle straps tight. We looked at each other. He raised an eyebrow; I nodded. Unsaid was the reason for Clyde's high-speed dash: the report of someone trapped inside a burning house. Minutes later we were drawing closer to the scene when my nose crinkled. I looked at Russ and asked, "What the hell is *that*? Smells like burned eggs, or...something."

Then we were there. Company 18's men had already advanced an attack line through the front door. Black smoke vomited from several windows. I heard glass breaking from inside. Though still a newbie, I'd gained enough experience to know one thing—that the fire's heat was making windows explode into lethal fragments.

The truck crew swung into action. Putting up ladders. Streaming into second floor windows. Searching for victims. I masked-up while shaking my head furiously. *What the fuck was that smell?* It did remind me of burned eggs, and anyone who has smelled burned eggs knows what that's like.

Bryan thrust a second attack line into my hands, and shouted, "Get your ass inside and upstairs, and stop the fire from spreading." Next, he jabbed a gloved finger at Russ and sent him to the rear of the house.

This wasn't my first working fire, and while it's true that only the foolhardy claim a lack of healthy fear, tonight was different—this fire had trapped somebody. Then there was that smell. Something was in there—a manifestation that I wasn't prepared to meet head-on. Yet here I was, alone and scared shitless as I started for the front door.

Although Company 18's crew had already knocked down the fire in the first floor, the inside temps were still hitting two hundred, and flashes of distant flames lit my facemask. As my breathing picked up, the air tank regulator's rubber diaphragm beat a staccato rhythm with every breath I drew. I sounded like Darth Vader, breathing heavily to signal his ominous presence.

Aw...purr; aw...purr. Aw...

My heart hammered my chest as I gripped the nozzle. Still trembling from the fear of an unknown ogre, I pushed on and had just reached the base of a stairway when I heard a whoosh. Someone—probably Russ—had opened a back door. Cool air rushed in at once and swept away the smoke. I could make out details. The walls were blackened, but not burned through. The stairs remained intact, although the heat had melted the carpeting that once covered each step.

Another breeze blew in and triggered that god-awful smell anew. I gagged and was working furiously to keep from retching when the hairs on the back of my neck stood on end. It finally hit me; I knew what that odor was. Then I saw its source, and I froze.

The poor guy was only five feet away. Atop a burned-up couch. On his right side. Completely swollen, with both arms drawn up like a boxer in a title fight. Fiery heat had drawn his legs into a fetal position. His lips were burned away, leaving two rows of teeth gleaming brightly through the diminishing smoke. He'd been burned to a crisp.

Then I literally jumped when I heard a voice.

"Oh, fuck. We got us a crispy critter, all right."

I turned. It was Bryan. He'd come in behind me. Crispy Critters was a popular cereal at the time, and it offended my juvenile sense of decency to hear it applied so callously. But there was no time for self-righteousness; we still had a working fire on our hands.

Together, we moved up the stairs with the attack line. But I found nothing to turn a hose stream onto; nothing to help me vent my anger, or to take my mind off that stench. So we did a secondary check for victims before Bryan led the way back down those stairs.

Later, I learned that the position of a burned corpse's arms is known to both criminal investigators and medical examiners alike as the "pugilistic stance," since the corpse does indeed resemble a boxer about to go a few rounds with Ali. I also discovered that I wasn't the only one to tremble at the sight of a fried human being. Other firefighters had, too. They had also brought in a set of Circle-D portable floodlights, and these naked bulbs now cast a harsh glare around the body. Everyone kept their distance, and I sure as shit didn't blame them. But as I stared at the face of a dead man that everyone was pretending not to see, I reached back into my ninth grade English lessons and recalled a line from Gustavo Adolfo Bécquer: *¡Dios mío, que solos se quedan los muertos!* (Oh God, how alone the dead are left!)

Then I thought of Matthew. I recited a silent prayer for him, then another for the corpse.

WE RETURNED TO our station three hours later. Only then did I learn that Clyde's break-neck speed in getting to the fire had been prompted by his recognition of the address. The victim turned out to be the twenty-seven year old nephew of Clyde's close friend. I also discovered that an investigator had already determined that the young man had put some food on the stove, and then stretched out on the couch for a nap that he never woke up from when the food caught fire.

There are victims, and then there are victims. I must have been in a mild state of shock from seeing my first crispy critter. But I was already growing a protective skin against future grisly sights. Unfortunately, I didn't know enough to talk to Russ or Tim about what we had all seen that night—although months later I did discover that they'd also been unnerved. Instead, I stood under a steaming shower for almost an hour, as if the driving water would purge the images. They didn't, and after turning off the taps, I pulled on clean clothes and went home with the idea of talking about it to my mom the next day.

Jesus, who was I kidding?

I FOUND MY mother at the kitchen table with the morning paper propped in front of her. I sat and said, "Mom?"

Without bothering to look up, she asked, "What is it?"

"Well—it's just that I saw this guy who'd been burned up last night, and I—"

"That's nice," she said in a voice without intonation or interest. I might as well have just told her that we were out of laundry soap.

"Mom, did you hear me?"

I had seen other moms show rapt, authentic attention to their kids even if they were only describing the fun they'd had with a new skateboard. My mom couldn't give a rat's ass that I needed to talk to her about. . .well, about a crispy critter.

She finally looked up. "Let me finish reading. Then maybe we can talk."

I got up at once and said, "Nah, that's okay." Then I jumped into my car and drove to the firehouse while the Stones blared from the radio speakers. I arrived, parked, and stepped inside just as the hot line rang. Report of a drowning. Bryan and I jumped into the ambulance.

Minutes later we screeched to a stop in front of a home in one of Glen Burnie's older neighborhoods. A hysterical mother pointed toward the back yard. I made a dash for it, and found an infant boy floating face down in a perfectly symmetrical swimming pool beneath a faultless blue sky. At first I wondered why the mother hadn't already pulled it out. Later, I learned that some people freeze when things turn south—even when it involves one of their own.

I leaped in and pulled him out. Still sopping wet, I started CPR. Bryan shouted, "Come on, Rick. Let's beat feet to the ER." So I scooped the infant into my arms and ran to the idling ambulance.

The siren growled as Bryan skillfully swerved around stopped traffic. In the meantime, I kept up the CPR. Deep down though, I knew it was too late. The boy's eyes reminded me of a doll's, fully open and staring into nothingness. Though still a child myself, I was determined to fight the good fight, so I continued the then-current ritual of one blast of oxygen for every fifteen finger-pushes against the boy's sternum.

We finally reached the hospital. Bryan jerked the rear doors open. My shoes went *squish, squish, squish* as we rushed the baby into the ER. The doc took one look and pronounced him dead on arrival.

Bryan and I drove back to the station in silence. After we made sure the ambulance was fueled and ready for the next run, I shoved dry hands into wet pockets and walked to the front ramp with my head hanging. Nelson Janz, a large and powerfully built paid man whom everyone liked and respected, was standing with an elbow propped against a bay door and staring through the glass while he smoked. Seeing me, he dragged at his cigarette and tossed it aside with a careless flick of a finger.

"What's eating you?"

We were on different sides. He was paid; I was a vollie. He drove the ladder truck that the powers-that-be wouldn't even let me ride yet. On the other hand, we'd both played high school lacrosse, and at least he cared enough to ask—that was more than my own mother had done. So I described the call, adding, "I feel so bad for the baby."

He grunted, stuck a fresh Marlboro between his lips, and lit it with a Zippo. After dragging deep, he exhaled twin jets of blue-gray smoke that went down before drifting up. After taking another drag, he caught my eye and said, "It's not your fault. The mother shouldn't have left it alone." His jaw worked silently until he said, "You did your best." He paused, dragged at the Marlboro again, looked sidelong at me, and finally said, "Get over it, Kid."

His manner had been, well, matter-of-fact. It hadn't been brutal. I understood; it was all about a reality of life. I didn't need counseling; didn't need an interventionist, nor an appearance before news cameras while a gushing reporter hyperventilated about a dead kid. Feeling grateful for the attention Nelson had given me, I nodded, drove home, packed some clothes, and returned to the firehouse. Once there, I had a word with the volunteer chief. By the end of the session, he had given me permission to live there full-time.

I'd found a home.

A DOOR LEFT OPEN

CHAPTER FOUR

The Quest in Question

I WAS SIXTEEN, I'd left home and moved into a firehouse, and I was about to drop out of school. I needed help.

Despite being a voracious reader, I'd never been more than an average student. History and English were my favorite subjects because they carried stories of adventure; of life on remote Pacific islands and faraway glaciers. Mathematics became my downfall, however. While the logic of math's problem-solving techniques appealed to my inner brain, I daydreamed during class and ended up with failing grades. Today, I understand that I did poorly in a subconscious effort to get my parents' attention.

In my mother's case, her lack of concern over my studies was a given. At the same time, Dad's latest job took him away from home for a week at a time. Besides, since they'd never supervised my activities in the past, I saw no reason not to redouble my efforts toward mediocrity. It's not that I was a deadbeat, or had copped an attitude. In fact, I was on the high school soccer team, we were unbeatable that 1970 season, and in March I made the lacrosse team until an injury sidelined me.

Feeling lost and with nobody to turn to for guidance, I dug in and became a slacker. I purposely failed math. But when that failed to spark a reaction from the folks, I enrolled in summer school and rode my bike to classes and did my due diligence with the homework. I passed the course, and this qualified me for entrance in a junior year chem course.

There was another problem plaguing my young and probably immature mind. Girls. I dated them, and when not seeing anyone on a steady basis, I met others at parties and urged them into quiet corners. Toward the end of tenth grade however, I fell head-over for a soul who could not reciprocate my feelings. Sure, we got together after school; did things on weekends. Then came rejection, total and absolute. I felt crushed. Self-pity took hold. I tried to make things better between us. But school ended before I could make another go of it.

I wanted to die. Thank God for my recording of Peggy Lee's, *Is That All There Is?* I played it endlessly.

And so it was that one month into my junior year, a series of trivial events conspired against me. There was the monotone home life, and friction between career and volunteer personnel had increased to where I felt unwelcome in the very fire department that I belonged to. Suffering a broken heart only added to my misery.

That's where things stood on a sweltering Indian summer day back before schools were air conditioned, when my fellow students and I filed into a hot classroom following lunch, and the English teacher stood and told us, "Now children. It's too hot and you've just eaten. So put your heads on your desks and take a nap."

Children? *Nap?*

By calling me a child, she had offended me to the core. After all, hadn't I been riding fire engines and ambulances for months? Didn't she know that I ran into burning buildings and gave CPR to drowned babies? There was also this: I'd also been sexually active since thirteen, and by sixteen—Maryland's age of consent—I'd enjoyed more than a few liaisons with older women.

Children? Who're you calling a child, Lady?

Feeling angry at the world—as if most sixteen-year olds don't—I told her to kiss my ass. Then I grabbed my books and drove home.

Later that evening, I sat down with my parents and talked them into letting me drop out of school.

When they agreed with no questions asked, their lack of concern troubled me even more. Yep, I was an angry kid. But how much of that had I brought on myself? I didn't know, although admittedly it nagged at me from some place deep inside my frazzled brain.

The next day I woke up feeling liberated. No more chem, no more class, and no more teachers to tell to kiss my ass. Then the curtain fell and I wondered, "What do I do now?"

* * * *

I ended up doing menial jobs, that's what. I bagged groceries at the base commissary. I cut grass and took on labor jobs. Yeah...I sure showed that teacher. So why did I feel such deep shame for ending up a high school dropout? The disgrace hit bottom one day when I entered a lunch diner with some other laborers, and spotted a friend's father seated at the counter. His son and I had played high school sports, and Mr. Barber always drove me home after practice when my parents couldn't be bothered. He stared at me. I pretended not to see him, too ashamed to admit that I was earning minimum wages instead of being in class with his son.

Gone too were any chances of following in my father's footsteps by enlisting, although by now I was thinking of becoming a career firefighter. After all, I loved it. Besides, what young man can deny the thrill of riding on big rigs at high speeds through town, with sirens and air horns blasting? How many teens routinely test their moxie by rushing into burning buildings to mix it up with hot, working fires?

But I could forget about that career, too. The county fire department wouldn't hire me without a high school diploma—not when other candidates had theirs.

Enter the friends. Russ Hewitt, Tim Doegen, and I were best buddies. Russ, slender like me, had been a classmate. I can best describe Tim as having the late actor John Candy's build and demeanor. Tim enjoyed a reputation as a ferocious firefighter, and he always had a gorgeous gal on his arm. One day about four months after I dropped out, they took me aside and told me to wise-up. "At least go for your GED," Russ finally said.

So I sat for the exam, and exactly one month later I got a letter from the state. I ripped open the envelope and was shocked—no, make that stunned—to learn that I'd earned the highest score in the state's history. Me, the slacker who never got more than average grades in school.

Feeling a resurgence of hope, I applied to Anne Arundel County Community College so that I could earn an associate of arts degree. They didn't offer degrees in fire science, so I chose their law enforcement program. However, they responded with a nasty-gram that claimed boys of seventeen were too young for college. I didn't see why that should make a difference. But in 1971 it did.

I mentioned this to my folks. When they shrugged and went back to watching TV, I called the college and asked for a sit-down with the dean of admissions. To my surprise, he granted the request, only to tell me after our very brief meeting to forget about it. His attitude left me angry, hurt and confused. The next morning I drafted a letter to my state representative seeking her assistance. If she refused or failed in her endeavor, I would reach out to the governor. After sliding the letter into a corner mailbox that afternoon, I went home and grabbed the phone book, determined to call the local newspaper for a human interest story. But as I reached for the phone, fate intervened when it began ringing.

I answered. The caller introduced himself as a senior administrator for the county board of education. He had learned of my plight, he began, and wanted to discuss my GED scores. After a brief conversation, he invited me to meet in person at his office. I arrived promptly. He asked pointed questions about why I dropped out of school, then wondered aloud what I would do with a two-year degree. After a few minutes, he thanked me for coming and walked me to the door.

One week later I got an acceptance letter from the community college, inviting me to enroll in the upcoming semester.

A kind and caring professional had shown me a door left open, and to this day I wonder if he'll ever know how many other doors he opened for me. This included other students, because my case had been a watershed, one that paved the way for anyone with a diploma or a GED to enter college regardless of age. It was a big deal back then. Society takes it for granted today.

* * * *

Yet another open door led to greater degrees of insight into life, since my constant presence at the firehouse exposed me to several surrogate father figures—rough and tumble men who spoke with a clear-eyed directness that I found refreshing.

Many decades later, I readily recall what one of the surrogates had to say about Life 101: "You can eat a thousand pussies," he began, "and nobody will call you a pussy-eater. But suck one cock, and you're a cocksucker for life." Yep, there it was. Life ain't fair, so get over it.

In an ironic twist, I also realized that neither the volunteers nor the paid men cared that there were gay firefighters throughout the county. Remember, this was 1971, and yet nobody gave a shit. For example, if a firefighter offhandedly-mentioned one of the gay firefighters by name, somebody would invariably nod and say, "Yeah, Ole Smitty. He might be queer, but I'll follow him into a burning building anytime, anywhere."

Or as many of the firefighters essentially said, "What do I care what puts the whiz in another guy's wick. The way I see it? The more guys who're gay, the less competition there is for the gals."

Some firefighters would even take colleagues suspected of being gay to one side, and talk in low tones. "Listen, I got a cousin coming into town next week. I think he's just your type. Maybe you'd like to meet him?" There was no malice. These were acts of friendship no different than when a guy sets up a friend with his sister.

These were lessons in life for a no-longer-so-clear-eyed kid, and I shook my head at the idea of men who didn't worry about what others might think of them—although imagine my surprise one day a few years later when a colleague took me aside to say, "Listen, I got this cousin . . ."

Furrows must have erupted across my forehead. "What're you talking about? I have a girlfriend. Hell, you've met her." It was true. I did, and he had met her. But this affable friend shrugged and said something about thinking I might be bi-, and then he dropped it. Did this anger me? Heck, no. There'd been no threat to my manhood, and it had only been a simple act of friendship—not to mention that he opened my eyes to greater ideas of acceptance.

I ALSO LEARNED that just because you don't like a certain person, you can still respect him or her; that you can admire them for their talents and gifts and learn from them, if only from afar.

As conflict between volunteer and paid personnel escalated into silent stares or bitterly uttered epithets, I clearly understood that the paid men didn't want me around. One of them, Dave Bond, worked the ladder truck and he typically kept vollies at a distance. But now and then he'd offer me a pat on the shoulder, or a word of advice.

One June day in 1971, he pulled me to one side. After looking me up and down—he was six feet tall, while I stood five foot seven and weighed 120—he rapped his knuckles against my chest. "Rick, we don't like you hanging around here. Why? 'Cause you've taken sides."

This was true. I'd made it known that nobody—not paid men or armies of academy recruits—were gonna run my butt outta there. For me, it was a matter of principle.

However, it should have been a matter of my greater willingness to yield and to open lines of dialogue. For example, I might have told the paid men that I wanted to "go paid," but add that I needed a place to live until then. They would have understood that the volunteer chief wouldn't let me live there unless I responded to fire and ambulance calls, and give me a free pass to a neutral corner.

But instead of mentioning this to Dave, I dug in and said, "You guys are not running me outta here."

He pressed his lips together. Several silent seconds passed. "Rick, maybe we don't like you, but for what it's worth we do respect you. You're not afraid to mix it up with hot working fires. You, Russ, Scott and Tim—you guys get in there. We admire that. Plus, you guys don't cut an' run when there's work to be done, the way most vollies do."

By work, he meant the laborious tasks of changing out the thousands of feet of hose that the engines carried. It meant cleaning and racking all that hose into hose dryers; it meant swabbing floors and cleaning toilets and waxing apparatus.

Dave had surprised me. I never would have guessed that the paid guys saw me that way, and I didn't know how to reply. All I could do was meet his eyes and nod. Well, the sad thing is that if at that point I had opened my heart and mentioned how badly I *wanted* to be friends with the paid guys, things might have changed. Had I expressed my desire for them to accept me as someone who meant well, maybe things would have been different. But I wasn't able to say those things. Not back then.

Even so, what Dave said to me that day was a beginning.

LONG BEFORE THAT talk with Dave, I had been making a point of watching LeRoy Wilkison go about his daily duties. To say that he and I didn't speak to each other would be an understatement. He was paid, I was a vollie, and that was that. Except for one thing: even rookies recognize consummate professionals when they see one, without being quite sure why the guy is such a pro.

LeRoy knew his shit.

I would watch him in the station, and pay attention to how he drove the apparatus. I kept track of his actions on the fire ground whenever I wasn't too busy myself, and tried to absorb his skills by osmosis. In time, whenever I saw him, I saw a hero. Only, it wasn't in me to tell him this. I mean, come on—we were a couple of guys.

At any rate, I didn't even know how to tell him. However, once I turned old enough to begin driving the engines, I found myself emulating LeRoy.

We did have some tough moments. Maybe what we really needed was to square off inside a boxing ring and go to Duke City, although winning the match wouldn't be the goal so much as it would be a chance to vent. In time however, he and I did loosen up. At first we offered grudging compliments to one another. Later, we made polite small talk. Eventually we began sitting down at a local firefighter hangout for drinks. In time, this evolved from acquaintanceship to friendship.

John "Buzz" Griner would also give me a wink or an encouraging word. Sure, we were on opposite sides of the career fence, but he still encouraged me; still slapped me on the back whenever I did a particularly good job on a fire ground. And it meant something to me because he was a great firefighter, and I always admired him for going the distance. Yep, Buzz showed me that small acts of kindness could be the keys a kid needed to grow into a better man.

I certainly can't forget Joey Rumenap, either. He was a crazy sort who manned the ambulance on weekdays, and everyone liked this ex-Marine. Joey told great stories, and his infectious laughter had us all holding our sides. Joey also readily offered advice, and he brought me into his circle of laughing at life's absurdities.

Steve Preslipsky had been a volunteer before coming to Company 33 as a daytime paid firefighter. He was full of mischief and fun, but he would charge into burning buildings so quickly that I felt hard pressed to keep up with him.

One of the older drivers was Calvin Sears, aka "Uncle" Calvin. He walked a fine line along the demilitarized zone between paid and volunteer, but he would also point a finger at us and say, "I'm gonna tell you boys something. . ." Then he'd launch into whatever he wanted to get across. At times he would even end his lesson with a smile.

Don "Hoot" Gibson operated the ladder truck. He was an old salt who usually kept to himself, but when he did break loose with a pointer or two, I always paid attention. Years later a couple of the skills I learned from him saved my life when I got trapped inside a roaring inferno.

As for that ladder truck, I regarded it as a shining pot of gold at the end of a rainbow, even if I still wasn't permitted to ride it. At least the reason why I couldn't was straightforward. Being a "truck man" required special skills, because a truck company's tasks are varied. They include search and rescue, laddering, ventilating a structure to let the heated air and gasses escape, plus salvage and cleanup. So when the county fire academy announced a "Truck Company Course," I ran to the head of the line.

The course was a challenge, especially for someone as scared shitless of heights as I was. Did I say, scared? I was petrified, thanks to a childhood accident that left me with a morbid fear of heights. But when the instructor raised the aerial ladder to its full height of one hundred feet and ordered me to climb it if I hoped to get qualified, it was shit-or-get-off-the-pot time. So I climbed, my knees turning to mush every time the wind pushed the ladder back and forth, and yet climb it I did—especially since I wasn't about to back down in front of everyone.

But Father God and Sonny Jesus, that trial by climbing definitely scared me into the next week.

We scaled a five-story building with ancient pompier ladders, and rappelled back to the ground. I also learned everything I wanted to know about ceiling hooks and ladders, but had always been afraid to ask. Then after two more days of evolutions and classroom work, the chief awarded me with the distinctive hook-and-ladder shield of a "true truck man."

A celebration followed, and afterward I rushed back to the station feeling thrilled by the idea of riding the truck on the next alarm. What a beauty it was, too. A 1970 Seagrave, sleek and fast and boasting a lion's roar from its 6-71 Detroit Diesel. It's what every boy dreamed of. Sure, I could pretend that this hunk of metal didn't send my pulse racing, but I'd be lying. Then one wintry Friday evening I told Tim, "I'm gonna drive this truck one day."

He scoffed and said, "In your dreams."

Yeah? Well, maybe this particular dream didn't sound like much to others, but it was a goal, and I vowed to turn it into a reality. One other thing: in an act of self-motivation, I decided that I would always announce my dreams to others as a means to keep the pressure on myself.

> *"What I've dared, I've willed. And what I've willed, I'll do."*
> — Captain Ahab in *Moby Dick*

Yeahhhhh, you bet your ass, Ahab.

Then again, Ahab had added, *"They think me mad...."*

CHAPTER FIVE

Strike the Box

P RIOR TO EVERYONE having phones in homes and cellular devices much later, citizens across America rushed to the nearest
street corner fire alarm box to report a fire. The boxes were painted
red—of course—and the older ones featured a hook behind a small
glass pane, along with an instruction plate that read: IN CASE OF
FIRE BREAK GLASS AND PULL THE HOOK. There was even a tiny
hammer hanging next to it. Pulling the hook sent impulses to fire
headquarters, where a receiver annunciated the impulses. Dispatchers then matched the box number against a master list, and
sent an engine to investigate the emergency.

If a responding unit found a building fire that was too large to
handle alone, the fire lieutenant went to the same box and struck—
or pulled—the hook again. This was known as "striking the box," and
even after fire apparatus became equipped with radios, lieutenants
still told dispatchers to, "strike the box" when they needed help. Because each subsequent strike required an additional alarm of three
more engines, a ladder truck and a battalion chief, the terms "second
alarm, third alarm," and "multiple-alarm fire" became part of the
lexicon.

In our county, dispatchers broadcast a "local alarm" over a radio network to send engine companies to automobile, brush, or dumpster fires. On the other hand, "box alarms" involved sending three engines and a truck to homes or buildings that are ablaze. If a local station responded to a dumpster fire, only to arrive and see that flames had spread into an adjacent building, the officer grabbed the mic and said, "Strike the box."

Yep, it's what firefighters said when they needed help.

LIVING AT THE firehouse came with an unstated price tag, one that all of us understood and accepted without argument: if you lived there, you had to answer fire and ambulance calls. That suited my friends and I. We not only fought fires, we rescued people trapped in wrecked autos, or pulled them from streams and lakes. About the only thing we wouldn't respond to were calls for a cat stuck in a tree. As one dispatcher famously told a caller who asked us to rescue her cat from a tall oak tree, "Lady, you ever see a cat skeleton in a tree? Trust me. Leave it alone an' it'll come down, wagging its damn tail behind it."

On a more serious note, we were challenging ourselves in confrontations with Mother Nature's elements of earth, wind and fire. But at least no malice was present in these stand & fight dramas. Nope, it was all reduced to the simple terms of you against the fire, with a simple goal of coming out alive. And if a firefighter got a small burn on his wrist, it was a badge of honor, one that signified that you leaped into the inferno and came out on top. Yes sir, it was definitely an attitude to be nurtured, and one that lent vitality to our unofficial motto: *You knew the job was dangerous when you took it.*

ON A SULTRY summer day in 1972, after a homeowner donated his two-story house for use as a teaching aid, local volunteer companies gathered for a "house burning." Volunteers routinely burned these donated homes to the ground in a series of stages, to teach rookies the basics of fire behavior.

My buddy Tim Doegen was in charge of exposing a clutch of sixteen-year-old newbies to the near-zero visibility conditions that they would encounter in burning buildings. To accomplish this, Tim placed a metal bucket filled with excelsior near a second floor window. Then he made sure the rookies had their masks in place before he tossed a match into the bucket.

The room filled with thick white smoke within seconds, giving the newbies a chance to experience zero-vis in a controlled environment. It's scary at first, but once you encounter it a few times and learn to feel your way to an exit, the loss of visual feedback loses its menace. The drills also stressed the need to guard against complacency, while keeping in mind the guiding principle of Murphy's Law, which states that if something can go wrong, it will.

This time, something did.

The rookies had already learned their way around the room by the third exercise, so Tim moved on to a different drill. But heated gases from the previous drills had accumulated near the ceiling. When he tossed the match this time, a flashover occurred and the second floor erupted in flames.

Earlier, Russ, Mike Schultheis and I had suited up with air tanks in place and a charged fire hose in hand, and stood at the ready near the open front door. We were the three-man safety crew, but when three giggly girls approached us, we naturally began chatting it up with them.

Then a whoosh overhead took my breath away. Frantic screams filled the air. Mike's jaw dropped. Russ said, "Holy fuck." I looked up—and masked-up.

A defenestration of firefighters followed, as bodies flew out of upstairs windows. Tim pushed two of the rookies toward the stairway, then began tossing the others out of the nearest window. When the rain of bodies stopped and we didn't see Tim, I bounded up the stairs while passing two newbies who were rushing down. Mike was behind me, and Russ brought up the rear with the hose.

The place was lit. But where was Tim? I couldn't see him from the landing, so I crawled further inside and found him in the middle of the floor. Flames were already lapping along his back and legs when Mike appeared at my side. As we tried to grab Tim the heat drove us back. But we were damned if we'd give up, so we did a full court press until I was able to grip Tim's ankle.

Once Mike grabbed his other ankle, we dragged Tim to the landing and bounced his fat ass down the steps, while Russ opened his nozzle and drenched us with water.

Once outside, Mike and I stood Tim up and we were checking him for burns when Tim began laughing. "Man, I was worried there for a second. I—"

"Tim," I barked. Then I looked him in the eye. "Tim. I thought you were dead."

He sobered up at once. Later, he told me that the look on my face said it all. Yeah, I had a reputation as a jokester. But I wasn't joking this time, and Tim damned well knew it. Seconds later, his legs buckled.

He'd sustained major burns after all, mostly on the backs of his thighs and on his rather ample ass (his words, not mine). Two of the rookies were also injured, so we loaded them into an ambulance for a rush ride to the ER. One of those rookies was Frankie Pleyo.

TIM NOT ONLY saved the six newbies, we also learned valuable lessons. Sometimes, that's what it takes. Sometimes it's enough, though not always. Years later, one of those rookies and I got trapped inside another conflagration. Only, it wasn't a training scenario. It was the real thing, it killed two firefighters, and the lad ensnared with me was none other than Frankie Pleyo.

AMONG THE OTHER volunteers who more-or-less lived at Company 33 were Nelson Pyle—not to be confused with Nelson Janz—and Russ Hewitt. Nelson had recently applied for a career firefighter slot, while Russ talked of going into law enforcement. Because the three of us were certified in advanced first aid and CPR, the paid guys tapped us for ambulance calls. Russ and I were still too young to drive the new SWAB "gut bucket," so that duty fell to the slightly older Nelson.

Those were older days, too—the days before paramedics. There were no blood pressure cuffs or stethoscopes or EKG's; no IV's to establish or drugs to administer or direct link-ups to ER's. Ambulances were only equipped to establish and maintain airways, administer oxygen, manage severe bleeding and fractures, and transport patients to medical facilities. We called non-serious cases "taxi rides," but the really scary ones were known as "scoop an' swoop calls," since all we could do was stabilize immediate life threatening issues, scoop the patient onto a litter, and swoop to the nearest ER at top speed.

We responded to everything from sick babies and heart attacks, to auto accidents with multiple-trauma victims. Yet Russ and I were not in the least intimidated. We knew our jobs, we approached each emergency as an academic problem, and with Nelson at the helm, the three of us saved lives.

A lot of lives. Imagine two sixteen-year-old boys in the back of an ambulance making life and death decisions on a daily basis with enviable calm, and almost always making the right call. ER personnel seeing us wheeling in a victim with a gunshot wound to the head would check our patient, see that we had crossed the T's and dotted the I's, and nod their approval. In some cases, they even expressed verbal admiration, an act that always left our chests heaving with pride.

But when the hotline rang one lazy Saturday afternoon, the normally taciturn Uncle Calvin ran wide-eyed from the alarm room and pointed to us. "A kid fell through a plate glass window. Dispatch said, 'hurry!'"

Hurry? Yeah, it sounded good. But traffic was heavy. So the usually cautious Nelson, possibly spooked by Calvin, floored the accelerator. The run took four minutes. We piled out. Russ grabbed the trauma kit. Nelson reached for the portable oxygen. I dashed inside. The hysterical mother pointed to a ground floor family room.

Only one word describes the scene I found inside: horrific.

A guy my age was lying in a pool of blood, naked but for blue gym shorts. The shattered remnants of a nearby glass door testified to the obvious: he had run into it, glass shards had slashed the right side of his neck, and at least one of them nicked the external jugular while luckily sparing the internal jugular. Otherwise, he would have been dead long before we arrived.

What can I say? He was a beautiful boy, tall and "imperially slim," as in the poem "Richard Cory." He was also what Michelangelo could only have *wished* David had looked like. Yeah, the kid was an Adonis, and perfect in every way. Well, he was perfect if you overlooked his utter absence of arms. In their place he had three tiny fingers protruding from each shoulder, fingers that hadn't developed enough to even be prehensile. Call them a mockery; sad ornaments of what might have been.

The sad fact was that he was a "Thalidomide baby," a child who had been born without arms because his mother used the 1950's era drug Thalidomide to curb morning sickness. I learned later that he only wore gym shorts at home to make it easier for family members to help him use the toilet. He went shoeless because his toes and feet substituted for fingers and hands. Yet despite all of this, everyone who knew him always shook their heads in admiration— "He's the happiest-go-lucky kid I've ever known," one neighbor quipped, only to burst into tears when he pictured what had happened to the boy.

And just what did happen to the boy? It seems that he had been playing grab-ass with a younger brother. At one point, while laughing and glancing over a shoulder as he fled the brother, he was trying to escape through a patio door that he thought was open. It wasn't. But without arms to stop or to at least shield himself, he ran headlong into the glass.

I knelt at his side. He was conscious, despite a colossal blood loss. And like Matthew, his eyes searched mine. Yet despite the curve ball that Life had thrown at him, he wanted to live and he wanted my assurance that we would pull him through.

"We're gonna take care of you," I told him.

He nodded. Talk about total trust. Vowing to live up to it, I slid my hand to the wound.

AIDS was an unknown entity in the early '70s. First responders didn't carry latex gloves. So I slipped an ungloved index finger into the gaping laceration, and damned if I didn't hit the severed blood vessel on the first go-around. The bleeding stopped.

I did not exaggerate when I said he was lying in a pool of blood. It had to be an inch deep, warm and viscous and slightly malodorous. The patient watched my face for clues. I winked at him. "You'll be okay. You're not alone. We're right here."

I had Russ roll a gauze pad into a cigarette shape. After taking it from him, I waited while Russ opened a bottle of alcohol and poured it around my finger and the laceration. Then I eased the finger out, and slid the rolled gauze into the wound. While Russ secured an oxygen mask around the boy's nose and mouth, Nelson went to get the litter.

That's when our patient turned south. He had been alert only seconds before, but now his pupils were dull, his respirations labored. We had our own term for this condition: we called it, "shocky," a nod toward a famous physician who described shock as, "a pause in the act of dying." I looked at Russ. Our eyes met. He nodded.

We weren't about to let our patient pause for anything, and this was definitely a scoop an' swoop moment.

I added an additional dressing and taped it securely in place to provide direct pressure against the wound, but not so tightly that I couldn't rip it off if I spotted seepage, since that would require sliding a finger back into the wound.

Then we were rushing the teen-aged boy from the house to the ambulance. Neighbors had gathered, and I heard multiple gasps as they saw the blood. It was everywhere—not only on this boy whom they all knew and loved, but also all over us.

We loaded him in. Russ and I climbed through the yawning rear doors and closed them behind us. I inserted an oral pharyngeal airway into our now comatose patient. Russ got the oxygen demand mask. Unlike the mask he had initially applied, this one had a button to force air into non-breathing patients. Russ put the demand mask in place, then triggered the button while Nelson urged the mom into the front seat.

We needed to determine blood perfusion. Was blood even flowing to the vital centers? I felt the carotid pulse.

"It's...okay," I said tonelessly. Normally, I would've checked the wrists next. But our patient had no wrists, so I reached inside his shorts to palpate a femoral pulse. Located deep within a crease near the base of the penis or the vagina, the femoral artery can be difficult to locate. But this guy was imperially slim, making it easier. "Femoral's there," I told Russ. He nodded and triggered the mask a second time. Next, I located the *dorsalis* artery atop our patient's foot. "Got a dorsal," I announced. "Kinda thready, though."

Thready or not, at least he had some perfusion. Moving on with my patient assessment, I pinched his big toe to check for capillary refill. The nail bed blanched as expected, but too many seconds swept by before it returned to a healthy, rosy-red appearance. I waited until Russ hit the button before adding in a conversational aside, "Poor cap response."

Meanwhile, Nelson whomped the transmission into gear and wheeled us around. Then I heard him calling the dispatcher on the radio. "Notify North Arundel (Hospital) that we're en route with a major bleeder." Seconds later he lay on the siren as we barreled down the street for a quick-trip to the ER.

Russ continued to administer oxygen while I reassessed our patient. Oh no, I thought. He had grown deathly pale. His pupils were dilated. We were losing him. We needed help. I wanted to grab the mic and cry out to headquarters—I wanted to tell them, "Strike the box!" But that flight-of-fancy wasn't an option. It was up to us.

I checked the *dorsalis* again. Nothing. I moved trained fingers along the foot in search of another pulse point. Couldn't find one. Checked the other foot. No dice. Looked up at Russ; an oblique look, almost apologetic, and then I grimaced.

"Try leg splints," Russ said from the side of his mouth.

I must have looked quizzical as hell before recognition dawned. We had recently attended a first aid seminar. A doctor had discussed experimental pneumatic trouser-like garments that medical personnel could wrap around a trauma patient's legs and abdomen. Inflating the garment forces blood from the extremities toward the heart, where blood is needed.

I drew a deep breath, said, "Fuck it," and reached into a compartment for the rubber-like inflatable leg splints. The splints have two chambers—outer and inner—and medics can place them around a limb and inflate them. By increasing the inflation, we could constrict the boy's blood vessels. So I wrapped those suckers around both of his legs, and filled 'em to the max.

Russ hit the oxygen once, twice, three times before our patient's breathing began settling into N.R.—normal rhythm. I assessed the femoral pulse. Not great, but not all that bad. I pulled my hand from his crotch. Checked my fingers. They were dry. That was good. He hadn't lost bladder control—and the bladder is always one of the last of the bodily functions to go.

By the time Nelson was backing the ambulance into the ER bay, a bit of light was rising in the boy's pupils like a dawn sun. Nelson raced around to the rear doors, flung them open and helped me pull the litter out, while Russ followed with the demand mask hooked to a portable oxygen tank.

Bystanders' eyes bugged as we swept past, our hands, arms and clothes drenched in blood. Russ kept up the oxygen therapy while Nelson and I barreled through the ER's swinging doors while yelling, "Coming through!"

Nurses took one look at us, then at our patient. One nurse put a hand to her mouth. A doc ran over, touched the inflated leg splints, looked at me and frowned, but abruptly nodded his understanding.

"*Good* job, guys."

"He gets the credit." I tilted my head at Russ, but the doctor had turned away to reach for latex gloves.

Russ and I transferred our patient to the gurney while Nelson wheeled the litter out from under him. Then we stepped back to watch. The poor guy had lost so much blood—so much in fact that while an anesthesiologist intubated him, the ER doc had to cut into the patient's ankle to find a vein viable enough to accept an I.V. catheter. It's called a cut-down, and doctors will only resort to it when a patient is in extremis.

A nurse applied electrodes to the boy's chest, and when we saw a ragged but steady rhythm on the EKG monitor, the three of us exchanged looks and blew air from our cheeks. Only then did we go to the scrub sink to clean the blood from our hands. It took a lot of scrubbing, but we finally finished and quietly wheeled the blood-stained litter from the room.

The kid lived.

We didn't need to strike the box that day. However, this young man's lesson on making the most of out of life haunted me into the night. And, his lesson would sustain me much later at a time when I least expected it—and when I needed it the most.

He's someone I would have liked to have had as a friend. To this day however, I still don't know his name.

CHAPTER SIX

Putting Wet Stuff on Red Stuff

W ET STUFF AND red stuff were providing passages that would unknowingly lead me to exponentially greater dreams in the near future. For now though, I was taking every available course in firefighting and emergency care. I took the University of Maryland Basic Firefighter program, and followed-up with pump operator and truck company courses. There were also flammable liquids management courses and many other schools—all the vital elements that work toward putting the wet stuff on the red stuff.

At age sixteen I was also watching medical examiners conduct full autopsies. Jesus, can anyone be ready to see one of these? The sights, the...yuck...the odors. But what better way to learn? I had also delivered my first baby by then, and what fascinating experiences all of these evolved into as I became one of the state's youngest first aid instructors. Soon enough, I was also among Maryland's earliest emergency medical technicians, or EMTs.

There was more. The fire chief promoted me to volunteer lieutenant, and I even stood in for the paid guys on the ambulance. That meant good money, along with some name-recognition once I applied for a career firefighter slot. Of course, getting that community college associates degree would also help.

I DIDN'T DO so well in college. Not that first semester, which was a shame seeing as how the college ranked among the nation's top ten. The campus was securely nestled within the embracing tidewaters of the Chesapeake Bay, and the school attracted students who could swim before they could walk. This led to a laid-back dress code that didn't require students to wear any footwear at all, which made it my kind of place. So I sold some personal items and robbed my bank account in order to scrape together enough money for tuition, fees and books.

Since I was the first county student to attend college full time when I should have been a high school senior, I gained bragging rights. Unfortunately, I had never developed good study habits, and I ran into trouble within the first week.

Three pop quizzes left me feeling dizzy and downright discouraged, at least until a very amiable science professor told me why I got a poor grade in his class. "You tried to bluff your way through the answers," he began. Then he arched an eyebrow. "On the other hand, you displayed a remarkable originality of thought. Yeah, I'm impressed." He paused. "Come see me after class. I'll help you find a tutor."

However, I failed to follow-up on his generosity; failed to break more than a C by semester's end. Even worse, I got two D's. Feeling discouraged and dejected, I decided not to return the next semester, and with no idea how to get out of the corner I'd gotten myself into. Deep down though, I knew that doing nothing would be the greater disgrace.

* * * *

I had never received a letter with a big red CERTIFIED MAIL stamped on the envelope. Even so, I kinda sorta knew what it was, and my hands trembled as I ripped open the envelope and read the acceptance letter:

> *Dear Mr. Anderson. I am pleased to convey that you have been appointed a "Probationary Firefighter" in the Anne Arundel County Fire Department. Your appointment will be effective...*

I pumped a fist in the air and shouted, "Yes!" Then I grabbed the phone and called Joyce.

MY ELDEST BROTHER Jim and his wife Jackie introduced me to Joyce Emge in 1973. She was a year younger than I, with long blonde hair and lively green eyes, and sunshine broke out from her face whenever she smiled. We were both full of mischief—another quality that endeared her to me, not to mention that she loved sports and adored nature. Joyce and I began a journey that saw great laughter, but also storm clouds that were the result of my own ignorance. Fortunately, she saw in me a thing or two that kept her working toward a stronger relationship.

Bobby Vinton's *Sealed With a Kiss* and Roberta Flack's *The First Time Ever* ruled the radio back then, and these songs among others became our anthems. Summers saw us hot and sweaty from hiking mountain passes, or shuffling through shifting beach sands. We also made frequent trips to Maryland's Assateague Island, where we marveled at the wild ponies that roam this enchanted isle. Winters brought us literally closer together as we huddled for warmth while walking beneath brilliantly star-studded skies. But no matter the season, we made a point of going to local hangouts to meet our friends.

Among the friends was fellow firefighter Scott Collins, whose parents were a couple of characters right out of Twain and seasoned by Faulkner. I grew to love his folks, and in turn they opened their hearts to me. It wasn't long before his family and I were exchanging Christmas gifts. Scott and I also had each other's backs during crises, and we were able to dump on one another.

* * * *

I had to move out of the firehouse before I could enter the fire academy. I also had no options but to move back home. Just my luck though, it was a temporary fix because my parents abruptly pulled up the roots they had finally put down, and moved into a new home. They also moved just far enough away that it became difficult to visit them without enduring a three-hour car trip. At least they gave me their living room furniture, along with some kitchen supplies for the small apartment that I rushed out to rent.

Otherwise I was on my own, with no idea how to reconcile a checking statement, do laundry, or use an iron. But I could cook, and I admired those who also knew how to handle a skillet. One time after a girl became interested in one of my friends, I described him to her this way: "You'll like him. He's a stud in the kitchen, and a chef in bed."

She blushed deep red but her dazzling smile brooked no lies, so I set them up on a blind date and they hit it off at once. As for me? Well, I don't know about the 'chef in bed' part, but my abilities in a kitchen were rather studly. However, while I didn't starve, I had to work long hours just to scrape together what I could in order to buy food.

MY FIRST ASSIGNMENT out of the fire academy was to Engine 27, in Maryland City. I had asked for Engine 33, but there were no open slots. Engine 27 was fine, though. The station was near my old stomping grounds in Laurel, and we responded there and to nearby Howard County for structural fires. Making the assignment better still, Nelson Pyle was an engineman there. Naturally, we wasted little time in busting each other's balls. But even while busting on him, I saw him as a winner and as the fire chief that he became.

I was earning the grand salary of $8,000 per year as a career firefighter, and whenever someone asked what I did for work, I laughed and said, "Who works? I get paid to do something I love."

Love would be an understatement; I adored my life as a firefighter.

I lived it morning, noon and of course at night. While on duty I studied street maps and gamed scenarios in my head; I talked tactics with others, and gathered the volunteers together to conduct planning inspections of the major structures and business complexes in our first-due area.

Whenever an engineman took off, I was first in line to fill in for him. This meant a whopping extra $74.00 on the paycheck for working a twenty-four-hour shift. The long hours weren't all that bad though—an unspoken gentleman's agreement between union and management acknowledged the fact that more often than not we slept for eight of those twenty-four hours. If it happened to be a busy day and you had to hump it for each and every one of those hours? Then that's when our motto kicked in: *Ya knew the job was dangerous when ya took it.* Anyway, by working extra shifts I met the monthly rent for my apartment, and still had enough left over for food and gasoline and dates with Joyce.

AT ABOUT THIS time my friend Scott told me about his college plans. "It'll open doors," he began one evening over a glass of beer. Then he looked directly at me. "So, Rick. Why not get your butt back into school?"

I nodded yet said nothing. However, a week later his dad invited me to their home, and after he poured some beers we clinked glasses. A second round followed before he turned to me and said, "Scott tells me you're considering college again." My gratitude toward him for showing even the slightest interest in my future knew few bounds. As we drank we talked, and with his encouragement I decided to get that two-year degree.

The next semester saw me working my regular fifty hours a week at Engine 27, while carrying a full course load at night. Each Saturday I drove a bus, and every Sunday I worked a twenty-four shift for one of the enginemen. All of this amounted to full-time school on top of an eighty-hour workweek. I wasn't being super human, though—I did have the luxury of being able to study while on duty.

So I put in the hours to earn a degree that among other things would dampen my history as a high school dropout.

Sadly, I ended up dropping out of my relationship with Joyce. She was the best thing that had ever happened to me, but we were having problems that were of my making. And when a major issue created an even greater rift between us, we said goodbye and walked away without looking back. Today I still ask myself, "How could I have been so dumb?"

"YOU'RE VERY INTELLIGENT." I stared at the words for a long time. They were written in red ink on the term paper I had turned in for a criminology course—words that mirrored those of the professor who tried to get me a tutor during my failed first attempt at college. *Intelligent.* Nobody had ever applied that term to me. Could it be true? I read those words again and again, even putting the paper away for posterity.

From that moment on I became a straight "A" student. I made every Dean's List, and eighteen months later I had an associate of arts degree in law enforcement, along with a partial scholarship to the University of Baltimore for a bachelor's in criminal justice. To this day, I shake my head in amazement at the amount of power that lies within three simple words: You're very intelligent.

I felt cockier than ever and didn't feel so alone anymore, although a few vestiges hung on like guests who don't know when it's time to leave. And just as Scott's father predicted, I now enjoyed greater focus. Well, I don't know about others, but focus for me meant pursuing the dreams that kept popping up in my sleep states. Among them were dreams of becoming a cop—and not just any cop, but among the best; I wanted to become a Maryland State Police Trooper.

CONSISTENTLY RANKED AT the top of the law enforcement food chain, the Maryland State Police enjoyed an enviable reputation of being firm but fair. Marylanders in general knew not to mess with "the man in tan," since it was common knowledge that before anyone could don the khaki shirts and olive drab trousers of a Maryland State Trooper, they first had to endure a grueling selection process. Assuming a candidate even got in, he or she faced a six-month long, live-in academy that former Marine Corps drill instructors ran like a boot camp. It was also the nation's most academically challenging and physically rigorous institution of its kind.

And while it is true that Maryland troopers patrol roads and highways as part of their job, they are not a Highway Patrol agency with very fine officers who are relegated to riding up and down various highways, but not much else.

On the flip side, a state police agency invests its troopers with a full array of duties. State troopers might patrol a highway one moment, respond to a bar fight the next, and investigate a homicide an hour later. Simply put, state police troopers are a combination of highway patrol, county sheriff's deputies, and city police officers.

In addition, the Maryland State Police (MSP) was on the ground floor of trauma medicine as the world now knows it. Prior to the late 1960s, trauma victims only stood a forty-five percent chance of survival. It didn't matter how efficient the ambulance crews were, or how close the patients were to a superior emergency room—the survival rates were dismal, and they remained so until fortune smiled in the form of Dr. R. Adams Cowley.

Dr. Cowley had served as a MASH surgeon in Korea. For all I know he might even have been the surgeon who saved my father's life. At any rate, Dr. Cowley never forgot the two most vital factors that led to phenomenally high survival rates of mortally wounded soldiers: a surgical team, and the medevac helicopter.

By airlifting wounded soldiers directly to a surgical facility where physicians and nurses worked in teams, and by using triage to assign priorities to the severely wounded, the staffs were able to address grievous wounds within one hour of the injury.

Dr. Cowley called this "the golden hour," and in the late 1960s he convinced Maryland's legislators to develop the first-ever Shock Trauma Unit. However, a trauma unit has little value unless helicopters are available to make it work. "If we can get trauma patients to our facility within that golden hour," Dr. Cowley told the politicians, "I will raise the survival rate to ninety percent."

The politicos granted the money, but the only helicopters available at the time belonged to the Maryland State Police. So they converted their fleet of Bell Jet Ranger helicopters into air ambulances, and trained the observers as medics. The program had barely become airborne when Dr. Cowley's predictions exceeded his dreams, when survival rates approached not ninety percent, but ninety-five percent

Following this success, the state trained the helicopter trooper-medics to a new level of uber medics, and the idea of becoming a member of this elite unit drew me like a glowing lamp draws moths. Why? Simple. I wanted a role with greater responsibility, and I wanted to be a "firm but fair" trooper who would treat others as I would want to be treated.

Once I decided on this path, I chose to hold myself accountable by getting together with Scott, Tim, and Russ. Then over beers I announced, "I'm gonna become a trooper and get on the medevac."

Scott nodded. But after Tim pointed out that there was a two-year waiting list for white males due to affirmative action, I shrugged and said, "Then I'd better get in that line." Left unsaid was that were it not for affirmative action, MSP would never have even given me an application due to my size, since troopers back then had to be five foot, ten inches tall. However, after the governor ordered the agency to hire females, the height standard went quietly into the night. Yeah, this turned out to be yet another door left open.

AFTER RIDING A high from those good grades, I did two things. First, I began seeing Teri Miller. She had long dark hair and a gleaming smile, she laughed at my absurd jokes, and I loved her mom. Teri was quite happy to go with me to union dances, and we both loved movies. One night we went to see Robert De Niro in *The Deer Hunter*. In one of this gritty film's more horrendous scenes, North

Vietnamese soldiers capture De Niro and his fellow soldiers and force them to play Russian Roulette.

Although that sequence had a power all its own, the scene toward the end of the film when Saigon was about to fall to the North really had me trembling. It's when De Niro slipped back in to find his best friend who had gone missing. As De Niro clings to the back streets of Saigon's shadow world while small fires burn all around him and men and women let out occasional screams, I thought, *What balls it must take to do something so utterly dangerous.*

And so naturally I resolved to live out that scene someday. I didn't know the how, where, or why this would take place, but I knew it would happen.

Soon after seeing that movie, I started the fall semester at the University of Baltimore. But this respected law school lacked the laid-back attitudes and relaxed dress code I'd enjoyed at the junior college. This left me feeling out of my element, plus the killer commute through Baltimore's congested streets also took its toll. Yet I pushed on and finished the semester with good grades.

In time, I received a promotion to the exalted rank of Engineman. Unfortunately, it meant a transfer to an engine company forty miles south of my home. The long drive made it difficult to go to school at the same time, so my first act upon reporting for duty was to submit a transfer request to Truck 33. If granted, it would send me full circle by returning to Glen Burnie and my beloved ladder truck—the very one I vowed to drive one day. Oh, one other thing—I also applied to become a Maryland State Police Trooper.

Then a horrible trial by fire nearly ended all my dreams.

A DOOR LEFT OPEN

CHAPTER SEVEN

Tragedy

P AT BAUER ALONG with his twin brother and their younger brother were volunteers at Engine 27. I'd become good friends with them, and came to know their parents. I also knew that Pat loved firefighting, and that he could think of nothing finer in life than working for the county, getting married and raising children.

In the early morning hours of December 26, 1976, Pat and I were among many others who were responding along snow-covered roads to a dwelling fire, when dispatchers notified all units that they'd received "multiple reports of people trapped inside."

People were indeed trapped. Flames, smoke and heat had forced a family of four into dark corners of their end-unit row house. We were still racing to rescue them when they began jumping from second story windows. The parents and the daughter made it out safely, but the eight-year-old son wasn't so lucky. He landed head-first on a concrete sidewalk, and he was bleeding profusely when we arrived in a huff of Diesel roars and the chuff of air brakes.

We could tell from the heavy brown smoke vomiting out of windows and billowing from beneath the eaves that the fire was in the basement. Pat pulled an attack line from the engine while Lieutenant Gibson—the old salt I'd known since my volunteer days

A DOOR LEFT OPEN

when he drove the ladder truck—ordered another firefighter to tend to the boy. Then while Gibson queried the parents regarding anyone else that might still be inside, I donned an air mask and took the attack line from Pat.

Rather than charge inside, we waited until Robert from Engine 32 joined us. The three of us discussed the smoke's behavior and concluded the obvious—the fire was in the basement. Pat mentioned the possibility of more victims inside, so we made rescue our priority and went through the front door.

Visibility was zero, leaving us bat-blind and relying on hearing, touch and even taste to find our way, the rubber diaphragms on our air masks making their rapid *aw...purr* sounds. But we had all done this sort of thing a hundred times before, and each of us automatically paused at times to sweep our arms across the living room floor, over furniture and even under the couch looking for victims. Finding none, we pushed on in search of a basement door.

Just as we reached the kitchen, a fireball blew across the ceiling. I opened the nozzle and knocked the flames back. Seconds later I was making a sweep for victims when I found a door to the back yard. I opened it and told Pat and Robert what I'd done, in case flames forced us into a hasty retreat. They both said, "Okay," although the facemasks muffled their words.

I rejoined them just as flames roared out of the basement door. Okay. Fine. At least we'd found the source. I opened the nozzle and we advanced slowly but calmly down the stairs, so confident in our ability to handle the fire that we sat on our butts and plopped from one step to the next while making casual remarks such as, "Yeah, we've got this mother beat."

Then the hose went limp. No prob; it's routine. It happens when pump operators change the water supply from the tank to the hydrant; a brief lag while he closes one lever and opens another. *No sweat; we've got this mother beat.*

But the lag is always brief; a couple of seconds at most. When four seconds passed, Pat told Robert to check for a kink in the hose.

60

Robert acknowledged. I heard him clunking up the steps. Two more seconds swept by. Something wasn't right. Then it got eerily quiet. Years of experience kicked in, and when the hairs on the back of my neck stood on end, I shouted, "Pat! Upstairs! *Now*."

We had just reached the top when I heard a whoosh, followed by a roar. An explosion knocked me to the floor. It blew out windows on the second floor and drove Robert through the front door. Flames filled the room with a dull orange glow, but heavy smoke kept our visibility to no more than an inch or two.

I figured there'd been a backdraft. It's what happens when flames deprived of air explode with greed the instant they find a new air source. The paradox is that we were depriving the fire of the oxygen it needed with our textbook attack—until the water stopped. Yeah, this wasn't supposed to happen, and now the flames were coming at us with vengeance. At least we had a way out; we had that back door—a door left open.

Then things got really nasty. The entire kitchen erupted in screams. Unknown to us, three young volunteers from Engine 34 had followed our hose line inside. They didn't know about that rear door. When one of them cried out, "We're trapped!" panic filled the room so completely that terror struck even me to my deepest core. I knew about that back door; knew we weren't trapped. And yet panic is contagious. All at once I thought, *This is it*.

In that instant, as fear took an even greater grip, I heard a flapping of wings. Then I sensed—I felt—those wings wrapping around me; encapsulating me; shielding me with their warmth. They were feminine wings; angelic wings. Don't ask me how I knew, but that's what they were.

But what were they? Vestiges of childhood religious training? Can anyone even answer such a question?

It didn't matter. What I felt was as real as the flames licking at my leather helmet, and all at once I experienced a great calm.

One more thing. I've never spoken of what I felt in there until now, on this very page.

Of course a more rational and more solid explanation might be that I'd felt grounded again after a volunteer pressed close to me and yelled, "Hey, man! What do we do, man? What do we *do*?" He was plenty scared and understandably agitated. Who could blame him? Surely not me.

The wings let go. I turned to the pressing business of survival.

"It's okay," I assured him, although the mask muffled my words. "You're not trapped. There's a door nearby. I'm gonna get you outta here. I—" All at once somebody stood and got ready to bolt. Fight or flight, that primal instinct, and someone had chosen flight.

I forcibly pulled him back down and pointed my arm at the rear door. Then, one by one, I brought their hands to my outstretched arm and said, "It's pointed at an open door. A *back* door. It's only a few feet away."

Then I heard scrambling—a lot of scrambling. Too much in fact, but the crackling flames and other popping noises made it difficult to pinpoint where the sounds were coming from.

All of a sudden one of the young men ripped his mask off, stood upright and yelled, "God help me! God, please help me!" But he abruptly put his mask back on, and seconds later I heard him get down and crawl toward the rear door as his regulator went *aw purr, aw purr, aw purr....*

Then Pat stood as if to make a run for it, until he dropped back down.

Micro-secs later I heard sounds of frantic cries and people crawling. Another volunteer crouched next to me. I held my arm toward the door; told him to grab it. He did; he escaped.

The noises stopped. I called out. "Anyone else in here?" Nothing. Because I'd been the nozzle man, by tradition that made this fire my fire, and I wasn't about to leave until the others reached safety. I called out again. No reply. Nobody else but me. Time to hit the bug-out trail.

I made a hasty retreat on hands and knees and literally fell into Lieutenant Gibson's arms. He had been perched at the rear door, waiting. I whipped my helmet off. Flames had melted the top part, and white smoke was still rising from its leather shield. I ripped my mask off next, and asked, "How many got through the door?"

"You," he said. "And one other."

"One? Only *one*?"

"That's it." He narrowed his eyes. "Why?"

"There were a bunch of us in there. Five, maybe. I—"

Then Pat started screaming, again and again and again, "Get me out of here! Get me out get me out get me out!"

He was still inside, and flames were burning him alive.

We still had no water; it didn't matter. I turned to Gibson. "I'm going back in. Follow me!" I put mask and helmet back on, then blasted back through that door.

Gibson charged in behind me. We made it to the kitchen. But Pat had already stumbled into the dining room. I found the attack line. It was still limp. Without water it was physically impossible to fight through the flames to reach Pat. I told Gibson, "We can't get him from here. Let's back out, and go in through the front door."

He and I went out and were racing around the rear corner when Pat abruptly popped halfway out of a window above us. But his breathing apparatus was wedged under the sill, leaving him hanging while flames blasted past him like a blowtorch.

As Pat screamed in agony, Gibson stooped down behind another firefighter and wrapped both hands around his ankles and lifted him straight up.

It worked. The firefighter braved the flames to grab Pat and yank him out. They tumbled onto the snow-covered ground. Two paramedics appeared. We stripped Pat's gear off—and we exchanged glances. Nobody had to say it. Everyone knew he would never survive these burns. Pat knew it too, and what he did and said next will remain with me forever, because he literally laughed in the face of Death as he wisecracked with, "Helluva way to lose weight."

Then he lapsed into unconsciousness while we loaded him into the ambulance. Halfway to the hospital though, he roused himself enough to ask the attending paramedic to join him in reciting the "Lord's Prayer."

That's courage—coupled with a spirituality that eludes so many people.

Unfortunately, one other thing also eluded everyone there. Still unknown to any of us, a sixteen-year old volunteer firefighter was still inside that house. In fact, he'd been lying semi-conscious just eighteen inches from Gibson and me when we were discussing how to reach Pat. Eighteen inches, man. But it might as well have been eighteen miles, because the thick smoke concealed him as surely as a Romulan cloaking device.

THE FIRE STILL raged out of control, so once the ambulance whisked Pat away, we got busy. Gibson requested a second alarm, and then a third. Six additional engines and a second ladder truck responded to the scene. What we really needed was water, though. However, the pump operators were hard pressed to restore it.

The flames that now roared out of the lower and upper story windows were so intense that we faced a real possibility of losing the entire block. When we finally got water several minutes later, three of us grabbed a hose and raced into the adjoining row house. Half an hour later we were still trying to stop the fire from spreading, when Firefighter Mike Schultheis appeared.

He had arrived on one of the second alarm units, and he was ashen-faced. Stepping next to me, he said in a hauntingly quiet voice, "They found a kid from Engine 34. Inside the house. Dead."

I all but felt my eyes bugging out. "*Whaaaaat?*"

"Yeah. Some of us were at the back door. We heard a bell go off."

He didn't have to elaborate. I knew what he meant. The air masks are equipped with a small bell that rings steadily when there are only five minutes of air left in the tank.

Mike pressed his lips tight and slowly shook his head. "We traced the bell to the dining room. Found him. Just a boy. Dead."

My shoulders slumped. I hung my head. It had been my duty to make sure—to be fucking sure—that everybody was out before I left that kitchen. Bad enough that Pat hadn't made it out. At least he was paid to do this job.

I mumbled, "We left him there. Alone—" I choked up when I wondered if he'd felt all alone when he died. Had he been conscious long enough to ask, "Why did they abandon me?"

In the case of Matthew, I had wanted to make sure his soul wasn't alone. Was this firefighter's soul left alone? All at once the poet Bécquer's phrase all but shouted at me: *¡Dios mío, que solos se quedan los muertos!* (Oh God, how alone the dead are left!)

PAT HELD ON until the following day. He had faced down Death by joking about his weight, and then he let go. But he showed all of us how to die, and he remains a hero.

I felt sick at heart after I got the news, and I stumbled through the rest of the day. That night I crawled into bed and had fallen into a deep REM state when a dream began nagging at me. In the dream, Pat's mom was calling to ask if she should see her son's body.

Ringggg...

I jerked awake. It was the phone. I checked the bedside clock. 3:00 a.m. I picked up the receiver and said, "Mrs. Bauer."

She gasped. "How did you know it was...?" After clearing her throat, she laid it out there. "I want to see Pat. Everybody's telling me not to. What do you think?"

"No. Do not look at him." I knew from experience how he looked by now—black, and so bloated by internal fluids that he would be unrecognizable even to his mother. I spoke a bit more, and then said, "Mrs. Bauer? Just remember him as he looked the last time you saw him."

She took my advice. Years later she told me that she'd done the research and realized how bad Pat looked in death, and how grateful she felt toward those of us who told her the same thing: remember him as he was.

GEORGE F. DRIGGERS, Jr. is the name of the young man we left behind. I didn't know him, but learned later that his family called him "Georgie," that his younger sister Theresa idolized him, and that everyone knew his infectious smile. He was sixteen, and as much in love with firefighting as I had been at the same age.

The fire investigators went into action. They found that stones and pebbles had clogged the fire engine's water intake. They theorized that someone—possibly children—had shoved those rocks into the hydrant we were using. But that wasn't the real culprit. In fact, we lost water long before the rocks travelled out of the hydrant and through 500 feet of hose to clog the pump, because unknown to any of us, we were still using water from the engine's tank. Worse still, two firefighters yanked additional attack lines from the engine without telling the pump operator. It happens. Call it, the "fog of battle."

Unfortunately, the engine only carried 300 gallons of water. Each of the three hose lines were flowing a hundred gallons of water per minute. The math is simple—we ran the tank dry and the damage was done before anyone opened that hydrant.

Investigators also determined that a faulty furnace gas line sparked the fire. Ironically, had we not lost water we might have gotten all the way into that basement. Then things might have been even worse, because if a tiny spark had reignited the gas, then the resulting flashover would have left six dead firefighters in its wake, instead of two.

I also learned that only one volunteer made it through that rear door. Georgie and a third young man apparently missed that portal to safety—totally understandable, since the zero vis conditions meant that even minute directional changes would lead to absolute disorientation. Combine this with the stress of a life-or-death struggle, and it was a recipe for tragedy. This is probably when Georgie— and we determined that it was Georgie—ripped his mask off and screamed for God's help. Then while scrambling to reorient themselves, he and the other volunteer ended up in the dining room.

One of them found a window through which he struggled to safety. But Georgie never found it.

As for Pat? In gaming what took place—and gaming sounds heartless, but the only way to prevent another tragedy is to examine it from all sides—many of us feel that he inadvertently veered from the path to that door-left-open just enough to also become disoriented. In that case he probably reverted to training and tried to follow the hose line out, because it will definitely lead you outside. Unfortunately, intense flames enveloped him before he could escape.

In Georgie's case, we now know that he ended up in a twilight zone. When his alarm bell began ringing, firefighters traced the sound to the dining room. Someone got a flashlight and swept its beam throughout the room, stopping after finding a lump that didn't compute.

However, the fire had weakened the floorboards so much that it made entry hazardous. So Jack Reckner, a highly respected old-breed firefighter, grabbed a fourteen-foot ladder and slid it through the dining room window. After guiding it to the lump—and after realizing that he'd located the source of the alarm bell—he and two others used the ladder to support their weight while they crawled inside.

They found a body; Georgie's body. The floor had partially given way beneath him, and the dining room table had collapsed on top of him. The young man was on his right side and at an angle to the kitchen entrance. More notably, he wasn't in a fetal position, which suggests that he didn't just give in and curl up to die. Jack and the others paused, and then went about recovering the body.

According to Jack, "His helmet was next to him. I can only conclude that the shifting floorboards coaxed it from his head. The mask was still on and appeared undamaged, and yet his turnout coat disintegrated to the touch. He wasn't burned up but he was, well, dark. Funny thing, though…he still had a full head of hair. He had long hair, too. But it wasn't even singed." Then this hardcore firefighter grew very quiet. His mouth opened and closed several times before he spoke again, this time in a low tone. "One more thing. I found something. I'd forgotten about it until now, while describing the scene." Jack paused. "The kid had a pocket Bible in his hand. He was clutching it to his heart."

On hearing this, the hairs on the back of my neck stood on end. Then I heaved a great sigh and said, "I guess he didn't die all alone after all."

"What do you mean?" Jack asked.

"Georgie realized he was *in extremis*. Trapped and alone, he didn't go fetal; he didn't give up without a fight. However, he dug into his sense of spirituality. He pulled that Bible from his pocket. He clutched it for comfort." I paused. "Don't you see, Jack? Georgie hadn't been abandoned after all. His soul was never alone. God was at his side the entire time."

SO WHAT DID happen to Georgie? He made a mistake. He ripped off his air mask for a few seconds, and in doing so he inhaled soot and smoke. While he did put the mask back on, he was already doomed, and also unable to speak due to the soot-irritated bronchi. Even so, he did his best to get out. But he hit a dead-end, and he was almost certainly still conscious when Gibson and I went back inside to rescue Pat. Georgie probably even heard us speaking. Only, he couldn't call out because he was already on a downward spiral. In short, he was done for.

What follows is conjecture, but it appears that upon realizing that he couldn't save his mortal body, the sixteen-year old volunteer reached for a pocket Bible that he got at a church camp the summer before, and this boy—this young man—clutched that Bible to his heart both for comfort, and to save his soul.

THE MEDICAL EXAMINER determined that smoke and soot inhalation killed Georgie. Soot filled his throat, trachea, large bronchi—even his ears. On the other hand, the heat hadn't seared his lungs, and they weren't filled with fluid. Although his body was saturated with twenty-four percent carbon monoxide—enough to render someone unconscious—it wasn't enough to cause death in a healthy young man.

The findings in any event were academic; no surprises there. But it's what I learned later that struck me to the core. Because in what I can only regard as a fluke of destiny, the person who taught the church camp that Georgie attended just a few months before his death—the man who gave him that Bible—was none other than Lieutenant Gibson.

Georgie's brother and sister confirmed this, adding that their brother had fully embraced his lessons. When I carefully told them that one of the volunteers in that burning kitchen beseeched me with, "Hey, man. What do we do, man? What do we do?" they both said yes, Georgie used that very phrase many times. So there it is. It turns out that he and I met after all—if only fleetingly—and I will carry a tenuous but no less intense connection with him for the rest of my life.

In the end, Georgie proved that there can be dignity in death. All firefighters, whether career or volunteer, understand that their calling is a deadly serious business, one in which people suffer cruel injuries and brutal deaths. Firefighting is also a tough, snotty and dirty job, unlike saccharine TV shows with fresh-faced, clear-eyed twenty-somethings strolling out of burning structures to prance and preen while cameras zoom in on the greasepaint that's been smeared across their rosy cheeks.

Georgie knew the dangers as we all did, and he accepted them. He was a brave lad who rushed into a burning house to render a service to his community. What transcends the academic though, are the links to spirituality that we try to embrace, and for me a sense of spirituality boils down to the relationship we have with ourselves, with others and with the universe. And so in the final analysis Georgie was never alone when he died. Not really. Because although none of us knew that he'd been left behind, we were still nearby; we were the community of firefighters that had drawn him into our ranks, and that bond is eternal.

And of course he had his Bible and his God alongside him.

JACK RECKNER'S DISCOVERY of that Bible in Georgie's hand went a long way toward healing his family's wounds. After more than four decades they now have closure, and they see Jack as a hero for making the connection between the boy, the Bible, and balance.

Earlier, I mentioned Pat's heroic acceptance of death. But I think Georgie is the greater hero. After all, he had plunged headlong into a nasty fire situation. He did it while alone. We can question *ad nauseum* whether he should have gone in, but it took balls to do what he did, and I'll always see him as a very brave young man.

In an ironic twist, the sole volunteer that I did succeed in pushing to safety turned out to be none other than Frankie Pleyo, the same lad who Tim Doegen pushed to safety during that training exercise years ago—the very exercise in which Tim suffered a blistered butt. Now here was Frankie after all, trapped in a similar situation but possibly saved by the lessons he learned from Tim. And in a post-script, Frankie recently told me that he often drives by the street where that fatal fire took place, and each time he does, he says a silent prayer for his friend Georgie.

The tragedy resulted in change. The county fire department re-viewed its procedures and called for new tactics. The hard-charging interior attacks we once took pride in making became a thing of the past. The chiefs also revised the command and control system, and hired battalion chiefs to provide guidance at major fires. Finally, the county enhanced the volunteer firefighter training programs, and formulated rules to limit what personnel did on fire grounds based upon their levels of training and experience. These were hard lessons, but we learned them.

CHAPTER EIGHT

Siren Song

TWO YEARS PASSED. My fire helmet still bore scorches from the flames that killed Pat and Georgie, and on a cold winter night I jammed it on for the last time after the radio blared an alarm for a building fire. Pressing my lips tight as the reality kicked-in that this was it, I climbed inside Truck 33's cab, stepped on the clutch, flipped the battery selector switch to "B," pressed both starter buttons simultaneously, and smiled as the 6-71 Detroit Diesel roared to life. The instant the tillerman signaled his readiness, I eased up on the clutch. Then while rapidly going through the Spicer transmission's gears (and double-clutching all the way), I roared down Crain Highway and made the air horn sing while Kenny pressed his foot against the siren switch to make the Federal "Q" growl. When another unit arrived and saw that we weren't needed, I killed the emergency lights, slowed down, and set course for the station. It was indeed my last time at the ladder truck's helm.

Ah, but in the two years leading up to that final call, picture DiCaprio and Winslet in *Titanic*, because it's how I felt. Yep, I was king of the world.

* * * *

Prior to ascending to the throne, my salary had jumped from eight grand a year to sixteen, and I'd never known such happiness; so much pleasure and satisfaction. I experienced a high that transcended anything I'd been told could be achieved through drugs. I lived, ate and breathed my assignment as a "truck man" on the county's busiest ladder truck. I felt, *Yes, this is what I was meant to do; this is where I belonged. No beer would ever taste so cold; no woman could be so alluring, and no—I will never feel alone again.*

After eight years beginning as a volunteer before moving into career status, I'd proved myself as a firefighter. Unfortunately, I also earned a reputation as a hothead of the dumbest kind—the type who thinks he knows better than the chiefs. They in turn gave me a cold shoulder. Can't say as I blamed them, either. However, the powers that be did honor my transfer request to Truck 33 and it was the best of all worlds: better pay, along with tremendous job pride. The truck required two drivers, so one shift would see me at the truck's helm while the other engineman operated the rear tiller wheels. The next shift, we simply switched roles.

John Riggin was the shift lieutenant. John was a Vietnam combat vet, a Marine's marine who rode the officer's position whenever the ladder truck responded to special calls. Otherwise, Engineman Kenny Bohn rode up front. He and I were close in age, had gone through the academy together, and he was a likeable, happy-go-lucky sort whom everyone admired. Kenny also filled in as a driver whenever I took a day's leave.

Although steering the trailer's rear wheels had its fun side, in truth I preferred the helm because I loved the mechanics of driving—the hands-on challenge of shifting and using the Diesel power plant to its greatest potential. There were also the air horns. Enginemen operate them like the San Francisco streetcar motormen that ring the streetcar's bell to their individual rhythm. In our case, we had air horns, and every driver tapped them out to beats of different drummers. Firefighters can even tell who is driving a particular piece of apparatus by the air horn melody, even when it's a mile away.

For me, my beat became an anthem; a choreography of clutch and stick-shift and horn that sent cars springing from my path. It became one of many wild demonstrations of myself, of myself in a job I loved; it was my *joie de vivre*.

To this day, I cannot count how many times I arrived at an emergency call only to hear a firefighter say, "Knew that had to be you!" It was more than a compliment—it was a degree of respect—an affirmation that I'd arrived, albeit on a small scale when compared to the world stage—but it was those small things that made me love the job so much more, especially when coming from stellar colleagues such as Mike Marsiglia, or "Crazy Dave" Hayes.

Oh, the humanity!

Yep, the horns were my anthem and my choreography combined, and they helped me find some inner peace. The hothead in me finally matured, and whenever I saw an opportunity to do a mea culpa, I approached each chief to admit my errors, while offering reassurance that my transgressions were things of the past. All but one chief nodded and essentially said, "Don't sweat it. Everyone steps on their dicks when they're young."

ENGINEMEN DROVE WITH windows wide open back then, with radio speakers amped-up and the roar of wind and sirens and air horns ringing in our ears. We also got to drive fast and blow past red lights. It's no surprise that most of us now suffer varying degrees of hearing loss. Long before the advent of GPS and Google Maps, enginemen also had to know their first and second due areas inside in and inside out—along with the location of every fire hydrant.

Altruism motivated us to varying degrees—we truly wanted to save lives and test our abilities for the sake of a fulfilling warm & fuzzy. The reality however was that it was an exciting job. Besides, this exhilaration is all any of us got out of the job, because the people we pulled from burning houses, or cut out of wrecked cars almost never—and I mean never, ever—stopped by to say, "Thank you for saving my life."

More on that below, and later.

ON A FRIGID SATURDAY in 1977, I was shooting the breeze with Scott Collins and two others when the hotline's shrill ring shattered the station's peace. But hotlines only rang for ambulance calls, so we ignored it until Lieutenant Dave Bond charged out of the alarm room.

"Rick," he shouted. "Mount up. We have a rescue."

Just then the dispatch speakers blurted the details: *"Rescue box. Engine 28 and Truck 33 respond to the Naval Academy Dairy Farm for a paratrooper in a tree—"*

I climbed into the cab and hit the starter button. Dave plopped onto the officer's seat while Scott and two others claimed the jump seats. Kenny took the tiller, and I stepped on the accelerator.

Dave explained as we got going that an army airborne unit making jumps into the Naval Academy dairy farm misjudged the winds. A tree had snagged a paratrooper in its branches. Dave added, "Headquarters said he's about to fall. Told us to hurry. That's why they used the hotline."

I nodded and turned south on Crain Highway to begin the ten mile long run on roads newly cleared of snow. I was picking up speed when the dispatcher called and uttered a single word: *"Expedite."*

Minutes later we were free of traffic and the road ahead was straight and true. I was pushing eighty when a beat-up white Cadillac pulled out of a side road directly in front of me. And then it stopped.

So many things flashed across my mind. We were in open country. We had lights, siren and air horn going. How could he not see us? Maybe he *had* seen us. Who knew? What really mattered was that I was bearing down on him, and that the laws of physics were clear: we were not able to stop.

Dave braced for impact.

There was a snow bank alongside the road. Thinking it would be better to hit the snow instead of the Caddy, I shouted "Screw it," and spun the wheel to the right.

So much speed; such a spinning of the wheel. The entire right side of the ladder truck lifted up. It wallowed, then settled back on all wheels. The snow bank was just ahead. Except for one thing—a kid was standing on it.

"Holy fuck!" I whirled the wheel hard left. This time the left side lifted. I was acting on autopilot now as I adjusted the wheel to keep from rolling.

The truck settled back. I straightened the wheel. Dave shouted, "Good job!" Then Kenny's voice came over the tiller position's hands-free intercom: *"Wahoo!"*

I wanted to strangle him. Instead, I stomped down on the accelerator and sped back up to eighty while my legs shook from the immense adrenalin dump.

We arrived, as they say in the cavalry movies, in the nick of time. The paratrooper was up a tree all right, and swinging from his lines like a rockabye baby—except this lullaby bough was about to break.

The air brakes huffed as I stopped and leaped outside. While I put the jacks down and raised the ladder, Kenny got ready to climb it and rescue the dangling paratrooper—one who, like a dangling participle, had nothing left to modify his life with.

I extended the ladder to ninety feet in record time, and I'd just touched its top rung to the bottoms of the soldier's boots when the branch gave way. He tumbled directly onto the ladder, and you can bet that he grabbed it with a death grip.

Hollywood could not have done it any better.

Kenny ran up the ladder and helped him climb down. But when the wayward paratrooper touched *terra firma*, he walked off without uttering a single word to any of us—not even a "go to hell" for risking our necks.

It happened that way sometimes. Good thing we weren't being altruistic.

SO IT STANDS to reason that a few months later when a major on the Maryland State Police interview board asked, "Mr. Anderson, why do you want to become a trooper?" I hedged my bet.

The board members had already asked me all the other questions—the ones about knowledge, skills and experience—and so far everything looked good. How I answered this question could be a deciding factor. The choices were to dissemble by giving a lame, "Because I wanna help people." Or, I could speak honestly. I chose the latter. "Why do I want to be a trooper? Because it's an exciting job."

The words were no sooner out of my mouth when the board members sat back in their seats with astonishment writ large across their faces. They looked at each other, then at me, and then the interview ended. I walked out of the room thinking, *I sure blew **that** answer!*

CHAPTER NINE

The Man in Tan

S OMETHING WASN'T RIGHT. The Maryland State Police had placed me at the top of the list of the applicants they wanted to hire, and that list was by no means alphabetical. A month later they offered me a place in the 79th Trooper Candidate Class, which was scheduled to begin in January of 1979. Although accepting the position would result in a fifty percent pay cut, I didn't care. They had hired me. That was reward enough.

The firefighters gave me a great sendoff, beginning with a special dinner that segued into a pie fight. I wouldn't have had it any other way. While cleaning up afterward though, it began to hit home: Jimmy Carter was still in the White House, our nation had double-digit inflation and unemployment, and I was about to leave a rewarding career position for the great unknown.

As if reading my mind, Lieutenant Steve Preslipsky pulled me aside. "Rick, you've got guts for venturing out into the cold cruel world. I gotta hand it to you, man. I'd never do it."

I thanked him while quickly pointing out, "Don't forget, I'm single. I don't have a wife and kids to worry about." Still, his gracious comment meant a lot to me, and I was now on fire to move forward in a world that didn't stand still for inflation or unemployment, but instead turned with the seasons and obeyed the concordance of tides. Viewed from this perspective, my soul saw a new light and a new future. But as so often happens, we conveniently overlook those other rooms in our souls, and as I emptied my locker and walked out of the station for the last time, I turned and looked back.

Never look back, they say.

If only I hadn't; if only I hadn't still been so in love with firefighting. How else to explain what happened next?

I'D ENTERED HELL. I can't explain it any other way. The instant I stepped foot inside the police academy, I felt that my soul had been lost, condemned to genuflect to the Devil's wishes, and the devil in this case was a sergeant who ruled over the academy as if it were his private fiefdom.

The fact that we had to live here full time for the next six months wasn't all that bad. Nor was it the harsh Marine boot-camp atmosphere that drove me to despair, or the daily white-glove inspections or even the "Midnight Olympics" sessions. That's when instructors barged into our monastic-like rooms at zero dark thirty to shock us out of a deep sleep, and shouted at us to strip the sheets from our waterproof mattresses and heft them to the communal showers, where the sergeant had turned every showerhead to its hottest setting. Once inside the shower room, we did military presses with steam-slick mattress while the instructors suppressed yawns until the sergeant finally yelled, "Now get dressed and assemble outside!"

After double-timing it to the parking lot, they marched us back and forth in the frigid night air, again and again at this citadel to law enforcement; this sterling palace of the "best gol-durned police agency in the Yew-nited States of 'Murica," the marching usually lasting at least an hour—or until the instructors grew bored.

No, none of these things were responsible for my fall from grace six weeks later. Rather, grief in all its manifestations took credit for being the responsible party. But as the commanding officer of that responsible party, I—and only I—should be held accountable for any subsequent actions. And they were not actions that I am proud of, although in confessing my sins it's only fair to point out that broken hearts can only exist inside those who have been blessed with souls; souls that still harkened for the music I made with air horns, while heralding a zest for a life as I once knew it...but could not yet put behind me.

The truly funny thing about all of it is that I was doing quite well. My academics were excellent, the tough and very demanding physical training didn't faze me, and I held my own against much larger sparring partners in the boxing ring—a venue in which the instructor made it clear that it was you or him, 'cause there just ain't no gentlemen's agreements in that ring. Either you put your opponent down, or the instructor put *you* down.

However, my heart ached and I asked for a counseling session with the Academy's lieutenant. He had a psych degree, he had been on my interview board, and was sympathetic to my plight. The lieutenant readily pointed out the obvious—that I was in mourning for a job that had seen neither a memorial service nor a burial ceremony.

"You're not the first trainee this has happened to, either." So he offered a bit of breathing space. "Anderson," he began, "you're an excellent trooper candidate. You were only one of two applicants with enough guts to tell us why you really wanted the job—not to 'help people,' even if that is laudable. But come on. Let's be real. We're all here for the excitement, we found your candor refreshing, and it meant a lot to us." Then he put an offer on the table: I could accept entry into the "setback program" and leave the Academy in good graces, with an open door to return with the next trooper candidate class.

He added a caveat: "Nobody knows when or if there'll be another class, because the Agency can never predict future budgets. Anyway, there it is and I can't tell you what to do. Only you can make the decision." He paused. "Look, you're locked in grief. Personally, I respect men like you who hold true to themselves. A period of mourning might be just the thing."

THE NEXT DAYS were a blur. After turning in my student uniforms and packing my bags, I drove home to an empty apartment and an equally empty life. I wasn't dating anyone at the time who could provide solace, and too many friends turned deaf ears to my explanation for leaving the academy, reasoning that I overextended my reach and should have stayed in the fire department. As for my parents, they just didn't understand—especially my father, who unknown to me had already taken to bragging about his son, "the future state trooper."

I was on my own.

* * * *

I finished packing for the trip, hung a camera from my shoulder, and carried everything to the '74 Gran Torino. Next, I made the short drive to Keith Hammack's house. After he tossed his bags into the trunk and plopped onto the passenger seat, we began the drive toward a distant sunset—in this case, we headed in the general direction of California.

We initially planned the trip as a sightseeing excursion. For me though, it would be an adventure. Going west had always been a dream, and my current state of unemployment made it logical to do the journey now, while time permitted. Keith was a friend and a highly respected firefighter who once told me that he also wanted to see the Wild West. So after I pitched the idea of a road trip to California and back, he said, "Sure. Let's do it. Anywhere is good, so long as we stop in San Fran to see some friends, and hit Iowa to see my folks."

The trip turned out to be the tonic I had hoped it would be. Although I'd lived in Europe as a child, had visited Texas and travelled up and down the east coast, I was now pushing the boundaries of new frontiers and loving every moment. We crossed the Mississippi River into Arkansas, crossed the Great Plains, and arrived at the Grand Canyon. With neither clock nor agenda to guide or contain our travels, we discovered that what others said is true—you really must see the Canyon in person, "'Cause photos just ain't gonna do it justice."

I was living for the moment, returning to happier days by shucking shirt and shoes and growing a beard. As the trip progressed, we stopped in isolated New Mexico towns for food and fuel. Keith and I took time to stare at the Salton Sea, and we discovered that San Diego really *is* Munchkin Land—meaning that it truly lived up to L. Frank Baum's description of that fabled land, when he penned *The Wizard of Oz* from his home deep within San Diego's embrace.

Later still, I saw that San Francisco's streetcar motormen did ring their bells in rhythms not unlike those I once played on the air horns. It was a time of decompression along with equal measures of discovery, and after returning from the month-long journey, I was ready to get back in the game.

* * * *

Six months later saw me perched atop an exam table at a walk-in clinic in Ocean City, Maryland. The doctor had barely given the Novocain time to kick-in when he leaned forward with a cigarette still dangling from his lower lip to suture the laceration on my forehead. Yeah, good old country doc. "Hold still," he said, his nicotine-stained fingers gripping a "needle pusher" as he initiated the first of four sutures.

Thirty minutes earlier I had been horsing around with friends at a water slide, when I shot out of the slide with so much speed that I skipped across the catch basin like a pebble and hit the concrete wall at the other end. I was bleeding, dizzy and laughing when my friends brought me to the walk-in for a quickie suture session.

It had to be a quickie because I had to be at the Ocean City Police Department in one hour for a job interview. After finding myself in need of a job, I applied for a police officer slot with this large department of some 150 personnel. I reasoned that this was a beach town and I was a water rat, so why not?

Minutes after leaving the clinic, I was straightening my tie and buttoning my jacket while my swollen, inflamed forehead shone like a red beacon light. However, to my surprise the board members were impressed that I showed up at all. From their perspective, my beaming noggin implied that I wasn't someone who calls in sick at the slightest sneeze. They also pointed to my high written and agility test scores. The prospect for employment looked good. Even so, I made it clear that I still wanted to be a state trooper. Ocean City hired me anyway.

One month later I was working a deep-cover assignment, since being a fresh face in town more or less qualified me for this instant promotion of sorts. It was a new experience, but not to my liking because it meant living a double life and hanging around with lowlifes. I also had to meet a plainclothes sergeant on lonely back roads to get my paycheck, and to ask any questions before he hurried away.

The investigation centered on a local doper with a penchant for snorting white powder up his nose, before sliding his schlong into whatever guy he had in his bed. It made no difference to me what he put *where*, so long as he cooperated by breaking loose with some names for further investigation. In the end, he probably ended up getting it in the end, after a judge sentenced him to hard time at one of Maryland's more notorious prisons.

* * * *

Once I went into uniform and started patrol activities, I began to enjoy the heck out of the job. I even decided that I would gladly make working for Ocean City a career if the state didn't rehire me. So I forged friendships with other officers, especially with Joe Rolles, who also loved travel and yearned to fly. He had recently bought a condo though, and didn't have any spare cash for flying lessons.

But I had the cash. So after publicly announcing my plans, I drove thirty miles to a medium-sized airport and signed on the line. Before the ink dried, I met the man who would be my instructor. John Lloyd was tall, gaunt and gray, and had learned to fly in 1917 during

World War One. Following the war, he flew airmail in the days when pilots had to peer out of open cockpits in freezing weather to find the landmarks that would guide them along the way.

John chatted with me for a bit, and then walked me around the two-seat Cessna-152 that we would be using. It was red, white, and brand spanking new, and while I ran a respectful hand along its wings, John held up a checklist.

"Pilots have a motto," he began. "In God we trust. Everything else we check." He narrowed his eyes. "Is that understood?"

I smiled. "Understood."

He wagged his eyebrows in response, and walked me through the list. We did a complete pre-flight check that included taking fuel samples from both tanks and the engine to ensure proper quality and octane. I liked that degree of attention to detail. But when we finally climbed inside the tiny cockpit, he pursed his lips and pointed at my feet. "Take off your shoes."

Having learned long ago that sometimes it's better not to ask questions, I removed them and had one sock halfway off when he shook his head.

"Leave the socks on, put the shoes there." He pointed a long bony finger at a tiny storage space behind the seats. "From now on you'll remove your shoes every time you fly." When I nodded without questioning this instruction, he smiled. "Good. You're a listener, not a talker. Now here's the thing. Aircraft *do* talk. The way to listen is by feeling their vibrations. You'll feel 'em from the control wheel, and through the rudder pedals."

Next, he showed me how to hold the control wheel. "Grip it with respect but hold it lightly, like a man holds his...well, you know. Yep, you're gonna learn to listen to her; to feel what she's telling ya. Learn to do that," he said while holding a forefinger aloft, "and you'll become a true 'stick and rudder' aviator...the type who flies instinctively." He peered at me. "It'll also make you a safe pilot, and eventually an old pilot."

Grinning from ear to ear, he repeated a celebrated phrase, "There are old pilots and there are bold pilots. But there are no old bold pilots." John paused. "You're not driving a fire truck to a fire. You're flying a machine through an airspace that can turn on you in a heartbeat. Aircraft also have motors that'll quit on you even faster. Always remember that."

Once he finished his briefing, we used the checklist to start the engine, check the gauges, and set the flight instruments. Then he let me taxi to the end of the runway, where we broke out the checklist again for the pre-flight run-up.

We finally took off, and John had me take the controls until we reached a practice area. Then he took over and demonstrated stalls, steep banks, and pitch and attitude changes. After "giving me the aircraft" again, he had me alter power settings while he also scolded. "Scan the gauges, but don't stare at 'em. Listen to the engine and airflow, instead. Remember to also look out the goddamn window, or you won't see the other planes that are out there at all times."

A few minutes later I was flying straight and level at 3,000 feet, wiggling my toes against the rudder pedals and feeling the vibes through my butt and smiling like a beer-chugging chimpanzee, when John abruptly reached over and pulled the throttle back. The engine died to an idle. The nose pitched down at once—and I mean, it pitched down. As we plunged toward Earth, I whipped my head around and said, "What the fu—"

"Where're you gonna land?" he asked in a low, measured voice.

"Huh?" The roar of rushing wind filled my ears. Sweat burst from my forehead; my pits felt slimy, and they instantly put up a god-awful stench.

John pressed his lips tight and calmly restored the power. After bringing us straight and level again, he said almost as an aside, "Back when I learned to fly, it wasn't a question of if, but when and how often your engine was gonna quit on you. That's another reason to always look outside—so you can constantly look for places to land. What you do when that motor conks has to be instinctive." He pointed to my shoeless feet and looked me in the eye. "Do we understand one another?"

I assured him that I did. However, it took two more flying lessons before I really kept an eye on what was outside and on the downside.

But what he said that first day would save my life six years later when an engine did quit on me, just like that.

* * * *

In the lessons that followed, John drilled me on the basics. "If you're forced into landing in a field, you can determine wind direction by observing grazing cattle, 'cause cows always stand with their backsides to the wind. That way they can see a predator approaching from the front, an' smell the ones that're sneaking up from behind."

John also made me practice touch-and-go landings, crosswind landings, and emergency landings. Sure enough, once I stopped worrying about things, I went from "white knuckles to cockpit cool," putting that Cessna down so gently that only the whirring tires revealed that we were already on the ground.

Then one day we were only halfway through the hour-long lesson when he told me to land. I thought, *Uh oh, what'd I do now?* But I didn't question him, and after landing, I taxied to the hangar and had a hand on the throttle to shut the engine down when he wrapped restraining fingers around it.

"Keep it running. And gimme your log book." He sniffed. "Takes most people nine lessons. You've had six. However—"

I handed over the log and watched him scribble something on a back page, before closing it and wordlessly handing it back.

Next, he undid his seatbelt, got out, and pointed up. "Why don't you take her out awhile? Spend some time in the practice area. When ya come back, do three touch-and-goes." Without even waiting for a response, he turned and walked away.

"Holy hell," I whispered.

Then I did as ordered. Damn, talk about being jazzed! Me, flying solo! However, I did bear in mind that flying is serious business, and after practicing my skills I keyed the mic and announced my intention to do three touch-and-go landings.

I made the final landing and taxied to the hangar. After I secured the aircraft and walked inside, John and the office personnel greeted me with a small white cake decorated with a red bi-plane and words written in blue sugar: First Solo!

Talk about walking on air. But a few days later a new development forced me to put the plane plans into a prolonged holding pattern.

THE CLASSROOM HADN'T changed at all since the first time I saw it. Now here I was at the state police academy again, exactly a year since I left and now a member of the 80th Trooper Candidate Class. This time, with all vestiges of grief finally and fully entombed, I got on with life and thrived.

There was this one thing, though. Everyone from instructors to fellow students made remarks about my size. I encountered this on the first go-around, too. Okay, I get it. At five foot seven and one-twenty, I'm a small man. Scrawny, even.

But my size never mattered during eight years of firefighting. I never even saw myself as being small. From my perspective, the fire department simply hired many others who were very big. Nor did size ever stop me from running up ladders to drape people across my shoulders and carry them to safety, nor was it an issue when battling flames.

However, it did matter in law enforcement—although the others regarded me with a new and different respect about a week into the class. One night while four fellow students and I were using the men's communal shower, six uniformed guys barged inside carrying a fully-clothed female classmate. My buddies bolted, but I shrugged and continued showering while the guys tossed her in. The water left her drenched but it didn't affect her eyesight, because she was pointedly staring—and smiling—at me while I calmly rinsed the soap from my bod.

Not that I'm an exhibitionist, mind you. Simply put, I was on my turf and not about to cut and run. Besides, I'd never seen anything shameful about being seen naked—no matter what my size. She flashed a final smile while I flashed one of my own. Then as the others cheered, they parted ranks and let her leave.

The next morning, everyone in the mess hall gave me a standing-O when I walked in, and this signaled an end to any issues concerning my size.

While on the topic of the mess hall, everyone always ate their breakfasts hurriedly so they could hustle back to their rooms and prepare for morning inspection. The inspections were all-inclusive, and the instructors would gig us for the slightest offense. A piece of loose thread peeking from a button? One demerit. Coat hangers in the closet not uniformly spaced? Two demerits. Instructors having a bad day? Figure on at least another demerit. Earn ten demerits within a week? Plan on spending the weekend at the academy while doing hard labor to purge your record of the week's offenses.

Each morning I got ready by donning shoes polished to a mirror-like glaze, and stepping up to a large mirror in the hallway for a self-inspection. One morning while I stood in front of the looking glass, a fellow student stepped up next to me to conduct his own self-exam. It was then, while I compared his height and build to mine, that it hit me: *Damn. I guess I am kinda sorta on the really small side. Huh, who'd have thought?*

Actually, I didn't need to give it much thought, because I'd always known a reality that many others apparently didn't. In short (pun intended) we've all seen grown men—big men—run from tiny yellow jackets or angry Chihuahuas. Why do they run? It's not the minuscule sting or the nipping at ankles that shoots fear through even very big men. It's the creatures' lack of fear that sends them running. It's why I always counted on showing a lack of personal fear to induce fear in others while enduring the ritualistic boyhood schoolyard fistfights. I became a yellow jacket and went wildcat whenever someone wanted to take me on. Now, I'd be going wildcat while wearing the uniform of a Maryland State Trooper, a trooper who also began to excel at judo.

Judo and boxing were major components in our physical training, and the instructor expected us to drive each other into the mats. Being nimble and quick on my feet, I took down colossal opponents with remarkable ease while the instructor offered approving nods— and that's always a good thing.

SIX MONTHS LATER I walked onto a stage in front of officials and families alike to shake the Superintendent's hand while he handed me a badge inscribed *Trooper - Maryland State Police*. Before I could step away, he handed me a coveted Superintendent's Commendation for completing the nation's finest academy at the head of my class. "But wait," he said. "There's more." The aviation division had also awarded me with an engraved plaque for my scholastic standing, and these honors would open other doors later on.

My parents and grandparents were there to applaud me, along with two brothers, an aunt and an uncle, and a handful of friends. Kenny Bohn and his wife were there, and Kenny took a photo while my father ceremoniously pinned the badge to my uniform. I now felt vindicated for my earlier double clutching, and when I walked out of the Academy this time, I walked out as a Man in Tan.

CHAPTER TEN

Working the Road

I WALKED THROUGH the door of the state police facility in Prince Frederick, Maryland with my Stetson at a jaunty angle atop my head, along with a big fat chip on my shoulder. Talk about feeling pissed. Angry. Bitter, even. Yeah, poor me. I felt put-upon because although the academy's top grad always got their choice of assignment, it didn't happen this time. I requested Berlin Barracks, which serves the Ocean City area. I penciled in Salisbury Barracks as an alternate, since it's only one county over. Instead, the agency sent me to their post at Prince Frederick, in rural Calvert County.

Calvert County is farmland and tobacco crops. That's fine, but there's no ocean. It's why I frowned and asked, "What the hell is this, anyway?" While the sarcasm mirrored my anger, it doesn't imply that this was a poor assignment. It wasn't; troopers saw it as a choice posting.

Part of the reason behind its status as "choice" centered on our reputation. We were the "Man in Tan," the troopers who wore Stetsons, khaki shirts, and olive drab trousers marked by broad black stripes on the seams. Our leather gun belts still had old-fashioned loops for twelve extra rounds of the .38 +P+ semi-jacketed hollow points we used.

Although the agency issued Smith & Wesson Model 13 .357 magnum revolvers, we could purchase and carry the S&W Model 19 Combat Masterpiece. I chose that option, and the academy firearms instructor engraved my name on it. Along with a revolver and the twelve cartridges in the gunbelt's loops, we were equipped with a set of speed-loaders, and handcuffs. They were it; we carried nothing else. No mace or pepper spray; no tasers or phasers or batons.

We worked with only the basics because we had a simple operating principle: if we couldn't talk it out, we would duke it out. And if the first two steps failed, we'd slap leather and shoot it out. While that attitude might offend some, this form of thinking is what keeps cops alive when backup is routinely thirty minutes away, and they're facing down bad guys who don't embrace the Marquis of Queensbury Rules. So it helps to have a confident attitude to set the tone, because cops fluent in street language succeed in keeping potentially violent situations from escalating.

More on that later.

The public also respected us because we wore our uniforms well and, well, uniformly. Regulations prescribed that we push the Stetsons low and slightly cocked over the right eye. Troopers could not leave a building or their cruiser without first affixing the Stetson onto their cranium, and woe to those who did not. Pens had to be concealed under the left shirt pocket flap. Badges, nameplates and collar ornaments had to be worn just so. We kept our shoes polished, uniforms sharply pressed, and our cruisers were immaculate.

Troopers salute each other, regardless of rank. Two troops driving in opposite directions render salutes. Troopers render this form of respect to supervisors when they encounter them in the office, and the supes return it with sharp salutes of their own. Our esprit de corps bonded us, and we were quick to correct citizens who said, "Excuse me, officer," with a curt, "I am not an officer. I'm a trooper."

It sounds petty. It's not. Those small pieces form an attitude of professionalism that garners public respect. Our 'tude also sent a message to would-be assailants: that cops who look sharp are probably on top of their game, and the image works. I know it does, after more than a few bad guys admitted that they didn't want to take me on simply because I *was* a Man in Tan.

Marylanders also respected our no-nonsense approach. We were polite, firm and fair; we "took no guff, cut no slack—we hooked 'em and booked 'em and didn't look back." What's more, in the state's rural regions we enjoyed genuine superstar status.

Rural regions were in fact the rule. MSP designates its facilities as posts until they reach a high-enough level of personnel to qualify as a barracks. As the term implies, the latter are equipped with beds, showers, and full kitchens for single troopers looking to save money by living there. Prince Frederick was a post, and not a barracks like Berlin. It shouldn't have mattered to me. But it did. I should have been grateful that the state even rehired me. Yet I resented management's decision to shunt me there.

The troop commander added insult to injury when he wouldn't let troopers commute with their patrol cars if they lived outside of the county. All troopers enjoyed the win-win privilege of using the state's cruiser even while off-duty. This provided a break on gas and maintenance for the personal cars, while it simultaneously increased police presence on the streets. But our troop commander didn't care about any of that, and denied that privilege to me and two other newbies.

His attitude not only left us with a sour taste, it angered others. Several troopers and even a few supervisors pulled me aside to say, "You got a rotten deal."

Naturally I agreed with them, but it's important to choose which battles to fight. Instead of butting heads, I quietly submitted a transfer request to Berlin Barracks, with Salisbury as a secondary choice. Taking that path was cathartic, and provided a chance to finally earn a pilot's license.

When I had that license three months later—another in a series of dreams-come-true—I called home to tell my parents. Dad was excited; Mom said, "That's nice," with the same dismissive tone she used when I wanted to talk to her about the burned-up body I'd come face-to-face with nine years earlier. Although her indifference took a bit of the wind out of my sails, I understood that we are all imperfect, and acknowledging this tempered my disappointment.

As for my father, well, in his view I could do no wrong. If I was off duty and went with him to the local American Legion, he bored the others by bragging *ad nauseum* about his son the trooper. Then again, I was proud to be the son of a man with three Purple Hearts and a Bronze Star for Valor. What's more, the other veterans at the Legion were not only aware of my father's combat record, they liked him. That's why whenever he momentarily stepped away from the bar, his friends would tap my arm and remind me on the off-chance that I'd forgotten, about how Dad felt about me. "Your pops sure does love you," they'd say.

I loved him in return. I also wanted to take him flying to demonstrate my newfound skills. I had to coax him, though. "We'll fly over your house," I promised. "Well? Whaddya say?" Dad appeared reluctant, but eventually gave a thumbs-up.

The next day he squeezed into the two-seater that I'd rented, and we flew along the coast before circling his house. Dad said, "Nice," but added little else until we landed, when he became talkative again.

What I didn't realize was that he had a great fear of heights, that flying in an airliner was one thing, but being in that small plane caused him a great deal of distress. But as my mother explained to me years later, "You were his son, and there was nothing he wouldn't do for you."

I SPENT THE next few months exploring my patrol areas and getting to know some of the disenfranchised and the dispossessed, just as Dad had done. More often than not, they kept to one side of an unspoken line of demarcation. They inhabited one society, while I represented quite another. Yet many of them magically appeared at bar fights or other disturbances to stand by my side while I restored order. "Hey," one of them told a belligerent drunk who was bad-mouthing me during a Saturday night altercation, "This is our Trooper Anderson, an' if he says for you to calm down, then get calm. Got that?"

Along the way I learned several other valuable lessons, chief among them is that there are always two sides to every story. Coming in at a close second, it became clear that the more preposterous the accusation, it's more likely that the truth will be found in the equal but opposite direction.

This bit of insight becomes especially vital while handling domestic disputes. One of my first husband-wife altercations involved a wife who accused her husband of beating her. I arrived at their home and found them standing on the porch, waiting. The husband was six-feet-four and two hundred pounds of muscle. The petite wife wore a scowl to highlight her black and blue left eye. I had just opened my car door when she pointed at her husband and screamed, "Look what the bastard done to me! Arrest him!"

"Hold on," I replied. "I plan on hearing what each of you has to say, but one at a time."

I figured the husband would shout a denial. Instead, he remained strangely quiet. "I'll get your story," I told him, "after I talk to your wife." I had him stand at the far end of the porch while I positioned the wife so she faced me. That let me keep an eye on him. After hearing her out, I had them trade places and let the husband say his piece. He said a lot, too—and most of it centered on their infant son.

When he finished, I nodded and said I wanted to see the child.

"Ya know," the wife suddenly began, "I ain't mad no more! I don't wanna press no charges."

"Hold that thought," I replied, "And come with us." She was still fretting as we went to their son's room, where I peeled the boy's diaper away and briefly examined his backside. After securing the diaper, I placed the wife under arrest and charged her with sexually abusing him.

It turned out that the husband had arrived home unexpectedly, only to find his wife using her finger to perform anal sex on the boy. When he moved to stop her, she shouted an expletive, grabbed a large kitchen knife, and came charging at him. He acted on instinct and landed a right hook on her left eye. End of story. Well, not quite. It proved to be a vital lesson in never leaping to assumptions or conclusions before doing a due diligence.

There's more to the story. As part of the investigation, I did some research and learned that ninety-five percent of all pedophiles are straight, even when it's man-on-boy. That's because pedophilia has nothing to do with sexual gratification, and everything to do with exerting power and control over helpless children. Unfortunately, although we can treat pedophiles, we will never cure them. Never. As in, not ever.

* * * *

Three other incidents burned their lessons home. In the first, I spotted a car going too fast on a busy highway. I decided to issue a written warning, made the stop, and positioned myself slightly behind the driver's door. This forced the teenaged male driver to twist around to see me. I explained why I pulled him over, mentioned the written warning, and said, "I need your license and registration."

I watched him open the glove box. Saw him reach for the small handgun sitting there. I don't remember drawing my revolver. I do recall jamming the muzzle deep into his ear canal while shouting, "Freeze!"

He grabbed his handgun anyway.

Time slowed. I saw him grip it harder; saw him swing the barrel in my direction. I thought, *This is it*, and began pulling my trigger. I had no qualms; I was gonna shoot him—hell, I was gonna blow his friggin' brains out.

And yet...and yet I instinctively clenched my other hand and drove a fist into his jaw.

He dropped the gun. I holstered mine; pulled him bodily through the window; drove him into the ground. Then I cuffed him.

That's when I realized that his handgun was a starter pistol for sporting events. It could only fire blanks. I shook my head and demanded, "What the hell were you thinking?"

He told me. His girlfriend had just given him the heave-ho. After sinking into a deep depression, he vowed to end it all. When I stumbled into the picture, he decided to get me to shoot him by resorting to what we know today as "suicide-by-cop."

However, had I shot and killed him I would not have felt any guilt. Survival is an instinct that recognizes no excuse for foolish behavior, and I've always taken comfort in the soundness of my gut feelings.

The second incident unfolded a month later, after four young men from Washington D.C.'s inner city piled into a battered green Chevy and made the hour-long drive to my turf. By the time dusk approached, they were cruising through a small town when they spotted a local cop sitting in his cruiser. Maybe they were bored. Maybe they were just being punks. In any event they pulled up next to the officer and pointed the business end of a shotgun at him. The officer ducked. They sped off.

The cop called for help. I started toward him, and found the bad guys driving down a dark and lonely road. As I fell in behind, the two punks in the back seat began staring at me through the rear window.

I was telling the dispatcher that I would tail them until other units could arrive, when the driver hit the brakes. I threw the mic to the seat, angled my cruiser behind their car, leaped out with shotgun in hand, and stood behind my door for cover.

The driver got out and faced me.

I leveled the shotgun at him and shouted, "Freeze!"

He stepped toward me.

This time I growled. "One more step, and you're dead."

He took that step. My shotgun made its iconic *thwack-thwack* sound as I chambered a shell, aimed for his chest and began pulling the trigger. At this distance the 00 buckshot would blow his head off. I was gonna do it...

...And the driver clearly realized this. His eyes bugged out and he threw his hands up and did not so much as blink while sweat streamed down his face.

I kept him and his three "associates" at bay until backup arrived. We took them down one by one, and as I snapped handcuffs on the driver, I found a loaded .357 revolver stuck in the back of his waistband.

He grunted and said, "Yeah. Thas' right. I was gonna shoot you dead."

It was a face-saving boast but I was in no mood for games. I cut him with my eyes and said, "No. You were not." Then I pantomimed chambering that shell in my shotgun.

The driver lowered his eyes. He knew.

I also learned a third lesson: that when you show up unexpectedly at a home to inform a parent or parents that a son or daughter is dead, the mother always know why you're there. She knows it the instant she sees you, whether it's twelve noon or twelve midnight, and while the husband is fumbling with eyeglasses or looking at you askance, she's watching your eyes.

From the very first, I never looked away as if ashamed of what was about to go down. I always gave the mother my eyes. It seemed the most dignified thing I could do, right before shattering both her world and the husband's by asking, "Is John Smith your son?" The father nods; the mother stares. I spell it out. "Your son was in an auto accident a short time ago on the interstate. He's dead."

That's it. End of message. End of their lives as they knew it. I remain long enough to tell them what hospital their child was taken to. Then I leave—but never before the mother silently nods her head ever so slightly at me.

I DID WELL enough at Prince Frederick Post to gain a fair amount of respect from the other troops. I also messed-up a lot. One evening while patrolling a shopping center parking lot, I spotted a young low-life stealing an elderly woman's coat. He saw me and took off running. I chased him down, and cuffed the poor excuse for a human being.

After taking him in, I secured one of his hands to a metal post near the desks. Then I took off my patrol jacket, but carelessly left it within his reach. Minutes later I was immersed in paperwork.

Once I finally dotted the I's and crossed the T's, it was time to bring him before a court officer for his initial appearance. I reached for the patrol jacket. My badge was missing. I began looking for it. But when I caught him suppressing a smirk, it became clear that he'd slipped it off the jacket while I was distracted. I finally found it beneath the desk he'd chucked it under, but only after he bent the badge's retaining pin.

"Smart," I told him. "Real, smart."

What else could I say? I felt humiliated. But since the exquisitely manufactured badges cost several hundred dollars apiece, I added a charge of M.D.O.P.—Malicious Damage to Property—to the paperwork. Then I vowed never to take my eyes off a prisoner again.

DURING MY ROOKIE period I also validated my theory that when confronted by a much larger man or men on a dark country road far from any assistance, the best defense is to go on the offense—and what better way than by becoming a yellow jacket. The tactic was doubly effective with that element of fine upstanding citizens who simply don't understand firm but fair, but do get it when faced with strength—one that you're willing and able to back up by the use of force.

Potential adversaries literally looked me up and down many times while gauging my slender frame, and I always looked 'em in the eye and taunted them by saying, "Feeling froggy? Then start hopping, motherfucker."

This almost always worked, since bullies back down when they see that you're ready, willing, and able to take 'em on. However, there are plenty of truly badass hombres who like to fight. The trick is in reading the eyes. Hardcore dudes don't look you up and down. They stare straight through you instead, and turn deathly quiet.

Yep, I've encountered the ones who'll go at it, and a couple of times I've had my ass handed to me. I even spent eight days in a coma after a child custody dispute turned violent. Over time I've also suffered broken bones, broken noses and broken pride. But despite all this, it never deterred me. Just as in the fire department, I knew the job was dangerous when I took it. Besides, in the end I always prevailed. That's because despite any injuries, my assailants always did hard time in the state pen, and I always went home for a cold beer. So what the hell, right?

MY ALTERNATE CHOICE on the transfer request I submitted months earlier came through. I would be going to Salisbury Barracks, which at least would be closer to the ocean.

Salisbury is the Maryland Eastern Shore's largest city, and in 1981 the population hit 20,000. It's the seat of Wicomico County, home to a state college, and a commercial hub for agricultural products. Salisbury has its own police force, and the sheriff's cadre of skilled deputies patrolled the county in partnership with us.

I said goodbye to my Prince Frederick buddies and rented a home in the same private community where my parents lived. After getting my furniture in and the utilities hooked up—I'd become an expert at moving by now—I reported to my new assignment.

Fortune favored me when I landed on a great team led by a young sergeant who everyone liked and respected. As for the corporal, he was a no-nonsense type. Finally, an assortment of veterans and newbies alike made up the rest of our group.

A month later I loved my job even more—especially when June came around and summer reigned supreme. I'd keep the window down while prowling back roads, the scent of honeysuckle washing past my nose so thick that it was as if I could swat at it. But no matter the season I always stayed busy, if only to remain awake and alert. Working hard also endeared me to the sergeant, and soon enough he recognized my enthusiasm by bestowing a macho-moniker upon my noble head.

Whether they'll admit it or not, all cops want a cool nickname—and I was about to get one simply because my very likeable sergeant and I shared the same first name. But whenever someone called out, "Rick," we both turned around. So after a couple months of this, he grinned at me and said, "This is getting ridiculous. So we're gonna change your name." Then the sarge mentioned the movie, Rocky, and as he surveyed my slender build he said, "From now on, your name is *Rocky.*"

The name stuck. Everyone at the barracks began calling me Rocky, or simply Rock. Did I mind? Are you kidding? Of course not. It gave me bragging rights, and to this day the old troopers still know me only as Rocky.

MARYLAND TROOPERS ROUTINELY conduct criminal investigations, and while investigating a burglary one day I developed evidence that pointed to "Smitty," the president of an outlaw biker gang. He was a tank of a man at six foot six and two hundred and fifty pounds of S.R.M.—Solid Rippling Muscle. And like a main battle tank, Smitty wasn't smiling when I knocked on his door and said, "I have a warrant for your arrest. Let's go."

"You ain't takin' me nowhere," he growled.

"Watch me," I replied with deliberate evenness.

He charged. I waited until he made contact, wrapped an arm around the big boy's waist, rose up on the ball of my foot, then shot my hip upward. Smitty cried out as I flipped him onto his back with so much momentum that I nearly drove him through the floor.

His mouth opened and closed like a blowfish for several silent seconds. Finally he looked me over and grunted. "Hmm. You must have one of them there black belts. Yeah, guess I'd be stupid to fuck with you."

I neither confirmed nor denied his assumption, because by letting suspects believe what they need to believe, it provides them with an "honorable out." And in a sub-society in which face is everything, a biker's friends won't put him down for backing down in the face of overwhelming strength. As a substitute for big and brawny, they'll settle for a trooper with a pocket-full of shock and awe. Or a name like Rocky.

Saving face or not, Smitty had still been honor-bound to resist, so I wasn't angry. In fact, I reached down and offered a helping hand. He hesitated, but accepted the "assist" and even put his hands behind his back so I could cuff him—which I did—and minutes later I was belting him into my patrol car. But once inside the barracks, he developed an attitude.

To nobody's surprise, Smitty did drugs. Yeah, *I'm shocked, shocked to know that there's gambling going on in this establishment.* When I saw him working his mouth while rivulets of sweat streamed down his face, I knew he needed a fix. After asking another trooper to watch my prisoner, I went into the next room and began plunking quarters into some vending machines.

A moment later I handed Smitty two Baby Ruths and a Coke—the real thing, with sugar. He wolfed down the bars and gulped the Coke. Then he stared at me with cruel eyes, and said, "Fuck you."

I showed no reaction and got busy with the paperwork. Two hours later I turned him over to the local jailers, and two months later Smitty received a two-year sentence in the state pen.

We would meet again.

CHAPTER ELEVEN

Trooper, Prankster, Flyer, Spy

THE TRANSFER ORDER came across the state police teletype, that staple of pre-internet secure communications, in terse language that held great meaning to me: Trooper First Class R.C. Anderson—Transferred, from Barrack "E" Salisbury, to Barrack "V" Berlin.

Saying that I was a happy camper is understatement. I would finally be working out of the barracks that oversaw Worcester County, with an area of responsibility that included the Atlantic coastal areas, the mythic Assateague Island and its wild ponies, and Ocean City itself. To celebrate my new assignment, I bought a pristine '67 Mustang fastback. It had a 289 engine, its candy-apple red paint job glistened, and it attracted a lot of looks from good-looking girls.

Of course, rain can come down on just about any parade. In this case, transferring from one barracks to another creates seniority issues, which meant I would get the assignments that nobody else wanted. Did I care? Not at all.

Then an issue that I thought dead cropped up. The "size matters" comments started anew, though mostly in jest. The Berlin troops knew my reputation from Salisbury, and they embraced my "Rocky" nickname. But one of them let me in on a dirty little secret: the assistant barrack commander had a "thing" about short troopers.

"Is that right? Huh, guess I'll have to do something about it." I thought I would discreetly point out that former high school football jocks who compete to become Navy SEALs are often dismayed to learn that they're regarded as second-stringers on the SEALs' playing field. Meanwhile, the guys who played lacrosse or water polo—guys who are my height and build—get sent to the head of the line. It doesn't seem logical, but the reason is simple: those two sports require exceptional stamina, combined with aggressive attitudes. I had played high school lacrosse, I knew what I was all about, and knew that a vast number of SEALs, members of Delta Force, or even para-rescue personnel are close to my size and build.

However, the next day I paid a courtesy call on the barrack commander himself, instead of the assistant with the fear of heights. But when I entered the commander's office, he screwed his eyes tight and pointed at my throat.

"What's that you're wearing around your neck? Looks like a medal, and the regulations specifically forbid jewelry other than wedding bands and watches that are visible to the public." He pointed at the open collar of my short-sleeved summer shirt.

While nodding, I reached inside my shirt and pulled out a small silver medal that I had thought was hidden from view. "A friend gave it to me. It's a St. Michael. Patron saint of police"

"Is that so?" He paused. "Are you Catholic?"

I bridled at first at such a personal question until curiosity kicked-in. "Yes, sir."

"Hmm. Okay." He appeared to be mulling it over before leaning back in his chair and smiling. "Now then, I have your personnel file and it's all very good. It's also superficial. Dry facts. That you were top of your class. That sort of thing. Why don't you take a moment to tell me about yourself?"

SOMETIME LATER THAT day I was chatting with a dispatcher when I idly mentioned the commander's comments about the St. Michael medal.

Her mouth puckered. "Don't you know by now?"

"Know? What am I missing? Come on. Clue me in."

"Maryland was founded by Catholics, *riiight*?" After I allowed that it had been, she continued. "Therefore my sweet, the Agency is run by Catholics...kinda like a secret society."

"Really?" I shifted from foot to foot. "Hmm, I never knew that."

"Well, now that he knows you're a Catholic..." She wagged her eyes and grinned.

Sure enough, things changed the very next day. Comments concerning my size ceased at once. The first sergeant reassigned me to a choice patrol area. He also approved a pending leave request. Yet another door had opened—or at least been knocked ajar.

NOT LONG AFTER that door cracked open I met Sally at an Ocean City nightclub. She was a successful businesswoman, we had a blast ribbing one another that night, and we became best buddies. However, she and I kept it at that level, never venturing beyond falling asleep in each other's arms on the couch while watching midnight movies.

She was full of beans, that one, and as our relationship deepened she began introducing me to local movers and players. We explored local restaurants, went for long walks along the beach, and talked. Among many other positive things, she polished my fashion sense, or lack thereof. "Rick," she would begin, "You can't wear black shoes with a brown belt. You just can't." Then she'd jabbed an elbow against my ribs and wink.

I always winked back. It wasn't that I was averse to fashion. I had simply been indifferent to what I was wearing. Once, when I was fifteen and working summer weekends bagging groceries at a military commissary, a slightly older co-worker named Bill pulled me aside.

"Dunno if you know this," he began, "But my folks have a place at the ocean. It's just off the beach, too." His smile lit the area. "They let me use it whenever I want." Then he pointed at a mutual friend standing nearby. "Ed an' me are heading there tomorrow. We figure on staying five days, maybe longer. Wanna come?"

"Say no more."

When Bill stopped in front of my house the next day and honked the horn, I told my parents where to find me.

Mom shrugged and said, "Be careful."

Dad warned me only half-kiddingly not to come home with the clap.

"I'll try not to," I said. After flashing a very male grin, I hopped into Bill's car while clad only in faded blue sweat pants and absolutely nothing else—no shirt, no flip flops; not even any underwear. After greeting Ed, I kicked back and beamed happily as we set off in pursuit of bad girls and good suds.

The next five days were a blur of sun, salt-scented air, creosote smells rising from hot boardwalk planks, and sizzled soles from said planks. They were days of breezes that blew my long hair into a tangled mess, while carrying on their backs a mix of suntan lotion scents and the ocean's murmur—all this as the surf rolled in and out, in and out. Coupled with the ocean's rhythms were bright-eyed girls with sassy smiles and sweet smells, and by the end of the trip I was exhausted, sunburned, and smiling.

And, I didn't contract the clap.

That was then. Back in the present, I absorbed Sally's fashion advice and routinely asked her to be my date at weddings and other celebrations. We also discussed the merits and demerits of prospective suitors—including those that I'd set her up with. On another level, I would be there for her whenever she needed to talk or vent or step into my open arms.

Sally was also a sweetheart by never chiding me for being a party animal in a festive town, one where unattached first-responders were fools if they didn't take advantage of the atmosphere of open attitudes and girls with playful smiles.

Of course, there are parties and then there are parties. With seven police agencies in Worcester County ranging from small town patrols to the much larger Ocean City—not to mention sheriff's deputies and state troopers—it would have been a crime, a total crime, not to party. After all, we were young and fit, and our police uniforms sent subtle signals to women over eighteen, signals that said, *You can go to any of our beds and not worry about being abused, beaten or more importantly, treated with contempt.*

They came by the busload, too. There were recent high school grads, and college girls looking for a few final blasts before settling into marriage. Many of the latter were blunt. "I'm here for the summer," they would begin. "And I wanna sleep with at least fifty guys before Labor Day." Of course, a few girls encountered a labor day of another sort nine months later, and cases of the crabs and the clap made the rounds among our ranks due to the indifferent use of condoms in these pre-HIV days.

A few cop parties also reached legendary proportions. In fact, they were little more than frat parties. It's why we held our bashes on deserted beaches, to keep from disturbing neighbors. Guests brought kegs and boom boxes and bottled-up energy, but had to adhere to an ironclad rule: drivers left their keys with a designated keeper-of-the-key, and those drivers had to blow into a preliminary breath-test device to get the keys back.

We played hard and loved hard. However, we also worked hard, and parties served a dual purpose by bringing in cops from throughout the county to meet over a beer and quench their need to socialize. We also traded information. Many times I passed along vital information to small town detectives, while officers tapped my arm and drew me aside to say, "I hear you're looking to serve a warrant on Joe Jerkson. So here's the deal. Go to Minion's Bar and Grille tomorrow night around nine. He'll be there."

Sure enough, the next evening I'd go to Minion's Bar and jerk Mr. Jerkson from his stool. "You're under arrest," I would begin. But this being a macro version of small-town America, they'd already heard that I was looking for them, and tell me to save the speech.

ANY GIVEN DAY or night might see me responding to a fatal auto accident, a burglary, or to fist fights that were almost always over a girl. One evening I rushed to a call at a local chicken processing plant, only to discover a young man lying on the floor with a very large knife sticking out of his ribcage. I quickly isolated the crime scene, questioned witnesses, identified a suspect, and arrested him within minutes.

After taking photos and collecting evidence, I took the suspect to the barracks and processed him. Then I brought him before a court official for the initial appearance, transported him to the county jail when bail was denied, returned to the barracks, and spent the rest of the night doing paperwork and processing evidence.

Although it sounds like a lot of work, it wasn't—not when this is what you loved doing. It's also why I can still claim, "I've never worked a day in my life. In fact, taxpayers actually paid me to do stuff that I almost would've done for free."

There is one activity that I did perform free of charge, and it involved flying—especially when I invited a girl to the beach to catch some rays and cavort in the waves. After we grew tired, I would take her on a scenic flight for a happy ending to a sometimes-perfect day. The girls loved the tours, I enjoyed building flight hours, and everybody was pleased.

Well, almost everyone. One day I was at the gym when I met a young woman named Cathy. We chatted it up, and when the vibe was right I asked her out on a flying/dinner date. "Whaddya think, Cathy? We'll do a scenic night flight, then we'll meet my buddy Dan and his wife Brenda for dinner."

I picked Cathy up at her condo just before dusk. She was a knockout in a pink blouse and black skirt, and after she complimented me on my business-casual apparel, we drove past cars filled with festive youths and distracted parents until we reached the airport, where she stood patiently while I grabbed a checklist and did a preflight. Once we were seated, I kicked off my shoes as always, got the checklist, and referred to it while performing the startup procedure. While all this was going on, Cathy sat silently at my side with folded hands.

After taxiing to the runway, I used the checklist for the engine run-up procedures. Cathy said nothing. Finally I stowed the list, taxied onto the runway, and firewalled the throttle. Once airborne, I leveled off at a thousand feet and flew over Ocean City. The night was clear and the town below revealed itself as a sparkling gem-stone; a city of old values and older sins; a long narrow strip of as-phalt and buildings and dreams. Cathy never spoke a word.

Although her silence puzzled me, it didn't stop me from pointing out various landmarks below, or mentioning how pleasantly the stars above us sparkled. She simply nodded, and that would be it. We flew for half an hour before I set a return course for the airport. My passengers have always stroked my ego by describing my land-ings as "kissing the runway." Tonight's touchdown was no different, but we taxied to the terminal in dead silence. Once there, I used the checklist for the shutdown procedures, going from item to item while Cathy sat at my side, still wreathed in stoic silence.

We drove into town. Silently. I glanced at her from time to time, hoping for a clue to what might be troubling her. Cathy always smiled back though, so I decided she was just one of those quiet people we all meet from time to time.

Dan and Brenda were waiting for us at a popular restaurant's gleaming cherry wood bar. A waiter took us to our table, and as I held Cathy's chair while she sat, Dan smiled engagingly at her. "How was the flight?"

"I, well—" She clasped her hands together. "Well I just don't know. I mean, I was so dreadfully frightened the entire time."

I narrowed my eyes and leaned closer. "What? I thought we had a great flight."

She avoided me and addressed Dan, instead. "I got real nervous when Rick had to use this instruction book thingy to start the engine. He needed it again to figure out how to takeoff. Then—" She paused and raised both palms to the ceiling, "Then he had to read how to turn the engine off."

While Dan shot me his best what's-with-her look, I touched my date's forearm. "Cathy, that's a checklist. All pilots use them. They're designed to ensure that all systems are functioning properly." Then I wisecracked with, "In God we trust. Everything else we check."

When her blank expression told me that the pilot's motto had been lost on her—as it had with one or two of my other friends—I changed the conversation's course to a new heading and we enjoyed a great evening. Later, she invited me to keep her company for what remained of the night. So what can I say? It became a learning experience, and after that I briefed all passengers on what I was doing before, during, and after each portion of the checklist.

BEING A COP also opens a door to pranksterism, and on one particularly sweltering June night in 1982, when Reagan was in the White House and the Cold War was still hot, I pushed a prank to its maximum acceptable limits.

It happened at the beginning of a graveyard shift. I'd no sooner gone in-service with my call sign of V-21 than the dispatcher said, "*10-4, V-21...and stand by to copy.*" Seconds later she hit her transmit button. "*V-21, with any unit to cover...report of a shooting, intersection of Route 611 and Antique Road, no further details.*"

The location was smack-dab next to the Ocean City airport, and after acknowledging her I stomped down on the accelerator. A K-9 trooper about to go off-duty got on the radio to say he would back me up. A sheriff's deputy also said he would be en route. Then to my great surprise, the barracks duty sergeant announced that he was also responding.

That almost never happened, because the sergeants are the only armed person in the barracks at that hour. For him to leave two civilian female dispatchers alone meant it must be a hot call, and that the dispatchers were reluctant to provide too many details on a publicly monitored radio frequency. So I stepped down even harder on the gas.

All four of us arrived simultaneously, pulses racing, and prepared to do battle with some major baddies.

But it turned out to be a false alarm; someone's idea of a hoax. Only, we were still amped.

The deputy, whose name I won't disclose, sighed mightily and said, "Damn. What're we gonna do now?"

We had all been primed for action, only to see the promise of going to battle yanked from under us. That's when I got an idea. "Listen, the airport's closed this time of night. But there'll be a summer cop on duty—"

Although the airport lies within the county, it belongs to the Town of Ocean City, and the city council had recently decreed that an officer should be there 24/7. The fact that two council members had just bought an airplane and were keeping it there was total co-incidence. As a result, police officers were taken away from vital patrol duties and forced to endure long lonely nights at a deserted airfield, while all of the action was taking place in town.

Meanwhile, the town itself faced a separate challenge. Its 140 full-time police officers easily coped with 12,000 off-season residents. However, the summer population would swell to 250,000 visitors, all bent on having a good time. Major holidays were worse, as 350,000 tourists clamored for a place under the sun.

The city compromised by hiring "seasonal officers" to deal with this annual onslaught. They were mostly college students enrolled in law enforcement programs, and visitors called them "summer cops," although not in a nice way. However, the seasonal officers were eager and they were sharp. They were also naive as hell.

So when I told my colleagues "there'll be a summer cop on duty," I waited until they leaned closer with hands cupped around their ears. "Okay. Here's the plan. We'll storm the parking lot with our emergency lights flashing." I faced the K-9 trooper. "You'll get out with your dog. The rest of us will grab our shotguns...and leave the rest to me."

In any other scenario, the sergeant would have nixed that idea at once. Not this night, however. He and the others broke into grins, and a minute later we rushed into the parking lot with lights flashing and doors popping open as we emerged with a display of force.

Seconds later a young officer charged around the terminal's dark corner with beads of sweat popping across his dark forehead. We'll call him Officer Jones, and he was clutching his portable radio while looking this way and that for signs of the trouble he had so clearly failed to detect.

Wide-eyed now, he asked, "What's going on, what's going on?"

"Wait," I said as I warmed to what should have been an Oscar-winning role. Then with one hand clutched to my chest while faking breathlessness, I explained.

I told him that a Russian submarine had run aground one mile away, that a group of sailors had come ashore, and we had been chasing them. "The last we saw," I rambled on, "they were running in this direction. Yeah, they probably wanna steal an airplane."

Well, good old Jones squinted at me, tilted his head to one side, chewed on it for a bit, and finally said, "Bullshit."

While my colleagues looked from one to the other, I held up a palm and said with great passion, "No, man. It's true. I...swear to God."

Jones's face went through all the gradations of shock to incredulity before he finally broke. But when he did break, it was with a total departure from logic, reason, and reality. "Um, okay," he began. "What should I do?"

He asked a question. So I told him. "All right. Listen up and listen good. We've done something nobody's ever done before. We've activated Search Plan Alpha Nine-Bravo—"

"Yeah, yeah," he chimed in. "I think they taught us that one at a roll call briefing."

"Good," I said with a great show of relief, while trying not to smile at his refusal to admit to having never truly heard of a Search Plan that never existed—at least not until just then.

Seconds later I was in the process of giving him all kinds of really stupid things to do in our search for Russkie saboteurs, when the unexpected drone of a late-night commuter plane sent me thinking, *Uh-oh, how're we gonna get outta this gracefully?*

That's when the deputy sprang into action. Ocean City officers had portable radios back in 1982, but none of us did. This lack of equipment worked for us when the deputy abruptly stuck his head inside the open window of his cruiser while pretending to listen to his radio. A few seconds later he reared back and shouted, "They just found 'em! They're at Stinky Beach! Let's go get 'em!"

Stinky Beach was half a mile north, and along a narrow bay that separates the mainland from Ocean City. With deliverance in hand, we slammed car doors shut, whomped transmissions into drive, floored accelerators, and spun off while leaving poor Jones in a cloud of dust.

Screeching to a stop at Stinky Beach a moment later, we fell out of our cruisers while clutching our guts as we laughed and laughed. Unfortunately for us, Murphy's Law had already kicked in. What we were unable to see from our redoubt was Jones, dashing into his office, and picking up the direct line to his headquarters.

Nor were we aware of the series of misunderstandings, miscues and mistakes that sent the local Coast Guard station's forty-four-foot launch speeding toward the location of the supposed Russian sub; nor could we see the shouting sweating men who were hauling large Coast Guard helicopters from hangars in nearby Cape May, New Jersey, and Elizabeth City, North Carolina, as the pilots brought the choppers' large turbojet engines to life.

We also missed NORAD's excited chatter as they spun the necessary dials that scrambled a pair of fighter jets from Andrews Air Force Base, and then vectored them to the rogue sub's last reported position.

In fact, it wasn't until the local Coast Guard boat swept past us with its emergency lights flashing and a Coastie in orange life vest and gray helmet manning a .50 caliber machine gun at the bow, that we collectively said, "Uh-oh."

Fortunately for all of our careers, calmer heads were already prevailing. Someone at the Pentagon made calls to double-check the facts, and they eventually reached the Ocean City duty sergeant—

one who knew us only too well. He explained it to the Pentagon this way. "No, no, no. Somebody got their wires crossed. We're conducting an exercise just in case such an eventuality should ever develop. Nope. It's all good on this end."

It turned out to be good on our end, too. Ocean City's police brass didn't care to admit that someone could dupe their officers so easily, and they pushed the incident completely aside.

Well, almost. Interview boards to this day still ask prospective seasonal officers a strange question: "If you're at the airport and state troopers arrive to tell you that a Russian sub has run aground nearby, what're you gonna do?" Then they press fingers against temples while adding the coda, "And please don't tell us you'll take them at their word."

Were our actions juvenile? Of course. Would there be dire consequences if we had pulled that prank in today's P.C.-drenched environment? Absolutely. Yet this and other stunts were the DNA that bonded us and made our job an adventure, rather than just a paycheck.

I COULD STOP by to see the folks even when working. They lived just half a mile away after all, and sometimes Mom invited me for dinner. Yeah, it all sounds good. Except that sometimes a dinner can turn to ashes.

One evening while I was slicing a piece of roast beef, my mom asked if I had heard about a recent house fire two blocks away.

"Sure, I know about it."

In hindsight, I should have feigned ignorance. Yet, how was I to know that she would make one of those off-hand remarks that you should leave alone but can't, not after you've endured decades of an adversarial mother-son relationship.

"Well," she began while ladling gravy onto her mashed potatoes, "If *our* house ever catches fire, I'll just run outside and get the garden hose, and put it out."

"Mom," I began in an easy-going, informative way, "Their entire living room was on fire. The place was lit. You can't extinguish fires like that with a garden hose."

She arrested the ladle's movement midway between the gravy boat and the potatoes, and narrowed her eyes at me. "Of course I can. Our hose will reach the living room."

That's when I definitely should have let it go. Instead, I described the dynamics of roaring fires that engulf entire living rooms. "Mom, it'll be six hundred degrees at the ceiling. Smoke will obliterate all visibility. You'd need a breathing apparatus and protective clothes just to get close to the flames." Then I provided a brief tutorial of the physics involved in determining the amount of water flow at such-and-such a nozzle setting to compensate for friction loss in order to fight the flames in a so-and-so square footage room. "You need an inch-and-a-half diameter attack line at minimum, with an adjustable nozzle capable of delivering a hundred gallons of water per minute. You would also need—"

"You don't know what you're talking about," she shot back.

Dad caught my eye and gave me a look that said, "Drop it."

But I couldn't. "Mom? I fought fires for nine years. I do know what I'm talking about."

"No, you don't."

The delicious roast beef dinner I'd been chowing down on turned acidic in my stomach. I excused myself and left the house, my anger so great that it obliterated the real issues—that she was mentally ill, and that sometimes parents can't bear the idea of their babies outgrowing them. So they grab at any ring that lets them believe that they still matter in their child's life. In this case, that child had recently turned twenty-seven.

Sadly, I didn't learn this lesson for many years to come. But by then the resentment had festered to a point where I avoided discussing substantive issues with her.

* * * *

However, somebody else began discussions. As my father had

done in Germany, he still lent a helping hand to people who had fallen on hard times. One evening he was at the American Legion when he noted a lonely figure seated at the far end of the bar.

The man was tall and powerfully built, with a florid face, a full head of white hair, and bloodshot eyes. His suit appeared to be out of the 1940s. So did his shoes. Even so, Dad thought he carried himself with a certain air of pride, even as he nursed a nearly empty glass of whiskey.

Dad bought him a fresh drink and listened to his story. When the gentleman said he was from Czechoslovakia (as it was then known), Dad perked up. "What a coincidence. My mother-in-law is from Czechoslovakia, and she's at my house as we speak." With that said, he invited the stranger into his home for dinner.

By coincidence, I'd gone to my parent's house earlier to chop firewood, and was about to leave when Dad arrived with his guest in tow. I gave the gentleman a cop's once-over and liked him at once. But when my grandmother entered the living room and saw him, she reared back in shock. Following a flurry of apologies in Czech, she stood before him and curtsied.

It turns out that the man—whom I won't name out of respect—was of noble Czech blood. His family fled the country after Hitler's annexation of the Sudetenland, and after going through his family's fortune he had turned to the bottle. It happens that way sometimes. People go from thrones to thorns to bottles. On the plus side, he was a great raconteur and an even greater friend to my father and grandmother. I also grew to admire him, and whenever the folks invited him to dinner, I stopped by to listen to his tales of foreign intrigue and adventure.

Over the course of a few months he began turning down Dad's offers to buy him a drink. His eyes became clear, his manner more robust, and his dignity re-emerged after being lost for so many years. A short time later he entered a hospital for some tests. When he got the bad news, my father remained at his bedside so he wouldn't have to die alone, and Dad was there when he passed away. Sometimes a greeting and an invitation to dinner is all it takes.

BAR FIGHTS TAKE on any number of characteristics, along with several similarities. There are the initial threats that soon fall flat. There are also those that escalate into flying fists. In both instances there's usually a lot of shouting. Fortunately, the combatants would cease and desist once we showed up. In fact, there's a good argument to be made that the antagonists secretly welcomed our arrival, since it gave both parties an excuse to stand down. There are exceptions, however.

At the dawn of the Great Summer of '83—and perhaps not coincidentally, about the same time of the mythical Russian sub—the new manager of an old tavern just outside Ocean City set out to attract his share of the enormous numbers of college kids who came to town each season. And what better way to do it than to offer a Wednesday night special of free hotdogs and dollar drafts. While he was at it, the manager came up with a name for those special nights. They would be known as, "Funk Night."

Yeah, sure. And let's call the tavern itself a blivet—a blivet being a five-pound sack stuffed with ten pounds of shit. Not that the kids were pieces of shit. Noooo. They were little angels, all of them— and every time you knocked one of them over the head with your nightstick, another angel somewhere got its wings.

Imagine a tavern set alongside busy U.S. Route 50—an old highway that stretches from Ocean City all the way to California. Next, picture a tavern designed to hold no more than sixty customers. Now visualize that tavern after word reached the college jocks that the hotdogs are free, the drinks are cheap, and the girls are fast.

The potential for problems grew after fuel in the form of too much testosterone combined with way too much attitude. Finally, add youngsters who would never dream of misbehaving in their hometowns, and an explosion was bound to ignite.

The first Funk Night began peacefully enough. However, by midnight hundreds of rowdy party animals were literally tumbling out of the sixty-person capacity tavern, and into adjacent parking lots.

When they began spilling out onto the highway, neighboring business owners called the state police.

The first arriving trooper had a reputation as the type who does not go gently into the night. Decorated for heroism and widely known throughout the region as an Alpha, he parked along the highway, turned on his P.A. system, and emerged from the cruiser with microphone in hand. Seconds later, his officious voice boomed forth. "This is the Maryland State Police. You are hereby ordered to leave this establishment at once."

The crowd answered with epithets, extended middle fingers, and a barrage of beer bottles and rocks.

Now thoroughly riled, the trooper called for the cavalry—and when this trooper called for assistance, every other law enforcement officer in the area just knew that something bad was going down. Now visualize them speeding to the scene like the cavalry of old.

Three troopers, four deputies, and six Ocean City officers came roaring in. Four K-9 units raced to the tavern. By now things had deteriorated to the point of men yelling, dogs barking and mothers pulling children from streets—especially after a deputy lobbed a tear gas grenade into the crowd. Teeth were knocked out, faces got bruised, and birds began having sex with cats.

The troopers and deputies eventually arrested a handful of the festive "yutes," and tossed them into jail for the night. As for the cavalry, there were two broken noses, a number of torn shirts, and more than a few sets of injured prides.

It was not a successful night.

A week passed. Another Funk Night revved up. Complaints poured in. This time the various police agencies formed a task force a short distance away. Once the players were in place, they proceeded to the scene and broke out the bullhorns, only to duck-and-cover when another beer-bottle barrage rained down of them.

The resulting melee was no different from the first.

On week three of the Funk Night hostage crisis, yours truly happened to be working. The call came out shortly after midnight.

"Berlin to V-21, disturbance at the tavern. Be advised, all other available units are tied up. We're calling Salisbury and Ocean City for assistance."

I acknowledged the call and drove to my destiny with Funk Night. But rather than park near the parking lot, I pulled onto the highway median strip. After watching a crowd of three hundred rowdy drunks hooting and hollering, I developed a plan. Let's call it, *Plan Ten from Outer Space.* After recalling how well my Soviet submarine ruse had worked, I felt certain that this gambit also has great potential for success. And so I got the crime-scene camera from the trunk, a Kodak Instamatic, the 1980's model that required film and flashcubes. I eschewed the former, and pocketed a handful of the latter.

Deciding there was nothing to lose, I aimed the filmless camera at the crowd and clicked the shutter. The flashbulb emitted a burst of white light. I edged closer. Pressed the shutter. A second burst of light. Next, I walked to the edge of the parking lot, clicked the shutter twice, put a fresh cube in place, waded into the swarming, squirming crowd, and kept clicking away.

It was about then that a slender young man sauntered over—just as I had hoped someone would—and with his head canted to one side he asked, "Hey, man. What're you doing?"

"Shucks, I'm just doing a safety survey." I lowered the camera and swept a hand at the parking lot. "You can see for yourself that there are a lot of people here." I smiled amiably and nodded rapidly until he instinctively nodded in return. "But there are *way* too many people and that's way too bad, 'cause someone might stumble onto the highway and get run over."

He stroked his chin, deep in thought. "Hey, I see what you mean."

"The thing is," I continued, "you guys should have a place where you can have fun without ending up in the morgue."

While he pressed his lips tight deep in thought, I brought the camera to my eye and clicked. The bulb erupted. I lowered the camera. "Yeah, I'm doing a safety survey. You know, to find a way for everyone to party it up but without getting hurt."

His face brightened at once. "Man, that's totally cool."

"Thanks. But, I'm probably gonna have to ask everyone to leave when I'm done, since it won't do to see a car hitting someone. You look like a leader to me, so you understand. Right?"

At this point I shut up and started a silent countdown. One...two... three....

"Hey," my newfound supporter-of-police said. Then he uttered the words I'd been praying for. "Listen, I can pass the word for everyone to leave. If you want me to, I mean."

I regarded him from the corners of my eyes and then offered a winning smile. "Damn. I'd really appreciate it if you would."

He walked off. I lowered my camera. Soon, distant sirens announced the imminent arrival of Salisbury's troopers and Ocean City's finest. Meanwhile, the crowd was rapidly dispersing, and the parking lot was empty barely five minutes later. Not a single party animal remained, having vanished as one due to the magic of word-of-mouth. Yep, I figured it was the greatest thing since canned ramen. And when I saw my newest best buddy standing in front of the tavern, I gave him a thumbs-up just as the cavalry came to a screeching halt along the highway.

Doors opened. Troopers stormed out of cars. A breathless corporal asked, "Where are they, Rocky?"

"Gone," I said while dusting my hands together, "Yeah, I ran 'em off."

Neither he nor any of the other troopers could contest the fact that yes indeed, the bad boys of Funk Night were gone. Better still, everyone called me Cocky Rocky afterward. Ain't life fun?

UNFORTUNATELY, HAVING FUN didn't prevent me from getting a bruising not long after that particular Funk Night. The barracks radioed me one Friday shortly after the bars closed. *"Berlin to V-21. At the West Ocean City 7/11. Report of two male subjects in the parking lot disturbing the peace."*

I keyed the mic, said, "10-4," and proceeded to the call, where I found a pair of clearly intoxicated twenty-somethings screaming obscenities and accosting any female within a hundred yards. I had arrested one of them a year before, and I knew the other. Their names were Bill and Ted, and they appeared determined to have a most excellent adventure.

As I edged closer, Bill took a swing at me. When he missed and stumbled, I put him in a restraining hold and cuffed him. Seeing this, Ted flew into a verbal rage that evolved into clenched fists, and soon the fight was on. A silent crowd gathered to watch me take Ted to the pavement, where we began trading punches while the handcuffed Bill repeatedly kicked my ribs. Luckily, my ballistic vest absorbed his blows.

It wasn't long before I had a bloody nose, a ripped uniform shirt, and split knuckles from punching the wannabe adventure boys. We were still going at it when a shadow obliterated the light from a street lamp. The next thing I knew, a huge hand gripped Ted by his neck, lifted him straight up, and held him suspended in mid-air.

My savior turned out to be none other than Smitty, the outlaw biker I'd put in prison two years ago.

Smitty wasn't finished, either. While still holding Ted by the neck, Smitty drove a fist into the nascent bad boy's face, and dropped him to the pavement like a pole-axed ox.

Then when Bill made the major mistake of trying to kick Smitty, the behemoth biker busted Bill in the jaw—a jaw that turned out to be made of glass—and he fell next to his brother, their most excellent adventure days now transformed into a daze.

Smitty reached down and helped me up, and then regarded me carefully while he spoke slowly. "I was driving by. Saw some pig motherfucker gettin' his ass kicked. I thought, 'good.' Then I seen it was you." He tilted his head. "I hated your guts for lockin' me away. But you done treated me like a man the whole time. You was righteous. Plus you got me that soda an' them candy bars. I never forgot that."

Smitty paused while his jaw worked silently. "So I decided to help you." All at once a huge grin spread across his face. "The best part?

I done got to punch out that punk-ass bitch you was fightin' with...
an' it was all legal! Haw, haw, haw!"

After I secured my other—and still unconscious prisoner—I faced
Smitty and said, "Thanks. I owe you."

"You don't owe me nothin'." He looked at me man-to-man. "It
wasn't like you needed no help. Looked like you was holdin' your
own with them boys. Still—" Then he winked at me, a gesture that
signaled a respect that amounted to yet another reason why I wanted
to wear a badge in the first place: to explore opportunities that
would let me deal with alternative societies that despite violent
tendencies, still respected those who aren't afraid to fight.

* * * *

After leaving my prisoners in a holding cell, I showered and put
on a clean uniform, processed them, took the brothers before a
court commissioner, and finally to the county jail.

It was dawn by the time I pulled into my driveway, only to find
Sally's blue Corvette parked in my regular spot. Not that it was a surprise, since we had keys to each other's houses. She greeted me at
the door holding a crystal tumbler containing two fingers of Johnnie
Walker Green Label, only to rear back after taking one look at me.

"*Rick*. Your nose. Ohh, baby. Let's see." She put cool fingertips to
my still swollen sniffer. But when I shrugged, she smiled and patted
my cheek and handed me the glass. "I know you're beat. So am I.
But we need to talk. Why don't we, um—" She took my hand and
guided me to the bedroom, where she peeled me down to my Calvin
Kleins. After easing out of her own clothes enough to reveal her
Victoria's Secrets, we slipped into bed.

Then while I sipped the scotch and idly ran the pad of my big toe
up and down her slender silken calf, she rested a hand on my naked
thigh and searched my face. "Rick? I have this friend. An attorney.
About your age, too. I think you two will hit it off. I might be wrong,
but I don't think I am." She revealed the attorney's name and added
brightly, "You both have so much in common."

I crunched the numbers, and once I realized the degree of her insight into my likes and dislikes, I traded a private smile with her and said, "Busted."

"Nah. Not busted. Boisterous, maybe. Energetic. Even enigmatic. But never a dull boy."

As she curled against me with a kittenish quality that I loved, I pecked her cheek. "Sure, go ahead and make the intros." When she smiled and winked, I gently elbowed her ribs before winking back. By unspoken agreement we kept things chaste as always, though we still had pillow talk that lasted long enough for me to polish off the scotch, get up and pad into the kitchen to refresh it, and return to my friend's side. Later, we fell asleep in each other's arms.

Yeah, she knew my tastes all right, because when I met the blind date a week later, I gave her a look the next day, one that said, *you certainly know what roads I like to explore.*

TWO YEARS LATER found me standing at the proverbial crossroads. That blind date—plus three others she arranged—never went beyond a few tentative dinners and movies. It's not that they weren't great people to be with, but we never really clicked, and in any event I'd begun dating Lauren. She was five years my junior, with an oval face framed not by night, but by dark brown hair that reached to her waist. Lauren had modeled clothes while putting herself through college, and now she had set her sights on law school.

We did make a nice couple. Even my mother loved Lauren, and praised her piano playing skills. "And," Mom said, "you two go well together. Why don't you marry her?"

I deflected my mother's not-so-subtle push toward matrimony by saying, "Neither of us are ready." What I didn't bother telling her was that Lauren's choice of law school would take her far from home.

Also at a crossroads was the love I felt for my job and for Berlin Barracks, where I saw plenty of on-duty action while eating up the off-duty social life. Even so, I still had unfulfilled dreams, and one dream in particular posed a problem, since pursuing it would force me out of my comfort zone and send me to the far side of the state. However, there are times when it's appropriate to say, "What the hell." This was one of those times.

The following day I filled out a transfer request to the Aviation Division. Now I could turn a boyhood boast into reality by joining the "best of the best" in trauma care. Yet I still paused before signing the transfer papers.

Should I go, or should I stay? That age-old question.

On the other hand, I could seek advancement in rank. I was a Trooper First Class, and the next big step was to get a corporal's stripes. It was the toughest rank to reach, since so many troopers throughout the state were competing for a limited number of slots. Make corporal though, and it would be much easier to make sergeant, and eventually lieutenant.

My chances were good. I led the barracks in criminal arrests that included homicides and rapes. I ranked near the top for drunk driver arrests, the public liked me, and my personnel file bulged with complimentary letters.

So I got in line and waited for the promotion process to grind away. It was a long one. Part of it included a trooper's official evaluation. The corporals prepared them, the sergeants endorsed them, and the barrack commanders received them. This posed a bit of a sticky problem for me, because the assistant barrack commander who had a "thing" about short troopers was now the barrack commander.

Meanwhile, back at the ranch, my corporal officially described me as a model trooper, and gave me the highest ratings possible in every category. These ranged from job knowledge, the amount and quality of work, and appearance. After reading it over and thanking him, I signed off on it and he sent it up the chain.

While working day shift a week later, my sergeant radioed me to report to the barracks. "Come to my office," he said when I arrived. He looked grim. I followed him inside and plopped onto a chair. He sat in his and released an audible sigh. "The barrack commander didn't want to approve your eval. He said you didn't qualify. Says you don't meet the standards for overall appearance."

"Whaaat?" I looked at him, and frowned.

"He said, and I quote, 'Anderson's too small to receive a high mark.'" The old breed sarge scowled as he looked in the general direction of the barrack commander's office. "I told him, 'Rocky's always STRAC.' Humph. He didn't even understand. I had to explain the military term for someone who is always spotless and squared away." The sarge rolled his eyes. "Jesus. It went right over his head. He even had the gall to quote a regulation that says 'troopers must project a positive image of the agency.' To which our illustrious commander added, "Anyone who is short can't project a positive image, and Anderson is short."

I bolted to my feet and clenched my fists. "Yeah? I wasn't too short the other day when I went in foot pursuit of that rapist and tackled his fat ass." I scowled and said, "I want to speak to him, as in right now. 'Cause if he's concerned about image, then he needs to know he's a horse's ass and that the good citizens shouldn't have to see an ass in public."

Sarge tapped my arm. "Slow down, Rocky. I've already taken care of it." He waited until I sat back down. "I told him that if he marks you down due to size, then I'll gladly appear as your witness when you sue him for discrimination." All at once he chuckled. "I'm not supposed to put him down, but damn...I can't believe how dense he is."

My gratitude toward him for standing up for me knew few bounds, and after telling him this, I added that deep down I felt sorry for the lieutenant. He was the type who always danced one beat out of step, and was doubly cursed by being socially awkward. So I wasn't bitter or down on the guy. But I got on the phone and started calling the old boy network. The time had come to put in that transfer request for Aviation. I had always wanted to be there for the right reasons, but now I amended those reasons by remembering that the division prized smaller people, because too much weight reduces an aircraft's abilities. To my great surprise, an order came through a month later transferring me out of Berlin, and into the sky.

CHAPTER TWELVE

Working the Sky

O RDERS ALSO CAME through for Lauren in the form of a letter inviting her to begin law school at The Catholic University. So on a warm Sunday morning, I helped load Lauren's things into her car, then took her in my arms and kissed her goodbye. We promised to stay in touch, and a minute later I watched her drive away until she turned a corner and her car blended with the Indian summer foliage.

A short time later I tossed my stuff into my candy-apple red Mustang, said goodbye to the neighbors, and drove to the Aviation Division Headquarters near Baltimore. It would be my home for the next three months while I underwent intensive paramedic training. After getting certified as an aviation trauma technician, I would report to my first assignment at Helicopter Five, located at Cumberland Airport in Western Maryland's Appalachian Mountains.

While settling in I greeted two other transferees. The three of us were already state-certified emergency medical technicians, but our instructors would train us to a level far above EMT—we would be Aviation Trauma Technicians, which is even a step higher than paramedic.

That exclusive certification was due to Maryland's pioneering and uncontested world leadership in all things related to trauma. State officials even wrote a book, *The Maryland Way*, and it became a bible of sorts for governments around the globe. For example, the state developed and codified unique protocols to define who did what, where, and when in trauma cases. By law, once we landed at a trauma scene we were the boss. Not even a physician could order us to perform a procedure contrary to established protocols. It was heady stuff, and now I would fulfill yet another dream by becoming one of the world's twenty-five best medics.

First, though, I had to earn those Aviation Trauma Technician wings.

THE INSTUCTOR DRILLED us on the basics of administering IVs, meds, and cardio shocks; he taught EKG interpretation, chest auscultation, and patient intubation; we did internships at burn units, neo-natal units and hand referral centers. And of course we spent time at "Shock Trauma," the Maryland Institute for Emergency Medical Services Systems, where among myriad other duties we assisted neurosurgeons as they performed delicate brain surgeries. We walked, talked, thought and slept "trauma medicine," with zero input from the outside world. Finally, after three months of rigorous practice, oversight and testing, the Aviation Division's commander pinned the coveted golden wings with a Caduceus emblem to our Class A uniform tunics.

I was now a Man in Tan, flying on a Wing and a Prayer.

CUMBERLAND IS ISOLATED from the rest of the world by both distance and geography. It boggles my mind to this day that a large city can be so cut-off from other doings. But what the locals lacked in geo-political awareness, they more than made up for in regional acumen. I learned this following a five hour drive from Baltimore, after I parked my Mustang in a general store's dirt parking lot. The store itself was a tired building of peeling yellow paint. Its windows had decades-old layers of dirt, the doorjamb bore scars from bored customers who had whittled their initials into it, and the floorboards creaked beneath my feet when I stepped inside.

I had never been to Cumberland, I was in civvies and driving a civilian car, all I wanted was a soda before going to the airport, and I'd stopped here on impulse. So I grabbed a Coke and went to the counter to pay, only to see the forty-ish cashier narrow his eyes and say without hesitation, "You're the new trooper for that there meddy-vac helicopter. Ain't that right?"

To say that I was taken aback would be understatement. Nevertheless, there was no arguing the fact that he was dead-on. So I told him that I was in fact that there new *meddy-vac* trooper. I also decided that I would probably hear the term *that there meddy-vac* quite often.

Boiled down to its essence, the locals had good reason to have a keen interest in their meddy-vac boys. We were the only advanced life support providers for portions of a tri-state area that included Maryland, Pennsylvania, and West Virginia—aka, West-By-God-Virginia. It also mattered to everyone that we could reach a scene far quicker than ambulances, by virtue of our ability to hop over mountains in our meddy-vac helicopter.

The helicopter was a superb one, too. If conditions permitted, the Bell 206 B-III Jet Ranger could carry two litter patients. It also had supplies and equipment that included a "night sun" spotlight that projected a 3.5 million candlepower stream of dazzling light.

The night suns weren't afterthoughts, either. We needed them to survey nighttime landing zones, to search for lost kids and criminals, or to highlight cars involved in high-speed pursuits.

The Jet Rangers were versatile, all right. They were also fickle and underpowered. There were times when we wanted to evacuate an obese accident victim from a mountain top on a hot summer day, but the laws of physics forced us to concede to their rule. In other words, "Ain't no way we're gonna be able to lift this bad boy off this mountain."

FROM ITS EARLIEST inception back in the late 1960s, the Aviation Division made a point of initiating liaison programs with volunteer and career fire departments throughout Maryland and neighboring states. These programs trained firefighters and ambulance personnel how to efficiently select and establish helicopter landing zones (LZs), because an LZ might be alongside a road, in a field or even in a parking lot. The program was a worldwide first back then, but it's commonplace today.

Of course as with everything, nothing is as simple as it might first appear. For example, just starting the helicopter's turbojet engine was a process, so pilots left the engine running while the medics attended to their patients. Meanwhile, the unheralded fire crews behind the scenes stood by with hose lines at the ready in case of a mishap, and to keep bystanders away from the whirling main blades and tail rotor.

Even so, accidents are always possible. It's why we wore fire-resistant Nomex flight suits and gloves, leather military boots and only cotton socks and underwear; if we did crash and burn we didn't want polyester fabrics melting into our skin. We had flight helmets equipped with earphones, mics, and two visors—a tinted one for flying under sunny skies, and a clear one for night flight—because a bird-strike could send a foul fowl through the Plexiglas, and a visor could prove to be a sight-saving measure.

Finally, we wore shoulder-holstered revolvers—after all, we were still state troopers, and there were legendary incidents in which medics leaped from hovering helicopters onto the backs of fleeing felons.

So there it was—the Division's history—and once I reported to my new assignment the section commander partnered me with Ed Hanna, a skilled pilot who liked the fact that I had a fixed-wing pilot's license. Better still, after Ed came to see that I also knew my job, he not only trusted me implicitly in all matters medical, he invited me to take the helicopter's controls during non-mission flights. He wasn't breaking any rules by doing this, either. Pilots were encouraged to teach medics how to handle the helicopter in case the pilot became incapacitated. Once I could fly and land safely, there was talk at headquarters of having me get my helicopter rating and transition over as a pilot—an idea that certainly appealed to me.

Ed also provided insight after I bought a small airplane, a 1972 Cessna 150-L two-seat commuter. It boasted long-range tanks, headphones and voice activated intercom, plus the bells and whistles that qualified it for IFR flights in zero-visibility conditions.

The interior and engine were immaculate. The exterior was another matter. In fact, it was so scruffy that I christened it *Belch Fire II*. Ed nodded approvingly while inspecting it, and afterward he looked sidelong at me and said, "Rick, I learned to fly airplanes when I was only fifteen. If you're up for it, I can show you a couple of tricks that I picked up along the way."

"What are we waiting for?"

Ed taught me many things—including how to start a plane's engine by spinning the prop—and doing it without assistance. "Propping" a plane is serious business, one that's fraught with hazards even when performed by two people. Picture the old WWI bi-plane as the pilot sticks his head out of the cockpit and shouts, "Contact!" Then a ground crewman grips the propeller with both hands and yanks until the engine catches and the prop spins smoothly.

This method worked well with trained personnel, and in the early days of aviation when airplanes didn't have starters, it was the only way. The Belch Fire had a starter, but it was a high maintenance item. So Ed showed me how to set the throttle and magnetos, stand outside the passenger door with the wing strut against my back, reach forward to grip the prop, and yank it down. The prop always caught at once, and I would climb inside to begin the engine check while letting the starter rest for a rainy day.

This system was eloquent by virtue of its simplicity, because on my days off the Belch Fire's simplicity turned an eight-hour road trip to Ocean City into a two-hour hop across mountains and meadows, and ended in a final approach to the shores that I called home.

ED AND I routinely responded to the worst of the trauma calls.

Most involved auto accidents, and upon landing I might find three or four dead victims, plus three others with life-threatening injuries. Each call provided a personal learning curve, while simultaneously giving me opportunities to build professional relationships with first responders and regional trauma center staff.

However, one call qualified as a true outlier when it came to working with others. It unfolded one day shortly before noon. Our hotline rang. *"Report of a suicide,"* a dispatcher began.

While I got the details, Ed fired up the Jet Ranger. Moments later we were skimming across mountaintops and arriving on-scene before other responders could reach it by road, only to discover that we faced a problem—where to land.

The suicide location was a house at the lower side of a narrow pass, and surrounded by towering hills. Leave it to Ed to find a spot—the three-foot high cement cover of a septic tank behind a house across the street from the suicide call. Ed gingerly set the skids down with only inches to spare all around. Not exactly a conventional LZ, but it would do.

After grabbing the trauma kit, I raced across the street just as a volunteer ambulance crew arrived. Suicides—both the successful and the not-so-successful—still pose a threat. Family members can become violent; a failed attempt might motivate the suicidal person to try again, or even take others with him.

I ordered the crew to take cover behind their ambulance while I investigated. Drawing my revolver, I cautiously entered the house and found the victim—a male in his mid-twenties. He was sitting upright on a couch with a large hole in his forehead. A revolver lay next to him. I checked his vitals. Nothing. I checked the rest of the house for anybody else who might be there, whether alive or dead. Finally I stepped outside and told the crew that they wouldn't be needed. "This is now a crime scene. But before you leave," I told one medic, "Would you go behind that house and tell Ed to shut down the engine? We'll be here awhile. No sense burning fuel."

Once the medic gave a thumbs-up, I stepped back inside to wait for the state police investigator. It was cold even inside the house, so I kept my division-issued brown leather jacket on over my flight suit. Then I found a kitchen stool, and I was still perched atop it when the investigator arrived half an hour later.

Eyeing me warily and without offering his hand, he said, "I'm Jones." Moving closer, he squinted at me and asked, "What're you doing here?"

I swept a hand at the interior and said in a friendly way, "It's a crime scene. Couldn't possibly leave, could I?"

"You haven't answered my question." He tilted his head. "Why are you here?"

I'm sure my face must have taken on a look of puzzlement. "I just told you. It's a crime scene."

At this point our discussion devolved into a "Who's on First" routine.

Jones frowned. "I can see that. But why are you here?"

Narrowing my eyes, I slowly enunciated the next words. "Because. It's. A. *Crime*. Scene."

He leaned-in on me. "But *why* did you come here?"

"Whoa. Back off, Jack. 'Cause I don't like the way you're closing the distance." He hesitated, but stepped back. I waited a second, then asked, "Okay. I'm confused. Whaddya mean, why did I come here? What kind of question is that?" I wanted to roll my eyes, but I checked myself and added, "We were sent here, after all."

Jones reared back. "We? I see no *we*. Just you." Before I could answer, he gestured at me and asked, "By the way, what're you doing in that get-up?"

"Get-up? *Get-up?*" Digging in, I glared at him. "It's called—wait for it, Jones—it's called a flight suit." That's when it finally hit me. Jones must have thought that I'd been home and heard the call on a scanner—which many people had in those days—and pulled on my flight suit and drove here in my personal car.

So I spent nearly half a minute trying to convince him that a Maryland State Police Bell 206-B III Jet Ranger helicopter was at that very moment sitting atop a septic tank cover. I even pointed across the street for him. "It's behind that house over yonder."

He snorted. "You don't really expect me to believe—"

That did it. I threw my arms up and said, "Wanna know something? I don't care *what* you believe. You're here, the crime scene's yours, and I am *outta* here."

A minute later, Ed had the helicopter's jet engine fired-up, and I was clicking my harness into place when a wide-eyed Jones appeared around the corner of the house. Once we were safely airborne, I told Ed what had happened. Definitely made his day.

I learned later that the dead young man had become despondent after his wife left him. As the days passed and his despair deepened, he confided in a friend that he couldn't endure the loneliness. Feeling unloved, unwanted and uncared for, he sought relief from the business end of a revolver. Such a pity, that feeling of being alone— and it's all the more pitiful because in the end, none of us are ever truly alone. Not really. Just ask that sixteen-year old volunteer firefighter, the one who died while clutching his Bible.

SIX MONTHS INTO my new job, a series of flash floods ravaged parts of West Virginia and Western Maryland. Ed and I flew innumerable rescue missions and evacuations, and we plucked five people from raging waters in five separate locations. At the end of a long and exhausting day, we finally landed and began the unheralded task of writing reports.

A week later we were doing some preventive maintenance work on the helicopter when someone knocked on the hangar door. I opened it. A young man who looked vaguely familiar stood there.

"Hello," he said, and held out a hand.

Cops don't shake hands with people they don't know, since it could be a set-up to a sucker punch. When I maintained eye contact but didn't take his hand, he pulled it away and said, "Sorry. Shoulda known better. Anyway, I came here to thank you guys. You know— for saving my life."

Ed appeared at my side, and I was giving him a *who the heck is he* look when I slapped a palm against my forehead and smiled at our visitor. "Of course. We pulled you from the river. You're the guy surrounded by the trees."

It was indeed him. Rescue crews standing along the shore of a roiling river radioed us about a victim in the middle of a copse of trees, adding that he had been in the water for at least an hour. They also expressed doubts that we could reach him.

They were right to think so. The trees surrounding him left little room for us to descend low enough to get the rescue harness to him. Despite the risks, we decided to go for it. It was a tough call to make, yet it really came down to mutual trust—I had confidence in Ed's flying skills, and he had absolute faith in my ability to monitor his blind areas behind and to the left of our Jet Ranger.

The helicopter came equipped with a yellow "horse collar" sling attached to a long nylon rope. I quickly rigged the collar and switched the intercom to "hot mic." This let us speak freely without having to hit a transmit button. Next, Ed gingerly approached the trees, bringing us closer and closer while avoiding their branches, since hitting even a small one would snap our rotors like a twig.

We were not there to be heroes, though. We would terminate the attempt at the first sign of danger to the ship. Luckily, Ed was able to remain clear of the branches while descending straight down until the victim grabbed the collar. Once he slipped it into place, we pulled the poor guy straight up and brought him ashore. I probably saw the young man for all of ten seconds before handing him over to the medics, and then hustling back to the helicopter for another rescue mission.

Now the guy was here to say thanks for saving his life.

I caught Ed's eye. After he arched a brow, we invited our guest inside and offered him a cup of coffee, which he eagerly accepted. But when Ed asked, "How are you doing?" he blushed and shuffled his shoes against the floor. Then he thanked us, sipped some coffee, and after an awkward silence he left.

Ed shook his head while we watched him drive off. "I do believe that he's the first person to ever say, 'thanks for saving my life.'"

"Ditto," I replied. Then after thinking about it, I realized that in nearly fifteen years of responding to a variety of emergencies, I had personally saved at least a dozen lives. That's not counting another thirty or so that I helped save as part of a group effort. Just three years earlier in fact, while on patrol I found a car sitting in the middle of a road. I stopped to investigate. A frantic mother rushed over.

"My kids! They're in the back seat. They ain't breathing!"

I called for assistance and raced to the car. Two girls and a slightly older boy were right where their mother said they were—and they weren't breathing, either. In fact, their pale faces and blue lips meant that they were in dire straits. Acting on instinct, I pulled them from the car and put them on the ground. The fresh air revived the girls within seconds, but I had to perform CPR on the boy before his motor kicked-in.

After the ambulances rushed the kids to an ER, I examined the car and found a faulty exhaust pipe. It had been channeling carbon monoxide fumes into the rear passenger seats, and into the kids' noses. It was an accidental incident, but I still tracked down the owner and issued a repair order to fix the problem. Later on the superintendent gave me an official attaboy. The mother? She never bothered to thank me for saving her kids.

Yet by tacit understanding, none of my colleagues or I ever sought gratitude for what we did. To us, it was all a matter of routine. Sure, we often wondered aloud about how people didn't think enough of their own lives to even say, "Go to hell," just as in my firefighting days when we plucked the paratrooper from a tree in the nick-of-time, and he never even bothered to look at us before walking away. It's why Ed and I were surprised by the expression of gratitude...and it's why we had no trouble accepting the accolades that followed.

WE WERE TOLD to appear at the Maryland State Police Headquarters in our Class-A uniforms on June 27, 1986. Then during a dignified ceremony, the Superintendent presented The Governor's Citation to each of us for pulling the guy from the river. The citations are Maryland's version of the Congressional Medal of Honor, and they ended with the words "...for true valor, undaunted courage, and performance which has been identified as outstanding and above and beyond the call of duty, with a definite risk of life—"

Ed and I received a handshake, framed citations, and black and orange ribbons to wear on our uniforms. But the ceremony only marked the beginning. Only days later, the Maryland Senate awarded us with Resolutions of Recognition for "selfless dedication in safely evacuating endangered flood victims," and the Shock-Trauma unit gave us their Certificate of Outstanding Contribution for "Heroic heliborne rescue and lifesaving efforts."

Not to be outdone, West Virginia's governor made us honorary citizens and offered ornate certificates suitable for framing. Next, his Secretary of State declared that we were now "Mountaineer Millionaires," which I learned is a highly respected honor among West Virginians, and the elaborate certificate that accompanied the declaration was also a candidate for framing.

Next, U.S. Senator John D. Rockefeller IV issued letters of personal thanks, and fire departments on both sides of the border bestowed a bevy of plaques and certificates upon us. Ed and I appeared at every ceremony, and we felt humbled by so much gratitude. Finally, two books were written that chronicled portions of our exploits. *Killing Waters* and *Killing Waters II* contained witness and victim accounts, along with photos of our rescues and some of our comments.

At that point I couldn't see how life as it was meant to be in my universe could get any better. I had earned respect within an elite unit that in itself enjoyed global admiration, my superiors were taking notice of me, and people on the streets pointed at me and smiled. I was wearing happiness like a halo, I felt on top of the world, and the stars were aligned.

But it all crashed down around me when I appeared at what would be the final award ceremony, the one where my eldest brother Jim and his wife Jackie came to see me receive a third award for heroism. My parents also showed up, and after taking one look at Dad, I wanted to die.

Maternal grandparents, parents and siblings in Kaiserslautern, Germany, 1958.
I am in the first row, second from left.

Erna Frances Mollari

My mother playing her debut recital in
1941 at age 16. Sergei Rachmaninoff
and Helen Hayes were among the
audience.

My father's Marine Corps ID card after he joined in 1939 at age 15.

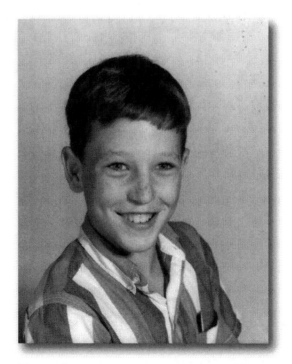

Me, age 9.

RICHARD CRAIG ANDERSON

Fire Fighter III-Engineman with the Anne Arundel County Fire
Department, 1976.

Truck-33.

LeRoy Wilkison helps Donald Gibson change air bottles during a 1972 building fire. Note Truck-33 behind them. (Photo by Keith Hammack, used by permission)

Me (*left*) and Kenny Bohn at a dwelling fire in 1978. (Photo by Keith Hammack, used by permission)

The rear kitchen door at the fire that killed two firefighters. Pat Bauer reached a window around the left corner. George Driggers' body was found near the middle window. (Unk photographer)

George F. Driggers, Jr. Known as "Georgie" to his family.

Patrick A. Bauer.

Dad pinning on my badge at Maryland State Police
Academy graduation ceremony, 1980.

In my state police summer uniform, my favorite
uniform, because "Summertime is Party Time!"

Taking a call for a medivac response, Maryland State Police, 1987.

The Belchfire, my 1972 Cessna 150, and me after the X-country trip. Note that my hair is growing back after I shaved my head bald as a joke.

The Belchfire's cockpit.

In my Class-A Maryland State Police uniform, 1987.

A DOOR LEFT OPEN

PART TWO

Abandoned

A DOOR LEFT OPEN

CHAPTER THIRTEEN

The Day the Earth Stood Still

D AD, WHO HAD always loomed large in my life, had a body shape that polite people once called "husky." Neither obese nor lean but somewhere in between, his build might best be compared to that of Alfred Hitchcock's. With only minutes to spare before the ceremony began, he entered the auditorium through a side door and approached the rest of us. The skin on his face hung like melted ice cream, and he had clearly fastened his belt to its last notch.

This man who successfully survived the Great Depression only to fight in WWII and Korea, and for whom an army chaplain administered the Last Rites while MASH surgeons fought to save him; this lifelong smoker of Luckies who dealt with PTSD blues, divorce, and all the other twitches that can threaten one's wellbeing—this man now had what John Wayne called, "The Big C."

Cancer.

Not just any cancer. We're talking cancer of the wildfire variety.

"I didn't want you to worry," he said by way of greeting, while Mom stood silently at his side.

"Dad. How long have you known?"

"Nothing's been confirmed," he said with a quiet calm that all but yelled *I am dying and I know it and I'm okay with it.* "Then again,

I've lost thirty pounds in the past month alone. But the docs can't find what's wrong. So—" His attention drifted momentarily before he rebounded and pointed at a dignitary who was taking the stage. Then he grinned and shifted gears. "Show's on."

ONE MONTH LATER I fired up my airplane, flew from Cumberland to Ocean City, and took a cab to my parents' home. My maternal grandparents greeted me at the door. So did my older brother Bob, who had come to get his bearings after a divorce that stunned all of us—not least of all him.

After greeting my mother, I found my father working away inside the workshop he had built behind the house. We talked without talking, and since he remained unwilling to delve into matters of death, I clung to the illusion that by giving him his space he might somehow surprise me with good news.

But it was not to be. After a sumptuous dinner marked by desultory conversation, I walked my father outside and shook his hand. He briefly locked eyes with me. Then he got behind the wheel of his Pontiac station wagon and drove off to Andrews Air Force Base, where he would spend a few days at the base hospital to undergo tests that the doctors hoped would determine whether he did indeed have cancer, and where it might be hiding.

Bob drove me back to the airport afterward, and I made a night flight to Cumberland. To this day I recall how vividly the stars appeared above the unutterably dark void of marshlands, farms, and sinewy rivers. However, those stars mocked me with their insistence that life is at all times finite, and although I accepted this reality within the logical portions of my brain, my heart rejected all of it. And while the band played on, I flew on.

The next day I flew several trauma missions, but before going off-duty I asked the section commander to put me on family sick leave for the next three days.

I woke up early the next morning, flew to a small public airport near Andrews, and took a taxi to the base. When the driver stopped at the gate, I showed my state police badge to the sentry. She was too busy doing her nails to even examine it, and simply passed us through.

Once the taxi driver let me off at the hospital, I raced upstairs to my father's room. My mother greeted me as I walked inside. Dad lay atop the bed covers, his skin pallid and sagging; his eyes rheumy.

He had no idea who I was.

But he did want to know where his Lucky Strikes were.

After making my peace with him, I telephoned my former sergeant at Berlin Barracks and asked for a car. He promised to leave his Cadillac at the airport for me, adding, "The keys will be on top of the left rear tire." I barely remember thanking him—or flying to Ocean City to prepare Bob and my grandparents for the inevitable.

The next morning, April 3, 1986, I stepped into the bathroom to shower before flying back to Andrews to see Dad.

I had barely lathered up when an urgent knock at the door sent my stomach flip-flopping. I rinsed off, wrapped a towel around my waist, took a deep breath, and opened the door. My grandmother was standing there. "The phone. It's for you." She didn't have to add anything. I already knew.

I picked up the phone. "Mom?"

Her voice filled with emotion for the first time ever. "Come here. Hurry!"

Ending the call, I dialed a local friend. "Pat? My dad's dying. Can you pick up my grandparents and drive them to Andrews? As in, now?" When Pat assured me that he would, I hung up and told my grandparents to wait for Pat. Then I turned to Bob. "Let's go."

We jumped into the Cadillac and raced to the airport. I slid to a stop. We ran to my plane. Always a stickler for pre-flight inspections and checklists, I ignored both. We got in, we buckled up, I fired up the engine, taxied to the active runway, positioned us on its centerline, and firewalled the throttle.

Leveling off at three thousand feet, I kept the throttle at max speed instead of reducing it to the normal sixty-five percent cruise setting. With chart and flight log atop my lap, I set a course for the small airfield I'd flown into the previous day. Ten minutes swept by. Then twenty more before we began crossing the Chesapeake Bay.

Minutes later, a quick glance at my chart told me that it was time to contact Air Traffic Control. I needed permission to enter their restricted airspace, and I would need the vectors that they would assign to let me reach our destination.

I made the call, received clearance to proceed, and jotted the compass and radio nav headings that they provided. Once I intercepted a radio beacon vector, I checked my flight and engine instruments and pushed harder on the throttle to increase speed.

We were crossing the Bay's halfway point when air traffic control called. *"And Cessna five two seven eight Quebec, come left to new heading, two six zero degrees."*

I acknowledged the controller and made the turn. Then while noting the time on my log, I stopped. Because I knew. I just knew. And so I reached for the throttle and reduced power to sixty-five percent, and when Bob looked at me askance, I pretended not to see him.

Ten minutes later I executed what is euphemistically called an "assault landing," which meant I came in at a steep angle and a higher-than-normal power setting designed to get us on the ground fast. After taxiing to the ramp and securing the aircraft, I pushed fifty bucks into the airport attendant's hand with instruction to drive us to the base hospital.

The attendant made good speed, and minutes later Bob and I stormed through the hospital's main doors. Following a brief search through hallways that reeked of medicinal smells, we found our mother sitting in an anteroom near my father's door. "He's gone," she said in a toneless voice that disturbed me even more than her earlier, impassioned one.

"How long?" I asked.

She shrugged. "Oh, I don't know. Thirty-five minutes."

I checked my watch. Those thirty-five minutes matched my log entry. Then I broke down.

I MEAN, I broke down completely.

I sobbed nonstop in my mother's arms until Bob eased me away and guided my head to his shoulder. I cried a bit more before drawing back and thanking him with my eyes. Then I turned to my mother and said, "I want to see him."

"I thought you would," she replied, and walked me across the hallway to his room. She pulled the privacy drape back and there he was, looking very pale and with his lifeless mouth hanging open. His inert tongue had collapsed accordion-like against the back of his throat, and taking one of his hands in mind and noting its cold touch, I kissed his forehead.

Later, after orderlies removed my father's body, I searched for his Zippo lighter. He'd carried it as a Marine during the Pacific war, and as an Army company commander in Korea. More importantly, he'd used it to light the Lucky Strikes that he would hand out to German laborers. I couldn't find it. Someone had probably stolen it. For me, it was as lost to eternity as my father now was.

"DETAIL, ATTEN-*SHUN!*" Remembering the warmth that deserted my father's body in death, I appraised the ranks of living soldiers. They stood beneath a stunningly blue sky on a warm spring day. Now they were ready to march in tribute to my father, whose flag-draped casket lay atop the horse-drawn caisson that would carry him from the Fort Myers Chapel to his burial site at Arlington National Cemetery.

I'd spoken from the chapel's lectern only minutes earlier, then joined my mother, sister and brothers outside as the soldiers responded with crisp movements following the order to come to attention. Seconds later the musicians began beating the mournful stutter of muffled drums:

Boom Boom Boom, Drrrr
Boom Boom Boom, Drrrr
Boom Boom Boom, Drrrr
Boom: Boom-boom-boom

It was repeated again and again, the drummers maintaining their beat while other musicians launched into *Onward Christian Soldiers*. Then the six matched-grays began moving as one after being spurred on by riders dressed in Class A uniforms, the horses taking up the slack until the caisson's wheels creaked and slowly built momentum as it bore Dad's casket. More soldiers, impeccable and resplendent in dress blues, their polished brass buttons glinting in the sunlight, fell into step, the tiny metal implants in their shoes' soles timing a staccato beat as they accompanied the casket to its final resting place, all this while a non-commissioned officer gave them their cues:

Left, right left
Left, right left
Left, right...

Our family followed in cars. Many of my father's friends were there, along with several of my firefighter and state police buddies. The procession followed the troops as they marched and played martial music amid the sheltering green trees and resplendent lawns that define Arlington Cemetery.

In time, the procession stopped and soldiers bore his casket to the gravesite while others fired a twenty-one gun salute. Then a bugler played Taps, the sorrowful notes rising upward to the blue sky. Finally, the honor guard executed quick practiced motions as they folded the flag and handed it over to an officer, who presented it to my mother.

Then it was over. Everything. Forever.

THREE WEEKS LATER my jaw dropped as the guests filed into Ocean City's Catholic Church for a memorial service. It dropped because they didn't just file in; they packed the place. My father, who despite his many faults of decades ago, had reinvented himself. And while it's true that young children and animals had always been instinctively drawn to him, those he touched later in life now felt compelled to honor his memory—and they did this by showing up in droves.

My brother Jim delivered the first eulogy. Then I got up to speak, the priest frowning when I bluntly described Dad as an agnostic. Yeah, although he might stand accused of many things, he had never been a hypocrite. However, the good priest's visage softened when I began reciting a prayer written by Johnny Gunther, the seventeen-year-old son of acclaimed author John Gunther. In "The Unbeliever's Prayer," young Johnny seeks balance in his struggle to come to terms with the cancerous brain tumor that would eventually kill him. Here it is:

> *Almighty God*
> *forgive me for my agnosticism;*
> *For I shall try to keep it gentle, not cynical,*
> *nor a bad influence.*
>
> *And O!*
> *if Thou art truly in the heavens,*
> *accept my gratitude*
> *for all Thy gifts*
> *and I shall try*
> *to fight, the good fight. Amen.*
>
> –John Gunther, Jr., May 1946

At the reception that followed, the drinks flowed, the stories gushed, and the priest was of good cheer after downing a scotch. Later, when he contemplated the martini I had in hand before flicking his eyes at the bartender, I said, "Careful, Father. These are nothing short of rocket fuel." The good father got one anyway and tested my opinion with an experimental sip. After he smiled and patted my shoulder, I couldn't help myself. "I'm gonna call you 'Rocket Man' from now on, Father."

He simply broke into another smile.

TWO MONTHS LATER I broke down while watching a dumb-ass

rerun of *Father Knows Best*. Who knows why? Certainly not me. All I knew at the time was that a breeze had brushed past an open window just as Bud wondered aloud if his father really did know best. For some reason still unknown, I asked myself, *What is this breeze? Is it the breath of God?* Then I lost it, clutching my belly and falling to the floor as heaving sobs rendered me inert. Hitching and snuffling awhile later, I considered calling a local Cumberland girl that I'd started seeing.

I even reached for the phone, only to put it down and tough it out instead of talking to her—or to anyone else, for that matter. Why didn't I call? 'Cause I'm a guy, and guys hold it together. More or less. At least that's what I convinced myself to be the case.

LIKE MANY IDEAS that sound great in theory, some fall apart while others do not. Maybe that explains why the notion of flying my two-seat airplane from Maryland to San Diego and back struck a chord as being a reasonable challenge. After sitting down with Ed to discuss my plans, I grabbed a phone and called my Ocean City Police buddy, Joe Rolles. "Hey," I began. "Feel like getting your ass kicked?"

Joe snorted, the sound clear even across the long-distance phone lines of the pre-cell era. "Think you're man enough?"

"Without a doubt," I countered. "Now here's the deal—"

After pitching my idea, I added, "It'll help take my mind off my father."

To keep our brains further occupied while turning a journey into an adventure, we vowed to do it the old-fashioned way, by shunning the modern navigation instruments aboard the Belch Fire II, and relying instead on compass, stopwatch and pilotage. The term pilotage is just a high-sounding term for glancing outside the cockpit to find one of the thousands of landmarks that pepper aeronautical charts. Therefore we would turn off everything except the transponder, since it would show our position and speed to Air Traffic Control (ATC). And when we did venture into airspace that mandated the use of electronic nav aids, we'd fire 'em up and call it a nod toward progress.

Joe and I also pledged to take our time; to sightsee along the way; to find remote desert locations to land at the end of the day and sleep under the wings beneath a halo of stars, just as the early pathfinders did. But when Joe pressed me to pack tools and other stuff, I drove the issue of *payload* home by shaving my head bald. "There," I told him. "No hair and no need for a comb. We'll reduce weight that way."

Ed graciously helped me plan a route that would take Joe and me from Cumberland to Arkansas to Tucson, and then on to San Diego. The return trip would include a stop at the Grand Canyon before venturing on via New Mexico, Missouri, West-by-God Virginia, and finally Cumberland. No sweat. Not a problem. Um, wait. I almost forgot. There were still those Rocky-damn-Mountains to consider.

* * * *

The journey began uneventfully enough on a warm bright day in May of 1986. After obtaining an FAA weather briefing, I did a weight-and-balance calculation of the storage space behind the seats. Then I stowed a gym bag containing an Aloha shirt, two T's, shorts, flip-flops and a toilet kit. I already had my business casual on to save space. After Joe added his carry-on, we loaded two lightweight sleeping bags and a slew of aeronautical charts.

Ed stopped by to chat and wish us luck, but when he turned away I kicked my shoes off, kicked the Belch Fire's engine to life, taxied to the active runway, and took off on a trip that would unexpectedly give us bragging rights for years to come.

AFTER LEVELING OFF at three thousand feet AGL (above ground level), we settled in for the journey. The winds aloft for May were predictably out of the west, reducing our airspeed until cars on the interstates below were traveling faster than the Belch Fire—and this was during the era of heavy enforcement of the fifty-five MPH speed limits. The slow going quickly grew tiresome, so we took turns flying. Besides, we had planned for the winds, and they were one reason why we set aside two weeks for the trip.

Unfortunately, the first day of headwinds began to wear on me. At times I would abruptly shout, "Fucking winds!" Joe understood my pain though, and pretended not to hear.

In Arkansas we landed for fuel at a public airfield that was literally that—a field. A *grass* field. After a brief taxi we found the fuel pumps, only to discover that they were unattended. Then Joe pointed to a sign above the pumps that read: HONOR SYSTEM. LEAVE CASH IN THE LOCKBOX BELOW.

Man, ya just gotta love it.

At Oklahoma City's Will Rogers Airport, we taxied to the general aviation terminal. A dozen executive jets were arrayed on the ramp. Many of the pilots were there, and clearly giving the scruffy-looking Belch Fire II a sneering once-over. Then their faces registered total contempt as I emerged from the tiny plane with a bald noggin, a green T, blue shorts and flip-flops.

Joe and I were social animals, so we shrugged at the wall of indifference and greeted the nearest corporate pilot. His initial response to our *how are you* was monosyllabic. But the terse tone and arrogant manner dissolved the instant we mentioned our cross-country flight, along with the compass-and-landmark-only navigation.

After expressing admiration—and following a quick inspection of our fully-equipped and spic-and-span cockpit—he jutted his jaw at two other pilots and tilted his head at us in a silent signal that said, *these guys are okay.* A crowd gathered around the Belch Fire. Then a thing of beauty unfolded when at least three corporate pilots asked if they could change places with Joe.

"You can always fly in my place as first officer," they each told him. "You know—work the radios. That sorta thing."

Joe demurred, and after refueling, we were two proud puppies when Joe took hold of the prop and spun it for an old-style engine start-up, all under the watchful gaze of the expert aviators.

The next day we crossed the Rockies just west of El Paso, a tedious and nerve wracking task that required a climb to 10,000 feet. We were fighting constant updrafts that had me cussing, and when absolute despair and weariness set in, I landed on a small runway sitting atop a mesa, if only to unwind. In hindsight, it turned out to be a wise decision. While walking around and stretching my legs I pulled up mental images of my father, and found a new peace of sorts. An hour later I told Joe, "I'm better now. Thanks. Now let's go."

* * * *

San Diego turned out to be a blast. This provincial yet cosmopolitan city nestled in the country's southwest corner is a gem that offers something for everyone. Joe and I played tourist for two days before beginning the return trip.

Upon departing San Diego International, we flew a northeast course and made a pit stop in Lake Havasu City, Arizona. Arriving too late to get fuel, we caught a cab into town to check out the London Bridge. Then we grabbed dinner in a local joint resplendent with hearty food and even heartier local characters. Finally sated with victuals and venturesome folks, we unrolled our sleeping bags along the banks of the Colorado River and slept beneath the stars.

Continuing north by northeast the next morning, we reached the Grand Canyon and saw that the big ditch remained as grand as it had been during my cross-country road trip seven years earlier. Luck favored us when we found two available rooms at the historic El Tovar Hotel, a place as grand as the canyon, and perched along the south rim. Joe and I spent the next day hiking and exploring and watching the canyon's vistas change in color as the sun climbed higher. And with these subtle changes in hue came an unburdening of grief as the journey finally began panning out.

For instance, I could now see how my ill humors had been making Joe miserable—even though he was too fine a gentleman to complain. So I took him aside and apologized for being a bit on the "testy side" as I modestly referred to it, and pledged to make the remainder of the trip more pleasant for him.

THE NEXT MORNING we made our departure from the Grand

Canyon. Its airport is 6,600 feet above sea level, with morning temps already in the '90s. This might seem like small stuff. It's not. Various aircraft perform differently, and our takeoff would require diligent planning.

Engine performance, runway length, altitude and temperatures conspire to create "density altitude," and careful pilots break out their aircraft's performance charts to check variables. Next, and prior to smart phones, pilots broke out a slide-rule like device to crunch the numbers and determine whether the aircraft can even make it into the air. Joe and I took all this in stride. After all, we were using this long flight to test our airmanship, and saw the challenge not as a chore but as an opportunity.

Working together, we checked the data, saw that the numbers were right, and contacted ground control for permission to taxi to the runway. After receiving clearance to takeoff, I stood on the brakes. Then while running the engine to full power, I adjusted the fuel mixture and noted the engine gas temperatures. Once I felt satisfied, I released the brakes.

The takeoff itself proved to be uneventful, and it turned out to be the easiest part of this leg. That's because as expected due to density altitude factors, it took the Belch Fire every bit of thirty minutes just to reach an altitude of 3,000 AGL, which showed on the barometric altimeter as 9,500 feet when calculated against the already high ground elevation.

At least we were up and eastbound, with Albuquerque slated as the day's final stop. To pass the time I cheerfully pointed out the stunning terrain that continuously unfolded beneath us. "Sure is peaceful down there," I'd say at times. It *was* peaceful, too. That leg, anyway.

IN THE MORNING I stashed my flip-flops in the storage space and executed a routine takeoff out of Albuquerque International. We cleared a high mountain ridge east of the city and leveled off at 8,300 feet—although by factoring in the mean elevation of 5,300, we were actually at a routine VFR altitude of 3,000 feet AGL.

We were blessed with "severe clear" visibility as I adjusted the fuel mixture and trim tab, only to find that the tailwind that a weather briefer told us to expect was better than anticipated. It gave us great groundspeed, and we settled in for a pleasant flight.

Thirty miles east of Albuquerque, I automatically touched a finger to the aeronautical chart atop my leg and noted a small airfield behind us, in Moriarty. Then, as John Lloyd had drilled into me since my first flying lesson, I craned my neck and found the field right where the chart said it should be. Just in case.

Barely a minute passed before I felt a faint vibration through my soles. All at once the Belch Fire abruptly belched. Then, dead silence.

The engine had quit. With the prop still spinning in the slipstream, I instantly turned the control wheel to the right and stepped on the right rudder pedal to make a one-eighty turn for that field. Then while my feet "read" the aircraft as John Lloyd always stressed, I established the plane's best glide speed and adjusted the trim tab. Upon stabilizing the aircraft, I checked the throttle, mixture, and fuel supply. They were fine. So the problem was with the engine.

Joe radioed ATC. Stopping short of declaring a mayday, he informed them in a voice that bordered on boredom that we had lost our engine and were making what he told them would be "a precautionary landing at Moriarty."

The wind rushed past, the once-favoring tailwinds now transformed into menacing headwinds. Otherwise, it was eerily quiet as the ground got closer and closer. Joe and I remained calm as we dead sticked it in. Finally with only a hundred feet of altitude to spare, we sailed over the clumps of arroyo and sage that peppered the runway's approach.

I made a smooth landing and the aircraft's momentum brought us to a taxiway. Stepping hard on the rudder, we turned onto it and coasted in silence for twenty more feet before grinding to a stop. We looked at each other and shrugged as if to say, *Whaddya gonna do?*, then got out. The first thing I did was look up at the pristine blue sky and give silent thanks to John. *Thank you so very much for teaching me to always have a place to land. May you forever rest in peace with the knowledge that you saved our skins.*

Now what? We were in the middle of the desert at a small airstrip with two hangars and a line of telephone poles that went thataway, until they merged with a distant horizon. That was it, other than two crows flapping lazy wings from high above, their sounds all but deafening in the silent and forlorn solitude. I didn't see an office or even any people, so we decided to walk behind the hangars for a look-see.

It's worth bearing in mind that I had shaved my head, and that on this particular day I had on an unbuttoned flapping-in-the-wind Aloha shirt over brown shorts and bare feet. Meanwhile, Joe was sporting a red T and blue jeans, and in the high desert where large hats and leather boots were de facto wear, we must have looked a sight.

At least that's what the two men probably thought when we turned a corner and surprised them. They were hunched over a tub filled with solvent, their sleeves rolled up and their hands holding various aircraft parts. One of them was a bearded fellow, and he stood and rose to a height of six-four. He clenched his fists—which prompted me to dub him, Grizzly Adams—then narrowed his eyes, not only at our sudden manifestation out of clear air, but also with a *what the hell do we have here* look as he overtly took in our appearance. Meanwhile, the other man remained seated. He was older and smaller than Grizzly, and dressed in a careful manner that made him appear to be nothing less than a gentleman. I christened him, Dapper Dan.

Grizzly finally spoke. "Where'd you come from? 'Cause I didn't hear no car drive up."

"Flew in," I replied, and pointed in a generally eastward direction. "Lost my engine. Dead sticked it."

He frowned in disbelief and followed us around the corner, where I swept a hand at the inanimate Belch Fire. While he looked us up and down again, I readily guessed what he was thinking—that he had a couple of yahoos on his hands—a feeling that he confirmed when he set his jaw and sniffed noisily. "All right," he mumbled, "Well, let's have a look at her."

"Look? You?"

"Yeah. Me. 'Cause I'm an A&P. So unless you wanna let it sit under the sun—"

A&P. Aircraft & Power plant mechanic. FAA trained and regulated. They enjoy high salaries and pilots' respect. I thought to myself, *And here we were thinking, why is there never an A&P around when you need one?*

While this was to our good fortune, Grizzly clearly didn't feel comfortable about us hanging around. Yeah, even a blind man could see that his offer to examine the aircraft was nothing short of, *I just wanna get you guys outta here.*

In a tit-for-tat, Joe pulled me to one side and quietly asked, "You thinking what I'm thinking?"

"That these guys are up to no good?"

Joe nodded. "I'm guessing drugs."

I thought it over and shook my head. "I dunno. Not with the aircraft parts they're working on." All at once it came to me. "This could be an airplane chop shop."

He drew a deep breath. "Could be. Let's be careful 'round this pair."

We walked back to the Belch Fire, only to find Grizzly warily watching us before he checked the engine. He finally opened the cowling, peered inside, and said nothing for several minutes. At one point he glanced up and skewered us with angry eyes, then did some more looking. Thirty minutes passed before he grunted and announced that both magnetos were cracked, and then he stuck his head back inside the engine compartment.

With nothing to do, Joe and I found a shaded spot where we could sit and keep an eye on this pair. Then, maybe because of the forced landing and the back and forth with Grizzly, the grief that I'd felt lifted from my shoulders at the Canyon returned. Why was God punishing me this way? I wondered why we were stuck way out here, instead of being grateful for our deliverance, even if in the form of a suspicious A&P. Yep, I should have been feeling upbeat. Instead, I was feeling sorry for myself.

Grizzly worked for another hour before pushing away and approaching us. "I need a break." He seemed ready to add something when he gazed off into the distance. Several silent seconds passed before he said in a barely audible voice, "The interstate's north of here. My kid brother is a New Mexico Trooper. I worry about him, working that highway."

"He is?" My mood brightened at once. "What a coincidence. I'm a Maryland State Police Trooper." When I saw his look of disbelief, I pulled out my badge and ID. "In fact, I'm in the Aviation Division." Then I smiled disarmingly. "I know. I must look weird in this get-up." I explained the shaved head and the trip we were on, adding that we were using nearly forgotten piloting skills. I finished by telling him that Joe was also in law enforcement.

Grizzly lightened up at once. "Is that right? Hmm." He rubbed his chin while he appraised us anew before abruptly asking, "You guys like to shoot?"

The instant we both offered thumbs-up, he turned on his heel and vanished inside the larger hangar, only to reappear a moment later hefting an M-14 rifle in one hand, and a target attached to a tripod in the other. He set up the target near the runway and took a few shots, then handed the rifle to me. I fired five rounds and offered it to Joe. He fired five, and after Grizzly checked the target and found that both of us had clearly outshot him by putting all our rounds in the bulls eye, he seemed satisfied that we were authentic manly men.

We admired the rifle a moment longer before he put it away. But after coming out of the hanger he ambled over to Dapper Dan. A quiet confab followed. Then both men walked over to the Belch Fire and went to work on her.

When they finished five hours later, I broke out my checkbook. I knew the job would cost at least seven hundred bucks—nearly three-week's salary for me at the time—and I turned to Grizzly. "Who should I make this out to?"

He grunted and waved me off. "Put it away. You guys are doin' our kinda flying."

Dapper Dan smiled pleasantly, but said nothing.

When I still insisted on paying, they shook their heads, and after Joe and I offered a flurry of thanks, they sent us on our way. We flew back to Albuquerque for the night, and as we settled in I conducted a low-key investigation. It turned out that Grizzly was a retired USAF pilot, former Alaskan bush pilot, and part time crop duster.

As for Dapper Dan? He was none other than Dr. Paul MacCready, the aeronautical engineer who designed the *Gossamer Albatross,* the flimsy human-powered airship that crossed the English Channel from England to France in 1979. He won the prestigious Collier Trophy for that achievement, he was enshrined in the National Aviation Hall of Fame, and three aircraft that he designed and built were on display in the Smithsonian Air & Space Museum, and they remain there to this day.

Even now whenever I think of "the day the Belch Fire belched," I say a prayer of thanks not only for our deliverance, but also for turning the journey into a rewarding encounter with two dudes in the middle of nowhere. Forrest Gump comes to mind: "And just like that..."

More importantly, if proof of karma exists, I found it that day. It's why whenever I feel the weight of the world now, I think back on the incident and take strength from knowing that everything has a purpose. In fact, all I really have to do is get out of karma's way and let it work its ageless process.

THE NEXT FEW weeks were a blur. Having grown bored with the simplistic Belch Fire, I sold it and got checked out in a Piper Arrow—a high performance plane with retractable landing gear and a variable pitch prop. That baby was fast, capable of "truing out" at 200 mph plus. Renting the Arrow cut the usual two-hour flight to Ocean City nearly in half.

I was settling back into a routine life when the division captain called on a sunny day in June. The boss had approved my transfer request to the Salisbury Section. "Great," I told the captain. And it was great; another dream was coming true, and my bosses had my back.

So what was that feeling deep inside my soul, whispering that I had been abandoned?

COCKY ROCKY WAS back on the shore and in his natural environment. I moved into an upscale rental home on an Ocean City canal, a serene location yet close enough to my mother's house for me to drop by and do chores for her. I would also be working with old friends again.

On a career level, I began work on my instrument flight rating. It turned out to be a grueling training regimen, one far more difficult than the effort I put in for my initial pilot license. I received high marks though, and got that instrument flight rating. Not only would the "IFR ticket" let me fly in zero visibility conditions, to my great surprise the division's upper management heard about my score. They mentioned helping me upgrade my license even further, and move me into a pilot's slot.

The brass also mentioned that I now had more decorations, awards and official attaboys than did any other trooper. Of course, if you work in the emergency field long enough the awards accrue almost by default. In any event the captain told me flat-out that the division was grooming me for rapid promotion.

In other words, they liked what they saw. But there were things about me that they did not see. Top among these was my taste in friends, which ran a gamut of diversity that would have met with official disapproval. I was also walking a wild side with greater frequency, which was also at odds with the agency's sensibilities. The thing is, I didn't care. I had just one life to live, and I was going to live it on my terms and not someone else's.

As for my romantic life, I had started seeing Denise. I liked her a lot, but her feelings for me didn't come close to the unconditional love I craved. Naturally, I didn't recognize it then, but what I really wanted was the love that my father had showered me with.

Life appeared to be full of promise one evening as Denise and I left a theater after seeing the Harrison Ford film, *Mosquito Coast.* The night was clear as only a crisp autumn night can be, and the stars shining above seemed painted there with a broad brush. All at once my breath caught. I felt the need to change paths in life—to search in different directions. Years later when I saw *Field of Dreams,* I instantly related to the notion that *If you build it, he will come.*

Back to what it was that hit me when I stared into the heavens. I had always dreamed of writing a novel. I had also fallen in love with San Diego, and what the hell...life is short. The next day I called everyone I knew and said, "I'm going to move to San Diego. And by the way, I'm gonna become a writer."

That afternoon I reported to work and handed the section commander my formal resignation. While he read it, I outlined my intentions.

After he finished laughing—I did have that reputation as a prankster—and saw that I was serious, he looked at me askance and waited. However, I'd said everything I needed to say. As for my mother, she shrugged and wished me well. I kept my own counsel on another aspect of my decision, though: I'd resigned once before, when I was six weeks into the academy. They took me back and I graduated with honors, but the agency had a policy: if a trooper resigns once, no problem. Resign twice? Don't come knocking again. I barged ahead anyway.

Were my actions thus far those of someone who had become unhinged? Well, *I* certainly didn't think so, and something I learned later proved that they were not. At any rate, two weeks later I turned in my equipment, packed my belongings into a rented van, and headed west. Was I scared? Sure. But as Bette Davis said, "No guts, no glory."

Or maybe what she meant was, "No brains, no fame." Because I sure as hell had no idea where I would live, or where the money would come from once my savings ran out. I only knew that the one person who had ever shown me unconditional love was gone. I also had no idea why it mattered so much. But it did, and ten years would pass before I made the connection that let me comprehend my need to run, and to keep running.

CHAPTER FOURTEEN

Sunny Sandy Eggo

TAKING COURAGE FROM what Firefighter Steve Preslipsky confided years ago, about how he admired people who left the comforts of great jobs and went into the great unknown (to which I replied, "Yeah, but it's easier if you're single"), I wasted little time in leasing a place near La Jolla—aka, "The Pearl"—San Diego's prime real estate for fame, fortune, and Mediterranean clime.

After settling in, I wrote the first draft of a literary novel. Next, I found the *Writers Haven Writers Workshop*. Fortune favored me, because the workshop enjoyed a sterling reputation, whereas most writer groups are overpopulated by frustrated authors who go out of their way to eviscerate other, more promising writers. But this group supported rather than shellacked their colleagues.

I fell into a workshop of fledgling writers who were not averse to telling you if the work you'd just read aloud could be likened to having a booger hanging from your nose. But I realized at once that they made their comments out of friendship, since nobody wants to see their peers appearing in public with hanging boogers. Of course, this was long before hanging chads, the point being that the workshop members pointed out errors and problems in order to help rather than hinder struggling writers. Then they would offer advice to fix the problems.

In my case, I had plenty of hanging chads—I mean boogers.

For starters, I had never studied creative writing. I simply took it for granted that voracious readers absorbed writing skills through osmosis. Jesus, what was I thinking? It's why the draft that I began reading in front of the group was not only not suitable for framing, but would have been put to better use for wrapping fish. After two months of seeing them shake their heads, I got that sinking feeling and wondered, what the hell did I do by leaving Maryland?

However, I pressed on while simultaneously reverting to earlier, more carefree days of indifferent attire and freedom from shoes. I grew a beard, wore beads, tried veganism, and made new friends. The friends included Betty Jurus, Jean Jenkins, and Howard Fischer. Betty had co-authored *Men In Green Faces*, a non-fiction story of SEALs in Vietnam that is considered required reading by members of that elite unit.

Howard turned out to be equally remarkable. As a boy, he'd worked as a "gofer" for the men at Ryan Air while they were building *The Spirit of St. Louis*, near today's Lindbergh Field. By the 1940s Howard was an airline captain flying DC-3s out of Los Angeles, and also a close longtime friend of aviation's legendary "Wrong Way" Corrigan.

I GOT CHECKED out on a rental airplane. I explored the region by air and by land, discovering birds-eye view landmarks and land-based tunnels that shamed anything the east coast could offer. There were clothing-optional beaches to enjoy, fine Mexican restaurants to embrace, and offbeat taverns where I could while away an afternoon.

San Diego boasts a first-rate zoo, Balboa Park was primo, and I became fascinated upon hearing that the author of *The Wonderful Wizard of Oz* had lived nearby when he wrote his classic story, and that his description of Munchkin Land was the mirror image of San Diego. But the rest of the country had yet to discover San Diego, which left me with a safe haven for relaxation and reflection.

A year later I had a polished draft of a literary novel. *Light...Precious Light* dealt with issues of betrayal and forgiveness, and the title was inspired by the Biblical passage where David finds his son Absalom's lifeless body, and cries out, "O my son Absalom, my son, my son Absalom!"

I had a novel, but I'd also gone through all my savings, and in 1989 I was a thirty-four year old veteran of two career paths that I had veered from—and there could be no return for one of them: the state police. I'd resigned twice. The agency had slammed the door shut. I didn't agree with their policy. It didn't matter.

At about the time I began wondering *What do I do now?* I stumbled upon an ad seeking former police officers who could work on a remote island in a far corner of the planet. The position required a security clearance, but it offered a generous tax-free salary, free room and board...and adventure. How could this be a bad thing?

Besides, who doesn't dream of living on a remote Pacific island? Although it meant leaving Sunny Sandy Eggo, what the hell? I'd already been running. Why not run even farther?

One more thing: during his World War II Marine Corps days, my father had been on that very island.

A DOOR LEFT OPEN

CHAPTER FIFTEEN

Partly Bali Today

P ARTLY BALI TODAY is a catch-all for my three years in paradise. Although I'd never stepped foot on that legendary island, its ideal resided deep within my imagination. Then there is *Treasure Island*. I had not been there either, of course. Yet it remained no less a place in the imagination of Robert Louis Stevenson. And so it goes with Kwajalein, except that it was not an imaginary place, and no less vibrant a place to me than Bali is for others in search of paradise.

* * * *

Kwajalein Atoll is a remote chain of coral islands buried deep within Micronesia, at a midway point between Hawaii and Australia. It's a genuine tropical paradise with islands that possess exotic, textured names—names such as Omelek, Gagan, and Illeginni. Coconut palms sway in balmy breezes, and furiously blue, green, and turquoise waters compete with talcum powder beaches for the eye's favor.

The islands are also a target. Once every two months or so, the United States test fires an Inter-Continental Ballistic Missile—an ICBM with dummy warheads—and aims it at Kwajalein, where the tracking and telemetry equipment that sprout from beneath palm trees possess equally alien appellations—Altair and Tradex and Super Radot among them.

Pacific atolls are named for their largest island, and at 800 acres Kwajalein took the local prize for length and girth. After invading Kwajalein during WWII, the U.S. established a military base there. A giant runway takes up half of its 800 acres. The remaining acreage supports 5,000 Americans in buildings that range from small homes to large dorms. There are also phased-array radar systems, elementary and senior high schools, a fine-dining restaurant, and great scuba facilities. Of the ninety-some islands in the atoll, the U.S. controls ten. Together, they form a ring of testing, tracking, and telemetry stations around the lagoon, becoming in effect a huge catcher's mitt for those incoming dummy warheads.

Geo-politics aside, Kwajalein remains an isolated lagoon, and isolation serves to buffer probing eyes. It's why scientists were conducting a huge chunk of Reagan's Star Wars R&D on "Kwaj," where things could remain out of sight and out of mind. It's also why civilian cops were recruited, since they're better suited for dealing with the civilian population of techies and entire families. As cops, we also provided high-level security for the secret facilities that dotted those tiny islands within the huge atoll.

* * * *

I stepped out of the cold interior of a U.S. Air Force C-141 Starlifter and blinked rapidly against the harsh glare of a noon sun bouncing off coral sands. When I stepped onto a black tarmac baking beneath a tropical sun, I had surely entered a sauna.

There was no jetway; a crewmember had triggered a set of internal steps that deployed in clackety-clack stages until it kissed that steaming tarmac. In fact, there were no jetways at all. I learned later that some new arrivals take one look at "the rock," and climb back aboard the plane. Others? They jump in to see what it's all about. I suppose that life itself can be that way. You either take the plunge or you get the hell outta the way.

At the terminal entrance a sign read: "Welcome to U.S. Army Kwajalein Atoll." Fellow passengers who were already residents went in one direction, while six of us passed through a door left open for us. Among "us" was Michael DuFour, a handsome stud seven years my junior, the type who could wear a burlap bag and still look great. He'd come to Kwajalein via the Washington State Patrol, and prior to that he served with an elite army jungle warfare unit. Although he and I had much in common, we had stayed at arms' length during the flight. Yet we were destined to become brothers-from-other-mothers.

As our group of newbies entered the Entry/Exit office, an armed police officer looked us over while checking our paperwork. He then issued IDs with clearances granting us access to all areas of the atoll. Following this, he delivered a simple security briefing: "Don't take photos of stuff you see around the islands. Don't do this... don't do that...." Then he added a relevant tidbit. "Be careful going outdoors until you're acclimated to the sun, 'cause that mother will fry you in fifteen minutes." Finally finished, he showed us to another room where a tall, tanned police lieutenant wearing a dark blue polyester uniform stood waiting with an open smile and an out-stretched hand.

After the introductions, he guided us into a white van and drove us along narrow roads teeming with bicycle traffic. In less than a minute we stopped in front of a white structure built upon crushed white coral nestled beneath the protective shade of broadleaf trees. Yep, I had it down by now—they painted everything white as pro-tection from the all-invasive sun, everyone got around by bicycle, and the few motor vehicles I saw were for official purposes only.

The building turned out to be the police headquarters, and when we walked inside my body seized-up at once. *Damn. I've stepped from a sauna into a meat locker.*

"Sorry," the lieutenant murmured as he rapped on the chief's door. "All a/c's are kept low. Sensitive electronics, and all that."

After the chief welcomed us aboard, we went back outside into dazzling sunlight tempered by tall swaying palms. Their green fronds offered a refreshing respite, blue and turquoise waters shimmered nearby, beaches beckoned, and I'd found a home.

I HATED THE place. Not really. However, a couple of things led to disappointment. In the first instance, it turned out that the recruiter had shown me photos of Holiday Inn rooms while claiming they were "the usual living quarters on Kwajalein." I ended up in a two-man room with zero privacy, located inside a military bachelor quarters building. The second and equally discouraging issue involved some of the island attitudes. Although we were sworn police officers acting under the authority of Hawaiian laws, residents from adults down to kids saw us as mall rent-a-cops. The dismal room and the bored attitudes alone left me feeling even further removed from the great home I once had in Ocean City, and the respect I enjoyed as a trooper.

I felt betrayed, just as I had felt when the state police sent me to Prince Frederick after I finished the academy. And just as with Prince Frederick, I was forgetting to be grateful for having this job in the first place.

Several days later found us qualifying with handguns, M-16s and shotguns. During a break, I was complaining about things until Michael DuFour shrugged and said, "Give it a chance."

I heaved a sigh. "Yeah. You're right."

One thing did temper my disappointment: an inverse fact of island life, one that troubled most of the single guys, but not me, or as it turned out, Michael. The reality was blunt—there were ten men for every single woman on "Kwaj." This posed a problem for some, but Michael and I agreed that most men are timid around women out of fear of rejection. At the risk of sounding arrogant, it didn't affect us. Michael and I had the gift of gab, and we viewed rejections as mere stepping-stones on the paths to acceptance.

We also agreed that a ready smile and honest laughter will open many doors, and neither of us were shy about grabbing a gal and getting on the dance floor—especially Michael. He had that kid-from-the-wrong-side-of-the-tracks rhythm that couldn't be ignored, and I couldn't help but admire his talents. His fluid movements definitely pleased the ladies, and they watched him with real interest. He had a steady girlfriend within a week, and I made short work of finding a friend of my own.

I ALSO GRABBED at the earliest opportunity to hop a flight to Roi-Namur. "Roi" is half the size of Kwaj, and fifty miles north. Twin-engine aircraft constantly shuttle workers and visitors back and forth at no charge, and a police detachment keeps the island's ultra-top secret facilities and its two hundred or so permanent residents secure.

After stopping by the detachment office for directions, I set off on foot for the trails that my father probably walked as part of the invasion force. Almost half of Roi's acres are jungle, and as I lumbered up one dirt path and down another, a sense of déjà vu swept over me so strongly that if was as if I could now see everything through my father's eyes. In some places the jungle opened to reveal massive Japanese bunkers still standing decades after the war, serving as silent testament to why three Marines received Medals of Honor during the invasion. In fact, I saw plenty of spent rifle shell casings everywhere, and wondered if some of them might've come from my father's rifle.

At the end of the day I jogged back to the airfield and checked in for my flight. With that done, I stood off to one side and looked at the nearby lagoon. A gentle incoming tide was kissing a crescent-shaped beach, and the whole was embraced by the ever-present green palms beneath an almost always deep blue sky. All at once a great calm descended upon me. I had to be here, I guess; I had to see a visible reminder of Dad's contributions. Finally refreshed, I flew back to Kwaj and got on with my life.

MICHAEL AND I had yet to go beyond being acquaintances. However, we were both quick to establish rapports with residents who had grown accustomed to stodgy, standoffish island officers. A good cop will stop, chat, and kid around with those they see, and he and I were determined to be good cops.

Our schedules were tight, though. The police department worked its officers six days a week, with at least one of those days devoted to a twenty-four hour detail on one of the outer islands. Those islands ranged in size from five to forty acres. Two of them had launch facilities, and sensitive telemetry systems and high-power telescopes studded the others. These facilities were crucial to Star Wars, so the Soviets were actively trying to put sailors ashore by submarine to steal secret data. It's why we were there, to stop 'em in their tracks—dead in their tracks if necessary.

"Island detail" personnel boarded Huey helicopters which flew them to the islands. There were also technicians on the flights, but they flew back each afternoon. With nothing much for us to do until the night's darkness provided cover for clandestine Soviet ops, we remained casual. In this case, being casual included doffing what passed as combat uniforms and boots, and donning shorts and flip-flops—the latter required for protection against the sharp coral and tiny land crabs that were everywhere. Once properly outfitted we could roam around, but always while still armed.

Later, when nighttime fell with a blackness that completely enveloped the atoll, we suited up and went on the alert. Although the islands were equipped with surface radars and motion sensors, we also patrolled on foot with night vision equipment.

Were there ever any encounters? A major network news show once aired a story about a Soviet submarine that entered the lagoon, but the reporter only provided the military's sanitized version of events. I was also involved in another incident that remains classified to this day, and will remain so for a long, long time. The bottom line is that we earned our salaries.

NOT ONLY IS Kwaj a speck within the Central Pacific, it's isolated further by the fact that people can't just go there. Only those who live and work on Kwaj can step foot on the island. To enforce this, armed police officers are present at the marina dock 24/7. They also meet the Air Micronesia flights that land for fuel and passengers, and officers literally stand in the doorway to stop anyone other than residents and authorized personnel from getting off the plane.

To counter the strict seclusion, the island boasts myriad activities. There are free movies at an outdoor theater—just remember to bring an umbrella along with your popcorn. There's golf, swimming, and scuba. Then there are baseball and basketball leagues, tennis courts, a two-lane bowling alley, nightclubs, and a superb restaurant. The bachelors eat their meals in a central dining room, where the food was free and fine. Two TV channels, a radio station, an island paper and a library kept us informed. Finally, two retail stores offer goods at PX prices.

On the downside, mail takes a month to reach the island, and phone calls to the Mainland must go through a central switchboard. You wanna make like E.T. and phone home? Fine. Just call the operator to provide your credit card number and reserve your time slot. Two hours might pass before she rings back and puts the call through—and they're limited to fifteen minutes. To nobody's surprise, calls are subject to monitoring by military intelligence.

For many of us, there weren't enough hours in the day. I didn't even bother buying a TV because there were so many things to do—especially for those who swim like a fish and love history. The atoll was the site of a major WWII battle, and reminders of the fierce fighting still litter the islands. Safety personnel teach even toddlers not to touch anything they find, since what appears to be a dirt-covered cylinder is probably an unexploded artillery shell or a hand grenade.

The U.S. Navy also sank several Japanese auxiliary warships and freighters in the lagoon, and they all but beg to be explored. On a somber note, some wrecks still contain human remains, so divers avoid the parts of the ships where they've been found. While the bones might be those of a former enemy, they died while defending their country and deserved respect.

And so among many other pursuits, I learned to dive and eventually got certified as a master scuba instructor. A small group of us plunged each day into water so warm that other than basic scuba gear, we only wore nylon running shorts. The underwater visibility could be up to two hundred feet, so every dive offered spectacular views of coral heads, reefs, and...sharks. Lots and lots of sharks. But as with all things in life, you either learned to co-exist with them, or you got a bigger boat.

Although a night dive that Michael and I made still stands out. We were eighty feet down on a moonless night, and using underwater lights to examine the coral reef. He was to my left, next to the reef. I had nothing but deep open water to my right. Then Michael punched my right arm to get my attention. I frowned. Something was amiss. Then the hairs on my neck stood on end as I thought, *Wait. How can he punch that arm? He's on my other side.* Sure enough, a quick area recon with my light exposed the six-foot long gray reef shark that had bumped its snout against me to do a "sniff test" during its search for dinner. Seeing it, I got *real* close to Michael, even as the academic portion of my brain shouted that this proved what we all knew—that for every shark you see, there are three others you don't see. This also showed me that since they were leaving us alone, we could swim with the sharks with at least *some* degree of safety.

There were also near-dusk excursions that saw us boarding small boats and skimming across lazy waves into deeper waters, the ocean translucent and the sky's summits altering from indigo to purple to pink. It was all so tranquil, until a strange buzz prompted all of us to abruptly stand upright and strain our ears at the sound.

Then they came. Flying fish. Ten and twenty at first; then hundreds followed by a thousand more, skimming atop the wavelets in their efforts to escape unseen predators beneath those waters, the flying fish encumbered not by fear but by instinct, which explains why they flew into us, their furiously flapping fins fluttering against our bare torsos as they sought survival, the dorsal fins of myriad sharks sluicing the ocean's surface in pursuit, while our mouths hung open in awe of this ancient order of Darwin's survival of the fittest. The surreal show humbled us while its ending reassured us, because it spoke of primordial accordance and innumerable millennia of karma's dictates.

Years later, while watching a flight of flying fish in Ang Lee's *Life of Pi*, I was instantly transported back in time to sea smells and sounds of wavelets slapping our boat's hollow hull, while thousands of fish took to the air to stream past us, their wings buzzing with unfathomable energy as they sought freedom from graceless deaths.

Later still, when I began to discover the reason why I happened to be in a tiny boat in a colossal ocean to see those flying fish, the facts behind my own flight left me reeling.

A YOUNG WOMAN whom I sometimes dove with discovered a Japanese submarine-chaser on the lagoon floor. The depth was a hundred and thirty feet and it turned out to be a virgin wreck, with all its weapons, supplies and equipment intact. There were also human remains, including a skull next to the forward anti-aircraft gun. When she asked me to accompany her on a follow-up dive, I eagerly accepted.

After going into the forward crew quarters, we found the complete skeleton of a sailor who had been pinned beneath a heavy beam when the ship sank. What made it more eerie was that his shirt, trousers and boots were still intact, encasing the bones as if shielding them from marine life.

She also found the captain's remains, along with a samurai sword still attached to the unbroken pelvic bones. Because these swords are family heirlooms, she retrieved it and cleaned the blade until she found some identifying marks. Using these, she tracked down the captain's family in Japan and offered to return the sword. However, many Japanese families want no reminders of the war, and this was one of those families. So their representative thanked her for the generous offer, and told her to keep it.

Kwajalein's location also provides unique travel opportunities. For example, I spent a month touring New Zealand with a friend I met along the way. We bungee jumped at Skipper's Canyon, fell into the festive nightlife in nearby Queenstown, and skinny-dipped in the frigid Tasman Sea. From Kiwi-land it was only a kangaroo-like hop to Australia, where I satisfied another boyhood dream by exploring that downright down-under land.

Our employer also flew us free of charge to Hawaii, Guam or Truk Lagoon. Truk, now renamed Chuuk, was Japan's Pearl Harbor, and in 1944 the U.S. Navy attacked Truk's airfields and shore installations. Next, the Navy fighters turned their sites on the more than seventy ships anchored in the lagoon. The ships carried tanks, ammunition—even tea cups—and today's divers consider Truk a Mecca of sorts. Divers fly there from all over the world despite needing up to three days to reach it. For us, it was a four-hour flight from Kwaj, which for some reason always angered the other visitors.

Well, that was their problem. Friends and I usually spent a week at a time there, diving in the morning and off-gassing in the afternoons to rid our blood of built-up nitrogen. Rather than remain idle, we rented motor scooters and explored Truk's mountain regions, where we would make friends with the kids. None of us spoke Trukese, they didn't comprehend English, but our openly friendly smiles always paved the way to further adventures.

More often than not, they gestured for us to park our scooters and follow them into the jungles. On one occasion, after we slogged barefoot along dank trails and creeper vines, we turned a corner where the kids proudly pointed to a Japanese fighter plane. This vanquished aircraft, known only to these children, still bore the bullet holes that caused its demise during a war, that like all wars was supposed to end all wars.

The kids also led us to cave openings that turned out to be entrances to tunnel complexes. The tunnel floors always felt slimy underfoot, and scores of bats hanging from the ceilings lent their own creepiness to narrow passageways. These Japanese defensive positions still contained crates of weapons, clothing, and food-stuffs—even a small dispensary that our young guides brought us to. I had read about these tunnels. Now here they were for real and in real time, so I said a silent prayer of thanks to the karma that led me here in the wake of unrelenting grief.

THE FORCES OF our universe also encouraged Michael to stop by my place one night, and over some beers he asked a pointed and very personal question. After I instantly confirmed what he suspected, he nodded and said, "I needed to know if I can trust you." He then proceeded to open his soul and unload his troubles—and unload he did. When he stopped talking, it was my turn to dump on him. We forged a deep friendship that night, and a couple of years later he asked me to be his best man. Later, he honored me again by giving his newborn son the middle name of "Richard."

Speaking of names, I became friends with a young firefighter whose full handle was, Ragnar Noel Valencia Opiniano. Known to all as "Opie," he fell in with our crowd and joined us for diving and dancing with the ladies at the club. The diving continued, although his dancing days were numbered after he fell in love with one of those ladies.

I had a wealth of other friends on Kwaj, and I remain close to a dozen of them decades later. It's why today, while walking along a beach in the half-light of a new day, I keep in mind that if I had stayed in the fire department I might never have realized so many other dreams. Nor would I have found the open door that led to a lifelong friendship with Michael.

KWAJALEIN REMAINED FOR me part Bali and part Shangri-La, an island that held its own mystic quality due to its isolation. And as was the case in Shangri-La, Kwaj could be anything you wanted it to be. Yep, it was Partly Bali Today, everyday.

Living there also opened paths to new adventures and travels throughout the Pacific. Moreover, I took advantage of this gift and saw those new places. By doing so, I learned things from diverse cultures while enjoying job satisfaction. After the chief promoted Michael and me to fill two sergeant's slots, he went to patrol while I took on a plainclothes investigator role.

Violent crimes are nearly non-existent on Kwaj. People leave their doors unlocked, and homicides and robberies are pointless to commit since a suspect can't flee the closely guarded atoll. Unfortunately, there were other crimes, and some involved a violence of the spirit.

That's why when the chief stepped into the Investigations Section one morning and beckoned me to follow, I got up and asked no questions. When he led the way into his office and pointed to a chair, I sat and waited.

"Rick, we have a super-sensitive criminal case on our hands. It's why I skipped the chain of command and summoned you personally."

That answered my first question, since police chiefs aren't known for bypassing their staff to personally hand out assignments to subordinates.

"Here's what's happening..." He described a problem involving a for-real rocket scientist who, an anonymous source claimed, was sexually and physically abusing his young son. After providing graphic details, the chief crossed and uncrossed his long legs and worked his mouth silently before releasing a pent-up sigh and locking eyes with me. "Tread lightly, Rick. There are deep issues at stake...national security issues."

My instincts shouted, *I'd like to skin Mr. Rocket Man alive.* But experience shouted back even louder, all the way to my days as a rookie trooper, when a wife accused her husband of beating her up. Only, it turned out that he had a different story to tell and I ended up arresting the wife for sexually abusing their infant son.

I'm not able to go into specifics in this Rocket Man case, other than to describe my actions. With my marching orders in hand, I put out a few feelers among my informants. I also literally camped outside the kid's bedroom window for three nights running, vowing to crash through the front door if I heard any signs of abuse. In the meantime, I collected evidence, listened to my trusted snitches, and drew some different conclusions.

The case turned out to be fake news in a job that breeds jealousies among co-workers. In this instance, a couple of ass-kissers engineered a story they hoped would yank the gifted and totally innocent rocket scientist out of the proverbial picture, and open the way for their own advancement. And so it goes.

In the rocket man case I uncovered the information and witnesses to save someone's reputation. But I also stumbled a lot, and in any event there were several police officers on Kwaj who were far better than I, and who taught me many important lessons.

A DOOR LEFT OPEN

CHAPTER SIXTEEN

The Incoming Party

I F MISSILES ARE ever made ready to fly from Korea or China toward targets in America, the residents of Kwajalein Atoll should
be on the talk show experts' short-lists. After all, in addition to the
Star Wars R&D, it's still on the receiving end of ICBM tests.

The end of the Cold War supposedly meant freedom from nuclear
death, but all that has changed. In the meantime, Kwajalein's isolation doesn't cushion the impact of current events, so the frequent
tests command everyone's attention.

The island paper routinely mentions each mission in a matter-
of-fact manner. "Warning," the announcements begin, "a hazard
area will be in effect in the lagoon's mid-atoll corridor tonight due
to incoming MIRVs." These MIRVs—Multiple Independently Tar-
geted Re-entry Vehicles—are the warheads, and up to ten of these
City Busters can be packed into a single ICBM. Just be sure to substitute dummy warheads for the real thing, and fire away.

"Open the pod bay door, HAL."

Because soldiers on battlefields yell, "Incoming!" to warn of in-
bound artillery, the mission announcements signal the formation
of "incoming parties." That's when groups of five or fifteen friends
lug ice chests and barbecue grills to the nearest beach. Once there,

they snap open beer cans while cooks slap hamburger patties down to sizzle. The talk is festive, and laughter mingles freely with the intoxicating blend of burgers and bougainvillea. Smiles on faces bronzed deeply by the constant sun are radiant, and the trades blow cooling air across the parties. Day-glo Frisbees and tattered footballs fly between leaping youths, while giggling children chase each other as watchful parents keep sight of them.

But as daylight capitulates to dusk and the time for the missile re-entry draws near, the athletics, the banter and particularly the laughter fade away. It's as if a Fourth of July crowd has grown silent in anticipation of that first cluster of iridescent reds, blues and shimmering golden spiders. The revelers search the sky.

Fourth of July crowds back home can see their rockets being launched. But Kwajalein's rockets are sent flying from California's Vandenberg Air Force Base. It's 5,000 miles away, so there's no whoosh on Kwaj, only an odd star that abruptly appears among the constellations. Then it blossoms into a super-nova with a heart-stopping jolt, and the partiers watch raptly as the MIRVs streak toward their targets at more than 13,000 mph.

There are no "ooohs" or "ahhhs."

As the MIRVs race toward their targets, streaks of white-hot vapor trail behind each; three, four...five of them, and all the natural similes are there I suppose—that an angry Thor has been roused from perpetual slumber, or that God Himself has thrust His hand into the great pickle barrel that we call the Pacific Ocean.

The MIRVs strike the lagoon with furious kinetic energy, sending up plumes of spray that reflect beads of moonlight. Sometimes in their wake there is a murmuring sound, a desiccated sigh that travels across the lagoon on the backs of the trades. That noise is haunting; it is every freight train or crying child or howling wolf that leaps, fleetingly, from the recesses of our memories.

The whispers eventually fade. A tentative burst of applause is followed by scattered talk of nuclear blackmail. The crowds move away. Conversations are muted. Many seem withdrawn, their faces grim. Mothers and fathers hug their offspring with something more than tenderness; they seem to engulf their children, as if their arms are protective shields. But the gestures, born of instinct, are so inadequate. The children, too, are hushed. They neither laugh nor shout as they had moments earlier, but look to their parents instead for a reassurance that does not exist.

It is *impossible* to not think of T.S. Eliot:

> *...This is the way the world ends*
> *This is the way the world ends*
> *This is the way the world ends*
> *Not with a bang but a whimper.*

The crowd disappears. The party, this one at least, is over.

A DOOR LEFT OPEN

CHAPTER SEVENTEEN

The Wilderness Years

T HE PARTY WAS indeed over. After three years of living in paradise, I stood between diverging paths. I could remain upbeat and content on a carefree yet isolated atoll. Or I could take my chances back in the real world. The question of whether to stay or go remains a common one on Kwaj, where large numbers of people who went there in the 1960s and '70s got married and raised children who went off to college, only to return and repeat the cycle.

Realizing that remaining in comfortable seclusion could easily see me still there thirty years later, I decided to leave. However, in doing so an unseen enemy leaped from its hiding place and hit me...hit me hard. For in the final analysis, the price I still had to pay in order to grow in another direction was as high as it was non-negotiable.

Before leaving, I walked Roi-Namur's jungle trails to say goodbye to my father by touching palms that had sprouted in places where he must have been so many years ago. After an hour of wandering I felt refreshed and at peace.

Except then I did something that my father would have found unforgiveable. Shortly before leaving Kwaj for good, I gave my firefighter friend Opie a dressing-down. He had asked a favor of me; I misread it. To this day I wonder why I didn't call and ask for clarification. Sadly, I didn't and I ended up being totally out of line. Not only did Opie not deserve my wrath, I threw fuel on the flames by writing a not-so-nice letter and sending it to him.

The things we do.

A month later I reached out to apologize. But when my repeated efforts were met by silence, I understood how much pain I had caused him, and how I had tarnished my father's memory.

$$* \quad * \quad * \quad *$$

In May of 1991, I flew the eight thousand or so miles back to Maryland and the house where my mother still lived, and where my father had spent what were probably his happiest years.

A day later I rented a four-seat Cessna-172 and spent about two hours aloft. Flying helped put things into perspective. It also kept my skills current, and after doing a few touch and go landings, I shot practice instrument approaches into Salisbury Airport.

One day after landing and securing the aircraft, I returned to my mother's house only to find a letter atop the kitchen counter. The return address was for a publisher's acquisitions editor. It took me a moment before I remembered sending him the manuscript for *Light...Precious Light*. After doing three years of rewrites while living on Kwajalein, I sent it out to several publishers. Now this editor wanted my book.

Literary novels have a limited market. Fortunately, my book saw a respectable debut. It was a regional bestseller within a month, reader reviews were generous, and Borders picked it up and distributed it nationwide. In an ideal world I'd have plopped my butt down on my mother's sofa and gotten to work on the next book. I would have, but I had to run.

I RAN TO Olympia, at least at first. Washington's state capitol offered reasonable rent and easy access to Port Angeles, where Michael now lived after the state patrol re-hired him, and from where he urged me to leave my comfort zone in Maryland and be a

Washington Trooper. "We'll work out of the same barracks," he said. "Live on the same street. Our kids will play together."

It sounded like a plan, so I bought a red 1983 Toyota Celica GTS with five on the floor and a souped-up engine. After tossing in clothes, toiletries and a desktop computer, I began yet another cross-country trek. This time I took the high road—Interstate 90—and motored through Wisconsin and South Dakota, stopping to see Mount Rushmore before easing onto a route that brought me beneath Montana's big skies. I sped through Wyoming and Idaho to reach Spokane, and after driving for two days through Washington's stunning high-desert country, I reached the superlative Cascades.

In Olympia I rented a room from a free-spirited gal. She lived next to Evergreen State College, aka Tree Hugger U, where student dress was pared down to the essentials and showers were to be avoided, and where many went shoeless even in the winter. Personally, I kinda liked the students. They were friendly and upbeat, and I learned a thing or two from them.

Within days I applied to the state patrol and began work on a new novel—a thriller this time. Then on weekends I set everything aside and drove to Port Angeles, to visit Michael and the girl he had fallen in love with. It all seemed so grand.

At least it did until the state patrol said they had no vacancies. That's when I packed my things and went back to Maryland—and that's when a friend sat me down for a talk.

Dan had been a Maryland trooper. When the new-home company he got going on the side took off, he realized the impossibility of having two masters. So he quit the state police and plunged full-time into his business. A multi-millionaire within three years, Dan clearly knew how to make money, and this is why I listened keenly to what he had to say.

"Franchises, Rick. They're the way to go."

We were in a gloomy Irish pub when this conversation took place. After squinting past my beer glass to signal our waitress for another round, I shifted in my seat and asked, "But what kind of business?"

"Maid service," he said at once.

I grunted. "You...want me...to be a maid? A friggin' *maid*? Tell me you're not just yankin' my chain."

"Come on, Rick. Cut the crap." Dan propped himself on his elbows and leaned forward. "You'll own a company that hires others to clean homes." He hesitated. "Yeah, you'll have to fill in for anyone who bangs in sick, but—" He banged a fist on the table. "Rick, I'm telling ya. It's a good deal." Leaning closer again, he locked eyes with me. "Look, I'll lend you the seed money. Zero-interest. You pay me back when you're able to."

If anyone other than Dan had made that offer, I would have turned them down flat. Pride, ya know? It was different with Dan. We had double-dated; we'd worked together and we had laughed together. "I'll think about it," I said. In fact, the tumblers were already tumbling.

A few days later I took my furniture out of storage, loaded everything into a rental truck, hitched my car to it, made my farewells, and drove back to Olympia to start a maid biz. I mean, who doesn't do things like that?

THIS TIME IT would be different, and to ensure against fickle behavioral patterns I rented an apartment and moved my stuff in. "There," I told Michael, who had stopped by to help me move in. "Yep. This is the anchor I need." With that pronouncement we high-fived it and hit a local pizza joint, and there we imbibed pasta and pints of the finest pilsner to celebrate the start of my new life.

MY NEW LIFE lasted all of three weeks. The change of plans began after a nationally recognized maid service flew me to Detroit to tour its headquarters. Tickets to a Michigan game followed, with seats on the fifty-yard line. The plan: watch the offensive linemen act offensively, then be swept away by a passively chauffeured limousine for dinner at a fine-dining restaurant. "Order anything you want," the sponsor said. Yeah, he clearly wanted me to sign on the line.

"I'll sleep on it," I said over coffee, dessert, and an aperitif.

He smiled graciously. "Most everyone does."

HOWEVER, AFTER RETURNING to Olympia, a case of the blues gripped me with such tenacity that I could barely breathe. On the one hand, I had no doubts about my ability to turn a house cleaning service into a thriving business. Even Michael's uber-successful future father-in-law encouraged me to take it on. Except that running a maid service just wasn't what I did in life. All at once everything that had once been my life reared up on hind legs like an angry stallion. I felt lost, and a week later I hit bottom.

I mean, I hit bottom not with a whimper, but a bang.

I REACHED FOR the phone. I called Michael.

"What's up, Toecheese?" He sounded so very full of life.

"Hey, brother. I, um—"

He must have sensed something, because he told me to stand by. Thirty minutes later he was knocking at my door, having made the forty minute drive in only thirty.

We talked. An hour later he swept a hand at the couch. "Why don't I stay the night, Barf Breath? Give us a chance to talk some more."

I wanted him to stay. But I also wanted him to be with the girl he had fallen so madly in love with. In the end I put on a brave smile. "She's the love of your life, brother. She's waiting for you. So you'd better get going."

Michael hesitated.

"Don't worry about me, Fungus Face. *Go.*"

Creases cut across his forehead. "You're *sure?*"

"Come on, man. Get outta here."

He met my eyes. Then he went to her. As he should have.

The next day I thumbed through the yellow pages and called one psychiatrist after another until I found one who could see me that afternoon.

I LOOKED OVER both shoulders before rushing across the parking lot and ducking inside the medical arts building. I didn't want anyone to see me. Yeah, I know—Michael, his girlfriend and her parents were the only people who even knew I'd returned to the State of Washington. It didn't matter. People like me just don't see shrinks.

I was seeing one minutes later, though. She was plump and comfortable in a dowdy dress, and she sat with both hands folded in her lap. I took a chair opposite her, and started talking.

Thirty non-stop minutes later, I finally shut up and watched her face for any signs of contempt.

First, she tilted her head sideways. Next, she began speaking. "You have every classic sign of deep grief. Everything you've done in the wake of your father's death—and I mean, everything—points toward a grief so profound that it renders you incapable of rational thought. You—"

"You mean, *everything*?" I edged forward and peered closely at her face for the telltale signs of a prankster. That alone is a symptom of the denial that characterizes the grief-stricken.

"Yes. Quitting a job you love? Moving to the opposite side of the continent? Changing your goals by becoming a writer? Moving back and forth across the country? Running away to a tiny remote island? It's all—"

"Running? *Running*? I...holy shit!" It all hit me full in the face. *Of course.* That's exactly what I'd been doing.

She nodded rapidly. "Yes. All classic symptoms, and all treatable."

"Wow." I sat back and stared past her for a long, long time. Eventually I said, "It's as if my dad abandoned me...right?" Then I hastily added in an effort to absolve him of sin, "Sure, I know he didn't. Not really. Only, it's how I feel."

She nearly whispered her reply. "Trust your feelings." Then the doctor unfolded her hands, pressed her lips tight, and gave me the plan. "This will sound ironic, but in order to do your best work for a full recovery, you must return to the place where you experienced your happiest moments with your father."

I didn't know whether to laugh or to cry. "You mean, Ocean City?" When she nodded, I thought for a moment. Finally, I said, "Okay. What else?"

"Therapy. With a psychologist. With a Ph.D. in psychology. And board certified."

I frowned. "I'm not following."

She explained the differences between psychiatrists and psychologists, and why only a board certified Psy.D. therapist could provide the most effective treatment.

Then something strange happened. I felt as if a tightly wound mainspring inside my chest had come undone. My shoulders relaxed. I exhaled loudly and saw brightness for the first time in years; not the brightness beneath Kwajalein's tropical sun, but a different sort, and I let go of everything—all of it—and when I looked at the good doctor again, I saw her watching, waiting, and affirming.

THE NEXT MORNING I called the Ocean City Police Department and asked for the personnel manager. I knew her from back in the day, and when she came online I uttered four words. "I need a job."

I could almost see her smiling by the way she cleared her throat. "As luck would have it, we do have a position available. You'll have to go through the hiring process...but I'll see what I can do for you."

After hanging up I recited seventeen-year-old Johnny Gunther Junior's, "The Unbeliever's Prayer." Then I called my landlord. "I'm breaking my lease. Don't sweat the deposit. I'll forfeit it. The apartment will be empty by tomorrow morning."

I spent the rest of the day packing, I crashed and burned that night, got up at dawn, and looked outside. It was a bright and seasonably warm April day in 1993. It was also my birthday. The start of a new life.

Imagine that.

A DOOR LEFT OPEN

CHAPTER EIGHTEEN

The Cavalry Has Arrived

T HE FIRST THING I did after settling into new digs was to pay a visit to a friend whose wife worked for a counseling service. After I revealed my reason for returning to the area, she nodded much as the psychiatrist had, smiled, and gave me the name of a Salisbury-based psych-D. "And yeah, Rick...he's board certified."

For my second act in this three-act saga, I pursued the cop job. The timing turned out to be perfect. I sailed through the written and physical agility tests, passed a polygraph exam, sat before an interview board, and two weeks later the chief swore me in.

The curtain opened for my third act when I reported as ordered to the patrol captain. We already knew each other professionally, and after I knocked on his door this admirable man invited me in and shook my hand. "Welcome aboard," he began. Then he got down to business. "Rick, I need a favor."

I smiled in that friendly way that's meant to maintain the respect that should always separate subordinates from their superiors. "Anything for you, Captain."

"I have an opening on the mounted unit, and a little leprechaun told me that you know how to ride."

"It's true," I replied, already knowing where this conversation would trot off to.

"I know your reputation. You're also older and more mature than many of my officers." He paused and made a tepee of his fingers. "We've been using the mounted unit to enforce the noise ordinances in the Robin Road area."

He meant a section of rental properties at the upper end of Old Town, where honky tonk bars merge with Gen X hangouts. But a slew of locals with lots of voting power felt caught between the pincers, and they'd gotten fed-up with partying college kids.

The captain collapsed the tepee. "We've tried everything. Arrests. Citations. A show of force. Nothing helps. So it's time to try a little experiment, and here's what I have in mind. I'd like to put you in the mounted unit, and I want you to amble over to Robin Road each night and be 'Officer Friendly.' The idea is to keep the parties from getting out of hand in the first place. That'll keep the neighbors happy, the dispatchers won't have to answer loud-party calls, and I'll be happy." Leaning slightly forward, he gave me the rest of my marching orders—or in this case, my galloping orders. "I don't want you guys making arrests if you can avoid it. No citations to appear in court, either. I just wanna see if being proactive in a neighborly way will make a difference."

"As I said, Captain. Anything for you."

"Good. I'll have the mounted sergeant team you up with Quenton Josey. He has your same level of maturity and sense of fairness. I think it'll be a good pairing."

"Like a fine wine and an aged cheese," I said at once, and smiled.

OFFICER QUENTON JOSEY leaped off his horse and held out a hand, his teeth bright within his coffee-colored face. As we clasped hands, he said, "I feel like I already know you. Yessir. All the brothers say you're righteous, so that's good enough for me."

"Louie," I said in my best Bogey, "I think this is the beginning of a beautiful friendship."

It was. Quenton, who quickly told me to call him "Que," always had a ready laugh to go with his insightful assessment of people both good and bad.

Since first things must come first, Que gave me a tour of the mounted unit's facility. It was next to an amusement park in the south end of town, with a small corral on one end and a wood frame building coated with beleaguered white paint on the other. The rickety building housed six stalls, a tack room, and a small office. Everything smelled of hay and manure and horse sweat, and I thought all of it was anything but bad.

At the conclusion of the grand tour, Que said, "Let's get at them stalls." He handed me a rake while he grabbed a shovel. "Here's your first lesson in mucking stalls."

He taught me the finer art of cleaning manure and urine-drenched stalls, followed by how to load the fetid mess into a wheel barrel. It took several loads before we dumped every bit of the yucky stuff behind the corral, where it would await further disposition. Next, Que showed me where the grain and hay were stored, and how much to feed each horse each day.

This was clearly a labor-intensive job—but as anyone who has mucked stalls will say, it's good for the soul. I certainly felt that way. Yep, I was going to love this assignment.

Later on the sergeant showed up. We were already acquainted, and he set me up with a helmet, jodhpurs, riding boots, and spurs. Next, he assigned the unit's most-recent addition as my mount.

Magic was a seven-year-old gelded quarter-horse who would try his best to bite my butt whenever my back was turned. He was an ornery cuss, the type of horse that riders have to "work" by using a combination of spurs and verbal coaxing. Yessir...*Keep them doggies movin', Rawhiiiide.*

But I didn't take Magic's malice personally. In fact, the surlier he acted, the gentler I became, usually by patting his shoulder and offering a carrot. I would also lead him to his stall and groom him, while speaking softly and touching him with respect.

A lot of good it did me. Nothing seemed to work. He flattened his ears and bared his teeth whenever I approached with a saddle. He also stood away from the other four horses, alone and forgotten, and I wondered what had happened to him.

The next eight weeks saw me arriving early each morning to feed "the boys." Once they all but inhaled their oats, I let them out to graze. But Magic, ever indifferent to me and to the herd, always went off by himself.

THEN THERE CAME a day when I entered the corral while the boys were at the far end. I whistled as always to get Magic's attention, and to my great surprise he raised his head and nickered, then came toward me at a trot with head held high. I pointed at his stall. He pivoted at once and ducked inside. I followed him in, patted his shoulder, and got busy grooming him while he nickered.

In time, I learned that Magic's previous owner beat him with a stick every day whether he thought the poor horse needed it, or not. By the time Magic came to us, he wasn't about to play the victim again. It's why it took me so much time to gain his trust. But trust I got, and from that day on I grew to love him, while he did whatever I asked of him with little more than a sidelong glance.

* * * *

Glancing over both shoulders as I had done in Olympia, I ducked inside the multi-story office building in Salisbury. After all, an acquaintance might spot me going inside, and discern that I was there to see a shrink. But once I checked the directory and saw that the building housed myriad businesses, I relaxed. Well, at least a little.

I liked the shrink at once. George Weaver III, Ph.D. was my age, clear-eyed, and friendly. Somehow, I sensed that kids and animals were probably drawn to him.

"Did you have any trouble finding the office?" he asked.

"No, Doctor. It's...really off to one side, isn't it?"

"Call me Toby." He smiled reassuringly and searched my face, then said matter-of-factly, "My office is in this building so patients won't feel ashamed about coming here for therapy."

I chuckled. "You've read me like a book."

"Funny you should say that." He gestured at a bookcase against the far wall. "I'll give you a reading assignment later. Now suppose you tell me a little about yourself."

A little turned into a lot. I spoke non-stop until he signaled me that the session had ended.

Toby smiled. "You'll do fine."

"Really?" It wasn't that I didn't trust his prognosis. What troubled me was that I would have to change some things, and that meant leaving a comfort zone. Sure, that zone had become a zombie apocalypse, but at least I knew what to expect from one moment to the next. Yet minutes later when I was leaving the building, I felt buoyed upon realizing that I didn't feel the need to check for others who might wonder what I might be doing here. It was a start.

* * * *

It had to end. Things were not fine. For starters, some people in the police department disliked me simply because they thought I didn't deserve to have the job.

"Anderson only got hired because he knows so-and-so . . ."

". . . He's got friends. That's how he got the job . . ."

Sure, it was public knowledge that I'd cultivated friendships with several employees, including one of the lieutenants. It's why that lieutenant publicly recused himself from any connection to my hiring process. So how did I land the job? I got it because I had the highest written test score, the best physical agility score, and very high oral interview marks. I also had one other advantage, an indelible one—I was already a trained and experienced peace officer, and this would save the department a ton of money that it would've had to spend to train me.

But facts made little difference to my detractors. Nor did it help that I had an Achilles heel, one that blinded me to the concept of jealousies—at least until one of the old-timers took me aside to explain the facts of life. He had left the department years ago to become a federal agent. However, he loved the city and so he returned—only to get the cold shoulder from fellow officers that he'd thought were his best friends.

"Rick," he began, "they won't cut you an even break. Some of 'em? When they see others leave for a bigger cut of the cake? It kills them." He grimaced. "Then when they see you exercising the freedom to return to a job that you love? It just eats at 'em; eats 'em up inside." He raised both palms toward the ceiling. "There's a line in the film, *Easy Rider*. 'Too many people here hate guys like you and me, because we represent freedom.'" This officer's mouth opened and closed silently while he stared at me and shook his head.

"Thanks for the scoop," I finally said. "I do love working here. Probably as much as you. I also want to remain on the job for many decades to come."

Armed with this insight, I felt it would be easy to put the problem to rest. It's why I sat tall in the saddle later that day as Que and I turned 'the boys' toward the Robin Road area.

Cool offshore breezes this evening tempered both the warm weather, along with the great amount of body heat that our horses were giving off. After a short walk that left us free of the corral's constraints, we broke into a canter to let them work the kinks out of their systems. I loved it, Magic enjoyed the "stretch," and as the mounts caught their wind, Que and I settled into our saddles.

While on the saddle topic, we rode English style with postage stamp-size saddles. They were easy to care for, and even comfortable when proceeding at a walking pace. Unfortunately, trotting required posting—the act of rising and sitting in the saddle in rhythm with the trot to absorb the horse's natural movement. It helps, but it's tiresome. Yet all of that changes once you go into a canter or a gallop, because then you're balancing the balls of your feet in the stirrups, and taking your weight off the saddle. Racehorse jockeys do it all the time.

In addition to being trained English style, our horses understood voice commands. I could dismount on a busy pedestrian thoroughfare and tell Magic, "Stand." He then became so still that if he twitched his tail while someone passed by, they invariably cried out, "Lord! I thought it was a statue."

Magic would remain rooted to the spot even if I walked a block away. But if I whistled and said, "Magic, walk," he came to me at once.

We also desensitized the horses against loud noises by pulling the unit's pickup truck near the stalls and leaning on the horn. Freon boat-horn blasts also helped, and sometimes we tossed firecrackers into the corral while they were grazing. Finally, we did our regular target practice from horseback, and I'm pleased to report that they never flinched.

So after leaving the corral this night and running the horses a bit, we proceeded to Robin Road to begin our patrol. Along the way a number of tourists sought plenty of photo ops, which we didn't mind posing for. The flash bulbs didn't bother the mounts, and the photo ops made for good PR. Later, after we made a second sweep of the neighborhood, we spotted the signs of potential parties as college kids carried cases of beer into their rental units.

That's when we sprang into action. Actually, we sauntered into action as part of a modus operandi that was simplicity itself. After guiding the horses to the far side of a street, we hung loose while the horses' odors filled the air. These odors were anything but unpleasant, and it rarely took more than three minutes before the collegians began stealing veiled glances in our direction.

In time, one of them would summon the courage to approach us, and on this particular night a young man came over to ask, "So like, what're you dudes doing here?"

I could have met what amounted to a challenge by turning my eyes into slits from too many days of staring into the prairie sun, and saying, "I ask the questions 'round these parts, pardner." But rather than play hard-core, I greeted him by peeling off a riding glove and reaching down to offer a handshake. "Hi. I'm Officer Anderson, and this is Officer Josey."

A hesitation—then he briefly pressed the flesh.

"What's your name?" I asked.

He shuffled his feet and said to the ground, "Um, Darryl. Yeah... I'm Darryl."

"Darryl, huh? Yeah, I knew another Darryl. Really cool guy, kind of like you." I shifted in the saddle. "Yep, we're just out riding. How about you? Where do you go to school?" By changing the subject and asking two questions at once, Darryl would either fall in line with *us*, or else he would still opt for trying to have it the other way around. He capitulated.

"Um, Georgetown." He watched my face.

"Wow. Great school. Congratulations." I smiled disarmingly and gestured at the condo. "I see you guys are planning a party. Hell, too bad my partner and I can't join all ya'll."

This was Que's cue to join the conversation, which he did. Then somewhere along the way we offhandedly mentioned the town's noise ordinances, and added verbiage about nearby families and seniors in search of a restful evening. As usually happened, Darryl was promising to make sure everyone kept the noise down by the time Que and I rode off into the sunset.

The good news is that after two weeks of using this approach a clear pattern developed: there were no loud party complaints when Que and I were on duty, while on our off-duty days the dispatchers were forced to answer never-ending noise complaints.

The bad news is that this is why I got into trouble.

* * * *

"You're supposed to dump your troubles on me," Doctor Toby said.

We had been exploring various schools of thought. Ever the Jungian, Toby constantly prodded me into a form of talk therapy that sought to reconcile the conscious and unconscious parts of the mind, with the goal of achieving balance.

Rather than answer, I changed the subject. "I bought that book you wanted me to read. The one on grief."

Toby smiled and nodded. "Good. Then you see why your history is much more common than you might've thought." He sat forward and narrowed his eyes. "The goal is to get beyond the past and focus on the future."

We would go back and forth like this with each succeeding visit, and after plopping into a chair for the fifth session, I felt myself beaming. "I was thinking about what you've been telling me, and about the books I'm reading, and the other day it felt as if I'd shrugged a terrible weight from my shoulders."

Toby smiled knowingly and guided me in another direction.

* * * *

"Let's go this way," Que said, coaxing his horse toward a side street. "I think I hear some action."

Two minutes later we settled into our saddles to watch a party-in-progress. It was a warm night with a salt-tinged offshore breeze fanning our faces. The low tide also made the air heavy with the primordial scent of shellfish exposed by receding waters, naked to the time-honored predators that roam the shore—the terns that step with patient expectation through the silt, along with the gulls, poachers of all they find, all of them prowling and gorging themselves on the fruits of this watery ecosystem, a confluence of odors as sweet as any nectar that's been ripened by golden sunlight.

I wasn't here to ripen beneath golden sunlight, though. My butt was here to work, and as Que pointed at a young woman pressing her face against a living room window, I watched her draw away from the glass and venture outside.

"What beautiful animals," she said while drawing closer. Then as almost everyone does, she asked if she could pet them.

"No sweat," Que told her. Then he grinned and patted his mount's neck. "See? No sweat. You won't even get your palm wet."

She laughed at his easy-going joke. With the ice broken, we felt free to discuss many things, including the need to keep festivities quiet. By the time Que and I finished our spiel, the woman nodded and thanked us for letting her interact with the horses.

But as she was walking away a marked patrol unit stopped next to us. The driver was someone I'll call Officer Flotsam. He got out and greeted us. "What's up, guys?"

Que pointed at a condominium and explained our method for reducing noise complaints. When Que finished, Flotsam gave a thumbs-up.

Then I stupidly added our ulterior goal. "The idea is to avoid making arrests by heading 'em off at the pass. This way the locals don't have to put up with noise if we're tied up with arrestees."

Que said, "No citations, either. Yep. That's the plan, all right."

Flotsam smiled at Que. But then he shot me a look before getting into his cruiser and drifting away.

* * * *

"You drifted away," Dr. Toby Weaver said. "The grief had become unendurable. So you ran from it."

I grimaced. "Makes me sound like a coward."

"Not at all. Grief is an unseen enemy." Toby paused. "Remember what I said when our first session ended?"

"That you admired me above all others? That you saw at once why ladies throw themselves at me, and why kids want to grow up to become just like me?"

Toby laughed. "That, too." Then he pinned me with his eyes. "The psychiatrist you saw in Olympia was spot-on in her diagnosis."

"Umm, I guess that's...reassuring."

"It's supposed to be. But you're not there yet, buddy boy. That's why I want you to enter group therapy."

"Group?" I turned the image over in my mind a few times. "Okay. I'll do it."

* * * *

"Don't worry. I'll do it," I reassured the lieutenant the following day. He wanted me to patrol different areas of town, and to do it on my own. Since none of the other mounties had been told to patrol Robin Road, I wondered if the supervisors intended to check for a spike in noise complaints. I also wondered why the lieutenant had jumped the chain of command; he should have given the assignment through the mounted unit's sergeant. In any event Que and I had our marching orders, and we prepared our horses for a night of solo patrol.

Awhile later I guided Magic to a grassy area near a convenience store, and after securing him to a stanchion I went inside for a soda, only to spot Officer Pete Jetsam. I'd know him for years, he always attended my parties back in the day, and we used to enjoy solving the world's myriad problems over cold beverages at a local cop hangout.

"Pete," I said, with outstretched hand.

"Fuck you," he said, and abruptly turned his back to me.

I chuckled. "Okay, Pete. I give. What's the joke?" When he replied by walking away, I pressed my lips tight and left the store. I had no idea what was going on with him, but it wasn't an appropriate matter to discuss in public.

Moments later, I was back in the saddle when I came upon a summer cop assigned to boardwalk foot patrol. I greeted him. He turned away.

"This is bullshit," I muttered. There were no other people nearby, so I caught up to him, dismounted, and blocked his way by standing directly in front of him. "You're the second cop who's done this tonight. Tell me what's going on." When he tried to turn away, I gripped his shoulder. "Nope. We're not doing this. You got the balls to turn your back to me? Then have the balls to talk."

He chewed on this under glowering eyes until he finally said, "Why don't you tell *me* what's going on, Mister 'I'm Not Gonna Do My Share of Work' Anderson. Yeah, that's right," he added when I squinted at him. "I got it directly from Flotsam."

"Really? Huh. Amazing. Tell me something, Boardwalk Boy. What exactly did Numb Nuts tell you?"

"He said you've been bragging that you're not gonna make any arrests this summer. Said you're gonna dump all the work on us. Said—"

"Hold on there, Hoss. 'Cause he's full of shit." With the reason for pulling me from Robin Road now clear, I explained what I really said to Flotsam without mentioning Que's name, since there was no reason to drag him into this.

The summer cop scoffed. "Yeah, right."

"Well, aren't you the objective, open-minded sort that every police department seeks." I made a sound and jerked a thumb over my shoulder. "You can resume your patrol, Boardwalk Boy." I remained rooted in place to force him into going around me. Which he did. Then he walked away.

* * * *

"You know by now that you can't just walk away." Toby uncrossed his legs and showed soft eyes. "By running from grief you only compound the pain."

"I see." After mulling this over, I handed over a piece of paper. "Maybe you'll want this. It's the letter you told me to write." During our last session, Toby explained how writing a letter to a dead loved one could help, and to write one to my father. It did help, because I sobbed while still only halfway through. I also felt much better afterward.

* * * *

Not every co-worker was treating me like crap. Others invited me out for beers, to their homes, and to social events. Some asked to go flying with me, and they all offered genuine friendship.

While on the topic of friends, Sally reappeared in my life. Always a great pal, she was now manna from Heaven. One night she had me laughing as before, but when she started to set me up for a blind date, I kissed her cheek and said, "Thanks. The thing is, I met someone. We're even talking about living together."

Sally was happy for me, bless her heart.

Yep, I had a new relationship going, and soon enough we were hanging out with Que and his future wife. Que had known "Law School Lauren" from days gone by, and he didn't blink when I introduced my new, below-the-radar lover. Que even told me in private, "Hey, if things don't work out between you two? I got this cousin I wanna fix you up with."

A few hangouts also offered refuge from self-righteous co-workers. Among them was an Irish pub at Fourth Street and the Boardwalk, the sort of place that smells of spilled beer, old wooden floors and even older stories.

The pub also boasted a trio of Irish musicians. The Gaels performed nightly, the lead singer was Pat Garvey, and he once played backup for the Starland Vocal Band. Brian played violin, while Mel handled the bass. I loved their shows, and they appreciated my ability to liven up a crowd by dancing a jig on the postage-stamp dance floor, my three-day scruff showing and my unbuttoned shirt flapping; sometimes getting a lass to join-in, other times springing onto a nearby table while startled customers reared back, the sweat streaming down my face as I showed off my footwork, only to leap off when the crowd cheered.

So after strolling inside the pub one August evening and catching a whiff of its odors, I got a Guinness and leaned against a wall to listen to The Gaels while I eyeballed the eye candy.

It seemed a great way to spend an evening, and when the band took a break, Pat made it an even greater night when he came over to greet me. "Rick, my friend. How're the horses?"

"They're doing good, thanks."

We made some small talk until Pat asked, "Say, when do you work again?"

"Tomorrow night."

"Yeah?" He smiled. "Hmm. Do you know that song we do? The one about a horse that pulls a beer wagon?"

"Of course." I drank some Guinness and waited expectantly.

"You know what would be great? If you rode your horse into the pub while we play the song."

Since I now roamed at-large, I shrugged and said, "Sure. I'll do it."

He slapped my back. "No, seriously. It'd be really cool."

"Seriously, I'll do it. What time do you want me here?"

He laughed. "Not that I expect you to show up. But...nine o'clock. Sharp."

We chatted about other things until The Gaels took to the stage. That's when I caught the pub owner's eye. "Greg, what do you think of the idea of me and my horse . . ." Once I finished relaying Pat's request, Greg chuckled and vowed to be at the main door at nine the following evening.

THE NEXT NIGHT I made sure Magic was clean both inside and out before guiding him to the Boardwalk, and then easing back on the reins when we reached the pub. The music—along with the crowd's cheers—carried easily, a sure sign of success for our planned endeavor. But we were early, so to pass the time I chatted with passers-by while Magic posed for the inevitable photos. Camera flashes never bothered him. He even stood taller whenever a camera clicked.

Meanwhile, I kept an eye on the pub's main door. Sure enough, the song about a horse pulling a beer wagon spilled forth precisely at nine. Minutes later, Greg appeared in the doorway, framed by interior light and grinning like an egg-sucking dog. As he waved me in, I made a "click-click" sound with my tongue and Magic began walking. I did have to duck low to get through the door, but once we were past it I rode high in the saddle.

The place was packed. We're talking SRO here, and the expressions on the revelers' faces were magical in their own right as I urged Magic on as he walked past them. Most of the men were holding beers, and they began doing comical double-takes while looking up at us, then staring at their beers with deep suspicion, and looking at us again.

The stage lights were blinding the trio, so they couldn't see me walk Magic onto the dance floor. But when I blew my police whistle the music ground to a stop and their faces were studies in stupefaction. Never one to keep others wanting, I shouted, "Who're the sons of bitches that're singing that song? Because my horse and I were blocks away when he came charging inside for his share of the beer."

Total silence. Then the room erupted in cheers and blinding camera flashes. The Gaels doubled over with laughter. People stood. Others still stared into their drinks. Then Pat spoke into his mic. "That's Rick Anderson of the Ocean City Police, folks. Now how about a big cheer?"

The applause began anew. Not wanting to push my luck though, I turned Magic around and rode off into the sunset—or in this case, the moonrise—as flashcubes lit the pub.

Hey, who says good PR has to be limited to dour officers delivering monotone speeches to Rotary Club crowds? Still, it was time for me and Magic to move on.

* * * *

"You've moved ahead in such a short time," Toby announced at the start of our next session. However, when I grew a smile that was too wide for his liking, he held up a hand. "Don't get too cocky. All it means is that it's time to take your healing to a new level."

"Sure. Whatever it takes."

"Good." He made direct eye contact—something he did a lot, and it was okay because he had nonjudgmental eyes. "I mentioned group therapy the other week. I'm putting together a group of four professionals. Physicians. Attorneys." Toby shot me a size-up. "Does this intimidate you?"

I smiled. "Thank you for not including me *out* of the group." Then I settled back into one of the leather club chairs as he began the session.

* * * *

The summer ended all too soon, segueing into a frigid winter while passing autumn's buffer. Tourists fled, shop owners boarded up businesses, hotels closed their doors, and the mounted unit followed suit as we traded horses for patrol cars.

The powers-that-be assigned me to the day shift, which I welcomed because the day sergeant and I were friends. He always supported his troops and showed up for cop parties. We even handled some mutual aid calls back in my trooper days. That's why I naturally assumed he hadn't subscribed to the myths that were still growing around me.

Shame on me for assuming.

The rest of the day crew were also old hands. But as I would discover, a couple of them had also bought into the rumors and rebuffed me. Their actions were unfortunate, all the more so because during the rest of that first shift and on almost every day that followed, I saw them hanging out at convenience stores for most of the entire shift while totally ignoring their duties.

I KEYED MY mic and said, "Seventy-three-oh-nine." Seconds passed while I waited for the civilian dispatcher to answer.

She finally got around to responding in a voice garnished by nothing less than contempt. "Seventy-three-oh-nine. What do you need now?"

I shook my head in disbelief. If a state police dispatcher had answered the radio like that, they would have faced instant disciplinary action. But in a department that had its favorites, she ranked among the untouchables. What lent even more acid to her attitude was that she had sought my friendship when I was a trooper.

That was then. This was now, and I needed a routine license and vehicle registration check. I keyed the mic again. "Seventy-three-oh-nine requesting a 10-27, 10-28. Ready to copy?"

Twenty seconds swept by before she answered in the same disrespectful tone. "All right, then. Go ahead with it."

I provided the data and waited to see if the driver was operating with a suspended license, bogus registration plates, or both. The dispatcher took her time, and once she finally told me that everything checked out, I wrote the driver a warning for failing to use a turn signal and resumed patrol.

WITH SO FEW people in town and so little to do by responding to the bar fights, strong-arm robberies and thefts that defined each summer, I stayed busy by attacking the clutter that always gets left behind in the summer's wake.

Then one day while scanning the local wanted posters, I found an interesting item: the residents of a condo just inside the Maryland border with Delaware had spotted a notorious burglar going in and out of a third floor suite. The poster added that the suspect was wanted by Delaware, and that he had violent tendencies—an unusual trait among burglars. Penciled notations showed that our detectives had been knocking on his door, but leaving after getting no response. Naturally, I decided to drive to the condo in question.

Nobody responded to my continued knocking—no surprise there— but while walking back to my car I noticed a boat trailer minus its boat parked along the curb. It had a Delaware license plate, and on a hunch I ran the plate not only to see if the trailer had been reported stolen, but also to find out who owned it.

A dispatcher replied seconds later. Bingo. It belonged to our friendly neighborhood burglary suspect. Well, well, well. Whaddya know?

The suspect wasn't an Italian *assassino*. Nor was he an international diamond smuggler or even a rogue. But he was here and he was all I had. I also had an idea, and it was this: the more I examined the trailer, the more convinced I became that it was parked farther from the curb than permitted by law. So I got my tape measure and checked the distance from the curb to the trailer's tire, and damned if it wasn't 1/128th of an inch too far away.

I keyed my shoulder mic. "Seventy-three-oh-nine."

The dispatcher replied at once. "Seventy-three-oh-nine."

"Requesting nearest reliable at—" I gave the location where I wanted her to send a tow truck from a list of reliable towing services. Then I added, "And start me a card for an impound." I didn't have to say anything else. She understood that I was impounding the trailer, and tapped her keyboard to start a complaint card listing me as the complainant. This would provide a case number for the report that would follow.

The tow truck arrived, the driver signed my form and took the trailer away, and I parked one block over to wait. It didn't take long. The dispatcher called twenty minutes later.

"Seventy-three-oh-nine. Report of a stolen boat trailer . . ." She gave the address, which of course was the one I impounded it from.

"10-4. En route and requesting back-up."

A few seconds ticked by before she responded with an edge of confusion in her voice. "10-4." Next, she sent the nearest officer.

I drove to the condo and saw a husky middle-aged man standing where the trailer had been. He matched the suspect's description perfectly, but I needed to verify his identity before making the arrest. So I got out and offered a friendly, "Good afternoon, sir," and listened to his impassioned plea that I please, please, *please* find his boat trailer.

"Not a problem, sir. I just have to make a report before I can broadcast a lookout." With pen and notepad in hand, I looked innocently at him and asked, "Name and date of birth?" He gave his full name and birth date. They matched. As a safeguard against Murphy's Law, I stepped away and asked dispatch to run a wanted check on him.

"Seventy-three-oh-nine," she began half a minute later, "subject's 10-99 for burglary, with a history of violence."

"Very well," I replied. When my back-up arrived a short time later, I placed the suspect under arrest and took him to police headquarters for processing. At the end of the day though, none of the other officers or supervisors acknowledged my making of a good arrest.

WHEN NOT CHASING down fugitive burglars, I did traffic work. After all, the town was paying me to make traffic stops among the other duties. It helped that I enjoyed doing this work, along with nearly every other aspect of the job. Better yet, being proactive made the time pass quickly. As a bonus, enforcing motor vehicle laws is so easy to do.

All it took was a quick pass through the mall parking lots, where off-season residents felt it was okay to park in handicapped spaces. I'd find five out of ten handicapped spaces taken up by cars that lacked permits, spend the two minutes it takes to write each citation, and stick it to 'em...under a wiper blade.

While looking for parking violators, I also kept an eye out for cars that hadn't moved in days. A quick check of their tags some-times came back as stolen or abandoned. In these cases, it took me about thirty minutes to impound them.

Then there were the residential areas with intersections controlled by four-way stop signs. I always parked in plain sight a short distance from the intersection, and then stood outside my cruiser to wait. When a driver blew through one of the signs, I flagged them down and issued written warnings or citations, depending upon how brazenly they blew the intersection.

In ten minutes I'd have six warnings and at least one citation. Easy peasy, as they say. That evening the motorists would spread the word and others would obey the signs for about a week while I worked other intersections. None of this equates to rocket science, but it's what I did, and I wanted to do what I did along lines of excellence.

However, I couldn't help but notice a not-so-subtle difference in the violators' demeanor. I was still Rick, with the same knowledge, skills and experience I'd accumulated as a trooper. But because I no longer wore the "Man in Tan" garments, the public related to me at a different level. Sure, they complied with lawful orders, whether it was signing a ticket or placing their hands behind their backs prior to being handcuffed. It's just that I needed to call upon my verbal skills in nearly all interactions. Yep, John Q. definitely has its prejudices, and a large number of them didn't cotton to being held to answer to a local yokel.

That was their problem though, because there were also speeding motorists, sloppy motorists, and snarling motorists. A written warning here, a citation there, and pretty soon we're talking a lot of paper to show by the end of the shift. There were also occasional calls from property owners who'd come to town to check on their summer homes, only to discover a break-in. Then I'd spend forty-five minutes jotting down information, taking photos, and dusting for prints. Later, I would park someplace and spend another fifteen minutes writing the report.

So imagine my surprise two months later when one of the sergeants called me on the radio. "Seventy-three-oh-nine," he said. He didn't need to provide his call number. Everyone knew his voice.

I answered him. "Go ahead, sir."

"Meet me behind Roses."

"10-4."

Roses Department Store no longer exists. However, at the time it was at the 94th Street Mall. I drove there at once and pulled alongside the sergeant with my driver's door next to his door so that we would face one another.

"How's it going?" I asked. I'd worked alongside him during my trooper days, and he came to most of the parties I'd hosted. Right now though, he was staring at me with his lips pressed tight.

"I'm supposed to have a talk with you," he began. "And get you to do some work."

My antennae went to red alert. I wasn't a rookie. I'd heard the drums beating, knew what was coming, and kept my voice neutral. "Go ahead, sir."

His chest rose as he drew a deep breath. "Let's start with traffic. We expect officers to do their share of work. You need to write more warnings and citations."

Contrary to popular belief, police departments do not have quotas.

They don't need them, simply because there are so many violations committed every day that it's almost impossible not to find brazen violators. While watching a homeless guy walking by and eyeing up a dumpster, I shrugged and said, "No prob, sir. How many do you want?"

The sarge gave me that same dismissive look. "You are expected to write at least five warnings and two citations." He sighed audibly before adding, "Per week, not per month."

I made a face. "Per week? Hell, I'm writing fifteen warnings and at least five citations a *day*."

"Bullshit," he said at once, then looked right at me and added, "You're a fucking liar."

"Whoa there, Hoss!" I leveled him with my eyes. "Ain't no man gonna talk to me that way. Are we clear? Now take it back or you and I are going to Duke City."

He looked away and worked his mouth silently until he said, "There's no way you're writing that much traffic."

"The hell I'm not. Here, check my books." I grabbed my citation and warning books and handed them over. He riffed through them far too quickly before returning them with that same condescending look.

"You didn't stop these cars," he said. "You parked somewhere and wrote these out to make me think you're working."

That did it. I blew up. "That's a fucking load of bull, and you know it! Christ, you know as well as I do that cops can't fake citations."

It's true. Each state regulates traffic citation forms. They're numbered and assigned to each officer, and must be accounted for. This makes it almost impossible for cops to fake a traffic stop by filling them out and turning 'em in, because the originals go directly to the local courts. While no system can be totally fail-safe, it would require more effort to pretend to be making stops than it would take to simply write genuine citations.

He knew this. Yet he looked at me and said it again. "I still don't believe you."

Now I threw my hands up in anger. "What is there to fuckin' believe? I'm writing twenty warnings and citations a *day*."

"Then why aren't we seeing them?" He shifted in his seat, and waited.

"Huh? What do you mean?"

"If you're writing 'em, how come we're not seeing 'em?" He was referring to the fact that officers turn in copies of their written warnings and citations at the end of each shift so supervisors can account for them.

"How the hell do I know?" Real anger was building in me as I stared at this supervisor who sat on his ass for hours at a time at a local Denny's, but had the gall to accuse me of being lazy. "I'm doing the work, I'm turning in the work, and I'm damned if you or anyone else is going to accuse me of lying." I narrowed my eyes. "Just so we're clear? I'm about to file an official complaint against you."

He sniffed and looked through his windshield. "There's only one way to prove this. Let's go to the office and check your file."

I bit off the next three words. "Yes. Let's do."

Ten minutes later I watched as he dug through the daily workload files. He pulled mine out and opened it. The damn thing was empty, and the look of triumph on his face was total as he held it aloft. I uttered four simple words that were huge in their implication. "This is a set-up."

He all but laughed. "See? There's nothing there. Proves my point. You lied to me."

That's when it hit me. I always signed my warnings and citations with my first initial only, followed by my last name: Officer R. Anderson. However, there was another Anderson on the department, with a first name that also began with the letter R. I pointed at the file cabinet. "Check the other Anderson's file."

"Admit it, Rick. You lied."

"Sarge? Check the other file and fucking do it ...or so help me—"

He laughed in my face—but he pulled the file out. Dozens and dozens of warnings and state citations fell out—more than two hundred of them. All signed, *Officer R. Anderson.*

Only, there were three significant points: every signature was in my handwriting; my handwritten I.D. Number appeared on each piece of paper; and as for the *other* Officer R. Anderson? That Anderson had been on light duty for several months, and would remain on light duty for several more months, making it impossible for the *other* Anderson to have written any of these documents in the first place.

Just as significant was the question of why the other Anderson's sergeant had filed all of those warnings and citations without wondering, "Wait. This officer's on light duty. So why am I getting all these traffic stops to file?" The answer? Pervasive laziness on their part, which they deflected by accusing me of being idle.

I told him all of this. What did he do? Instead of resolving the issue in my favor, he said, "Well...you're still not doing what you're getting paid to do."

The look of pure contempt on my face couldn't be mistaken for anything other than what it was. Except that it actually might have been lost on him, because he's what I call a "night owl," because the more light you shine on night owls, the less they see. I turned on my heel and walked out without waiting to be dismissed.

THE NEXT MORNING a dispatcher sent me to Roses for a shoplifting complaint. The plainclothes security officer pointed to the very good looking young man that he'd apprehended for stealing a green parka. The silent, handcuffed suspect was in his twenties, his dreadlocks hadn't seen shampoo in months, and his frayed clothes reeked of pot. The threadbare hoodie on his equally barren sweatshirt was of little value for the frigid outdoors, and his sneakers were literally falling apart.

After the security officer removed the cuffs, I told the suspect, "I.D., please."

He sighed and handed over a tattered Virginia license.

I examined it and said, "This is expired."

He shrugged. "Don't matter much. I ain't got no car. No money. Not even no *ganj*."

Before running him for priors and outstanding warrants, I plugged an earphone into my radio since it's never a good thing to let suspects overhear something a dispatcher might say.

A moment later the earphone chirped. "No wants, but subject's known to Parole & Probation."

That was good to know; it provided me with leverage. I gestured at the suspect. "Up against the wall."

He stood and placed his hands flat against the wall, walked his feet back, and spread his legs. He knew the drill, all right. I frisked him thoroughly. He was hard-muscled and could have put up a good fight had he wanted to. It's why I used the earphone, in case he panicked and went nutso on me.

"Okay," I said. Once he was standing normally, I asked the security officer to excuse us. The instant he stepped away, I pointed a finger at the suspect. "You've got two choices. I cite you, and you take your chances with Wild Bill Yates." Judge Yates was a notorious hanging judge, and I saw the suspect frown. "Or, you can work for me."

His brown eyes turned serious and he studied my face until he asked, "What do I gotta do?"

"You gotta give me names. You—"

"Names?" His face turned ugly. "Fuck you, dude. It ain't happening."

I turned hard eyes on him. "Cut the shit, *dude*." I opened my citation book and got ready to write out a criminal summons.

"Okay, okay," he blurted. His shoulders slumped. "I'll do...whatever."

"Too late," I said. "Where do you live?"

He spoke in a near-whisper. "An apartment. Above Lee's Store. Me an' my girl."

Lee's store was a dump, as were the low-rent apartments on its second floor. I touched my pen to the citation book, about to begin when he touched my wrist.

"Please don't write me up. I...I'll do anything you want. *Anything.*" He hung his head and waited.

Having already guessed his past by what he'd tried to steal—warm clothing, rather than CDs or the era's popular Walkman, I spoke quietly. "You'll do anything, huh? Let me guess. You were a street kid. You turned to prostitution to survive...didn't you?"

He looked up with something akin to hate in his eyes. "Whaddya want me to do? Spell it out?"

"No." He was clearly against the ropes with no place to go. I closed the citation book and said, "The only thing I want are names. Dealers. Their hangouts, their connections."

"You want me to be a rat. Can't do that, man."

"Fine. You'll do hard time."

He grimaced. "I did six months in county. It was bad enough. Can't do no state pen, man." He looked at me with sad eyes. "Give me a chance. *Please?*"

The young man wasn't a bank robber. He wasn't a murderer. He was cold and practically shoeless. "I'll give you a chance, if you come up with some names."

He instinctively glanced over his shoulder. "You won't tell no one?"

"Nobody will know you're working for me. That's a promise."

When he looked away and nodded, I summoned the security officer and asked him not to press charges. He arched an understanding eyebrow and showed us out of his office.

"Follow me," I told the suspect. After picking up the parka he tried to lift, I led him to the shoe department. "What size?" I asked.

"Um, nine?"

He watched with great curiosity while I selected a modest pair of sneakers and handed them over. "See if they fit." He sat on a nearby bench and slipped them on. "Good. Now put your old ones in the new box." Next, I grabbed a fistful of socks and pressed them into his hand. Then I pointed toward the front of the store. "Take the box, the parka and the socks to the checkout girl." I checked the price tags. Forty bucks for the parka, twenty for the shoes and ten for the socks. I pulled three Andy Jacksons and a pair of Hamiltons from my wallet. "Here's eighty." I gave him the cash and followed from a discreet distance while he paid for everything. That way he didn't lose his dignity by coming across as a charity case.

Once we were outside he offered me the change. It amounted to three bucks and coins after the sales tax. "Keep it," I said, "And name a time and a place to meet tonight."

He answered at once. "Nine o'clock. The vacant lot behind the city sanitation works. Do you know it?"

Sure, I knew. It was a short walk from his apartment. "I'll see you there. Now go home."

I waited until he was gone before notifying communications that there wouldn't be an arrest. The same female operator who had previously been nasty to me replied with a sarcastic, "Ten-nine?" The code meant, "Repeat your transmission," but the tone all but shouted, "Are you friggin' kidding me?"

No. I wasn't kidding. I'd used police SOP—take a stand, then extend a hand. It's how cops develop informants, it's a no-brainer, and it's why agencies give officers wide latitude in the decision-making process concerning suspects. It is also definitely not a civilian dispatcher's job to interpret or second-guess what an officer has chosen to do.

* * * *

I was wearing civvies and driving my personal car when I went to the vacant lot that night. As I got out a westerly breeze brushed past my nose. It smelled of the estuary and the assorted creatures that lived within its myriad roots, from tiny anemones to hulking horseshoe crabs, all of them searching for tiny footholds on life.

I was also searching; so was the suspect. He showed up precisely at nine wearing his new parka and shoes. After licking chapped licks and checking left and right, he began talking.

When he finished, I had a list of people and places of interest that I would turn over to narcotics. One other thing. He had said nothing when I paid for the parka and sneakers. Now he shuffled the shoes against the dirt lot. "Listen," he began. "Ain't nobody ever done nothing for me. Not never. Even my girl ain't been as nice to me like you was, an' she's about to have my baby. What I'm saying is, I know you got a job to do. An' I'd of understood if you'd come down hard on me. Busted me, that is. Only, you didn't." He swiped at a sudden tear, then flicked his eyes at mine. "Anyhow, thanks for...you know."

"It's okay," I said. It didn't take a genius to realize that he'd never had a reason to thank anyone, not ever, and he didn't need to lose whatever dignity he still clung to by doing it now. I handed him the number to my work voice mail. "Call me if you need any help. Anything, no matter what. One more thing. Go to Shore Seafood. Ask for the owner. Tell him I sent you. He'll give you some work. He pays well and he gives his employees good bennies."

Unable to speak, he bobbed his head and briefly locked eyes with me. Then he looked away at some unseen thing and spoke quietly. "Back when I was a kid. When I took off to get away from my step-dad. When I was on the streets an' needed money, I'd turn tricks. With guys." His eyes flashed with defiance. "I wanted to kill myself after each time. An' now here I am. So who knows? Maybe there's hope after all." He grunted. "Hey, that'll be my kid's name. If it's a girl, I mean. Hope. Yeah. I like that." He glanced sidelong at me and smiled a shy half-smile.

We left it at that, and I watched this father-to-be who was trying to make it in a cold world walk away until he blended with the night. Call it fate, karma, or whatever, but I made the right call when I didn't arrest him for shoplifting. And a few days later when I responded to yet another shoplifter at Roses, I also gave that suspect a break in return for his promise to be my snitch. Maybe it's not pretty, but it works that way sometimes.

ALTHOUGH I WAS assigned to patrol the city's north end the following day, I realized soon enough that I'd been given the All Over Patrol, this epiphany hitting me upside the head some ten minutes after starting the shift. To kick the event off, my friendly communications operator began sending me to call after call—calls that ranged from newly discovered burglaries to complaints of malicious destruction of property. Only, I was the only unit getting calls—calls that were located throughout the entire ten-mile length of the town—even though there were nine other officers on duty, and the calls were in their patrol areas.

Gee. A pattern had developed. I called the shift supervisor and asked for a meet. He brushed me off; said he was too busy. I tilted my head. "This isn't the end of this."

The topper came around noon. I was handling a noise complaint at the extreme north end of town when the dispatcher sent me to the extreme south end of town for an auto accident with injuries. I told her, "Send another unit. I'm still up north." I added that there were units fewer than three blocks from the accident.

But the dispatcher said, "It don't matter. You have to respond."

Auto accidents with reported injuries are serious business. Letting an injured person sit and wait for help when other units are much closer amounts to criminal negligence, and sending an officer with lights and sirens on a ten-mile journey with the potential for having an accident is downright unforgiveable.

I wasn't about to tolerate that type of crap, and once I handled the accident I filed an official complaint. When the higher-ups promptly swept it away, I announced my intention to bring my complaint to the state's attorney and the media. That's when someone saw the wisdom of assigning me to the shift headed by Sergeant Ron Haslam. As usual, he and I already knew one another, and the first thing this fine man did was to sit me down for a face-to-face.

"Rick, I find it so difficult to believe all the negatives I'm hearing about you." He ticked off several items on his fingers, and then invited me to give, as Paul Harvey always said, the other side of the story.

I explained everything, beginning with the lack of criminal arrests the previous summer. "The captain wanted to do an experiment with the Robin Lane noise complaints." I left Que's name out of it, but told the good sarge about the fugitive burglar I nabbed, the informants I developed, and the quality information I'd given to Narcotics. I didn't try to validate my decision about how I handled the shoplifter, since that would've marked him as my snitch. Finally, I briefed Ron on my tete-a-tete with the day sergeant over my traffic stops.

He smiled and offered his hand. "Don't worry, Rick. I have your back. If anyone gives you any more grief, come see me." He lapsed into a brief silence, and then frowned. "Listen. I tell you this as a friend. You have no future here. No matter what you do, it'll never be right." He mentioned the cop who returned after going to the feds. "The guys here hate you for the same reason they hate him. Personally? I should have left long ago. Now it's too late."

"Sarge? Am I God's gift to Ocean City? No. Of course not. If anything, I learn more from watching other cops here than I ever learned before. But . . ."

We left it there, and Sergeant Haslam held true to his word and did his best to help. Even so, it wasn't enough.

IT DIDN'T HELP matters when I got a burr up my butt at the third group therapy session. As Toby had warned, the other four men in the group were physicians and attorneys. Me? I was a local cop with nothing beyond an associate's degree, and when one of them said something nasty to me during the third session, I told him to kiss my ass. Then I turned to Toby. "That's it. I'm outta here."

"THAT'S IT. I'M outta here." The police chief leaned back in his chair. I'd known him for years—what a shock—and he had hired me on the promise that I would stay at least two years. But at this point I'd only been there thirteen months. He asked, "What's the problem, Rick?"

"It's not working out." I saw no need to delve into specifics. Besides, he was no village idiot. He had to know.

There was more, of course. I had always loved Ocean City; had loved working in concert with the department during my trooper days; had loved partying with its officers and loved knowing that I had a home. Only, it seemed that Ocean City had abandoned me.

That's why I found myself at a lonely crossroads, after returning to what I thought was my home to do the intense therapy that the Olympia psychiatrist suggested. By now I'd done that hard work. But Ocean City had stopped being my home, and I saw no reason to remain in a place where I clearly wasn't wanted, and where no matter what I did, the old timers would twist things into a negative.

It's not that I was letting a small cadre run me off the job. I had proven that point with the day sergeant. There were also a ton of great and openly-friendly officers. But I no longer had any good feelings for the place, and this threatened to diminish my motivation to be a consummate cop. I also saw that Ron Haslam was right, that I had no future here. However, on the theory that it's always best to get a second opinion, I sought out the former fed who had returned to be an officer again.

"Rick," he began after I approached him, "I'm not happy here, and never will be. Not with the hostility I get. Maybe it's only coming from a small number of the guys, and maybe if I were single I'd be outta here. But I'm not. Now I'm stuck."

It was time to move on.

Where to go, though? It didn't matter. I had reinvented myself several times already: firefighter, trooper, and medevac medic; author, Kwaj cop, and scuba instructor. I had even been a cowboy in one sense, since Que and I tended to let loose with some yahoos while cantering the horses.

Trooper, Prankster, Flyer, Spy. Hell, by now who knew? I might still end up a spy.

The sum of the parts had fallen into place, and they were leading me to another door through which I would either find a new path in life, or else engineer one to my liking. Only, this time things would be different. This time I could leave without spinning off-course from grief-induced mystification. After all, I had resolved my issues. Or so I thought.

A DOOR LEFT OPEN

CHAPTER NINETEEN

Still Lost but Not Forgotten

I PUT MY furniture into storage, stuffed some clothes and personal items into bags, and went to Sally's. After dinner and a movie, a trail of our clothes led from the couch to the base of her bed, where we made love for the first time ever. It was good, it was healthy, and the union sparked a stronger personal bond than the one we'd always had. Better still, during the pillow talk that followed, she promised to visit me.

At dawn she walked me to the door. "Better get going. You have some driving ahead of you...and I have to call my gal pal Gail and tell her about our little adventure." She wagged her eyebrows in a way that said, it's a girl's prerogative to kiss and tell.

I smiled and touched her cheek, then kissed her and turned away.

Sally dropped dead two weeks later, victim of a weak heart valve. I flew home for the funeral. Her friend Gail spoke quietly to me and touched my hand. When I finally found myself alone at her open casket, I whispered a final goodbye to one of my best friends ever.

* * * *

Then I caught a flight back to Sunny Sandy Eggo. Its Mediterranean clime, provincial charm and cosmopolitan outlook had always appealed to me. Now these virtues served as a salve while I grieved Sally's death, which I did in part by visiting the high-end shops in La Jolla, the scenic spots on Point Loma, and San Diego's sparkling beaches—including the clothing-optional Black's Beach, which was popular with college co-eds on weekends. I went to the latter partly because I knew that in her unselfish way, Sally would have wanted me to relax. At the same time, what can I say? I'm a guy, so yeah—mea culpa.

I also camped out in a friend's guest room, since I had little money to rent a place while job hunting. In time I saw an opening for police dispatcher in National City, a medium-sized bedroom community just south of San Diego. It's next to a large naval base, the department boasts a cadre of professional cops, and the dispatcher's starting pay was notably higher than what I'd been earning as a cop in Ocean City. I developed a plan: land the dispatch position, and use it as a stepping-stone for a police officer slot. With this in mind, I submitted an application.

One month later I took the written and practical exams. An interview followed. Then, nothing. I called personnel, but they were tight-lipped. Jobs were scarce, and with no real work prospect, I decided to fulfill another dream—to live in Hawaii. I was single, so if anyone got hurt it would only be me. As Sally also proved, we can drop dead at any time, life is too short, so...

...So within a week I'd sold my car and bought a one-way ticket to Honolulu.

"I AM HOME." It's what I whispered after stepping off the plane. Frangipani graced me from open concourses as it had done on innumerable previous visits, and red and yellow bougainvillea wound around the support columns. Beyond the terminal there were green hills, tanned faces with bright smiles, and a sky so blue it reminded me of Kwaj.

I'd heard from plenty of people who moved here from the mainland that they left after only a year or two, citing "island fever" as their reason. "It's so small," they would say. "I felt locked-in with nowhere to go."

But after living on an 800 acre speck of coral for three years, I couldn't get a grip on their gripe. When compared to Kwajalein, Oahu was continental.

And so I stepped deeper into my new home, hailed a taxi to Waikiki, and found an affordable room within minutes. Luck favored me again the very next day when I ran into an old friend who had lived here for years. He invited me to stay in his guest room. It was a no-brainer; I moved my stuff in at once.

I also fell into the island lifestyle at once, and quickly adopted the local pidgin dialect. Just add "yeah?" to the end of every third sentence and you're halfway there. So when a friend drapes an arm around your shoulders and says, "*Hey, bumbai we be pau hanna. Then we go getta beer, yeah?*" he's really saying, "We shall reach the end of our working day in a surprisingly short time. Perhaps we can retire to an establishment that offers cold beverages at a reasonable price. How does that sound to you?"

Yep. Hawaii was definitely my kinda place, yeah?

But with free-thinking attitudes and a free place to stay notwithstanding, I still craved meaningful employment. So after investigating openings for police officers and firefighters and coming up with nothing but dead ends, I landed a job with an undersea tour company that had a submarine equipped with *plenny* portholes, yeah? The sub carried thirty tourists for undersea tours along Waikiki's shore. The highlight was a "waterbatics" segment, with scuba divers on submersible scooters doing underwater antics to the passengers' delight while they snapped photo after photo.

In between shows we sunned ourselves atop the boat. What a way to earn a buck...and the company paid a lot of damned fine bucks. Yep, things were looking good.

THE JOB WASN'T the only thing that looked good. I'd found a favorite evening hangout, and one night after ordering a rum and

Coke, I'd just settled back when a young man asked if the chair next to mine was free. He was tall and slender, with black hair that reached to his waist and clothes that would be the envy of rock musicians. Any of my friends judging him by outward appearances would surely conclude that he was my complete opposite.

Yet I saw in him a kindred spirit, and I invited him to sit.

Nathan was from Brazil, he lived in San Francisco, and he'd been en route to Sri Lanka when he decided to spend a few days in Hawaii.

We became instant friends. The next day we pooled our money to rent an apartment a block from my job site. All seemed well, at least at first. Then both the Honolulu police and the fire department announced that they couldn't hire anyone for at least a year. Nathan couldn't find a decent job, either. Then karma intervened in the form of a letter from National City, offering me the police dispatcher job.

There are dreams to be lived, and there is prudence. Once I chose the latter and accepted the job, Nathan asked to join me in San Diego. We made the move, found an apartment near the city's famous zoo, and celebrated two days later when Nathan landed a well-paying job as a fine-dining waiter. The next day I reported for work with the National City Police Department.

IT TURNED OUT that dispatching presented some unforeseen challenges. The police department handled a high-crime area, so calls came in fast and furious. Now pushing forty and unaccustomed to so much activity, the pace wore me down well before each shift's end.

But I adapted, and made new friends. One of them was Levi Hart. He was only twenty, and I was shocked to learn that twenty is the minimum age for California cops. But Levi carried himself as if he were thirty. He was in fact a consummate cop with a ready smile, and when too many calls left us swamped in dispatch, he would appear almost as an apparition to lend a hand. Levi had also played varsity water polo, a sport that—along with lacrosse—requires tremendous stamina and aggression. But something else about him caught my attention, and that was his name.

"Levi," I began one night when he walked in to help us out. "I have a Jewish uncle who calls me a true mensch. I say this because I have to ask. With a name like Levi Hart? Are you—"

"Jewish?" He threw his head back and laughed. "I get that all the time. But, no. I'm not. Besides, 'Hart' isn't my birth name. I was born, 'Levi Bailey.'" Then he added while sitting at a console, "Straight up, though? I won't deny that I've let suspects think I am. Sometimes it works to my advantage."

I told him that his name intrigued me, that I'd written a book, and was putting together ideas for another novel. "Levi, would you mind if I use your name for a main character?"

"Sure, go ahead." His smile lit the dark room. "Wait until I tell my girlfriend."

A YEAR PASSED. I felt blessed. The money was good, I was on the verge of applying to become an officer, and the cops liked me. Nathan and I now had an apartment in a trendy part of town, and my circle of writer friends had grown.

So why did I abruptly resign my job and move to the former Yugoslav countries of Bosnia and Croatia?

A DOOR LEFT OPEN

CHAPTER TWENTY

Crawling through Caves in Croatia

"**W**ANTED: CURRENT AND FORMER police officers to serve as a United Nations Civilian Police (CIVPOL) officer in Bosnia and Croatia," the job announcement began.

"Wow," I said after reading it. "This is something different."

"You think?" Nathan asked.

"Stop being a wise-ass." I pointed at the most relevant item. "Look. $87,000. Tax-free. For a year's service. Plus per diem, and a bonus after completing the mission. What can be so wrong with that?"

What was wrong? I hadn't resolved my grief issues, that's what. At least not enough, and this explains my need to take flight again. It's why the announcement sent my pulse racing and my mind spinning, while I missed the clues and dismissed the portion of my brain's logic center that was shouting, *Knock it off!*

I had already missed so many other signs, beginning with that night when I got pissed-off during group therapy and walked out. Compounding the error, I missed Toby's phone call urging me to return. Nor did I pick up on the clues when family and friends looked at me askance after I mentioned leaving Cold Cruel Ocean City for Sunny Sandy Eggo—*again*. In short, I'd come toe-to-toe with the issues that plagued my grieving mind nearly ten years previously.

Unfortunately, the idea of new adventures overrode my common sense. Hey—maybe it proved the saying that if common sense is so common, why don't more people have it?

I thought I did. In truth however, I didn't even have the common sense to see that I didn't have it after all.

The final nail in the coffin I was building for myself came after I rationalized that spending a year as a UN Peace Officer in a war zone would make me a more attractive candidate for the National City police job. What I couldn't see through the proverbial forest was my record for not remaining on one job for more than three years. Even Levi asked, "What's with you, Rick? Can't you stay in one place?"

It was a proper question. Had I thought to answer Levi, I might have said that an inner voice was whispering something akin to, "If you build it, he will come." In other words, I felt driven to follow that path. Not that I could tell him this, of course. And yet, why not go? Hadn't Toby urged me to follow my gut? "Your body knows," he kept repeating. Then again, perhaps I might've calmed down if the current apartment lease wasn't up for renewal in only three weeks. Talk about a door standing ajar.

FOUR WEEKS LATER I stepped out of a commuter jet alongside two dozen other fledgling American CIVPOLs, and entered Zagreb International's terminal. We'd just made a grueling red-eye from JFK to Zagreb, an ancient city as far from Kwaj as one could get. All of us were exhausted and isolated from all we knew. Yeah, talk about isolating myself again.

Naturally I brushed it all aside because I had larger issues to deal with. For example, we were now in a region that a month ago was a war zone, and the United Nations expected us to resolve myriad issues. Did they even have a plan? Yes, and no. In any event we had "landed on Utah Beach" to act as transitional police, along with police officers from around the globe.

The idea itself was sound and based on a simple reality: war zones create vacuums, and unless other nations fill the vacuums with qualified logisticians, government experts and law enforcement professionals, everything ends in chaos. Why send civilian cops? The reason is also basic: local populations view military police units as occupation forces, while civilian patrols don't come across as a threat to their sense of home and family.

This was the case during an earlier crisis in Cyprus, when far-thinking politicians proved that sending cops who knew how to talk to people and acquire snitches would work pretty darn well. It did work, too. However, CIVPOL officers are never more than a temporary deployment, and once CIVPOL rebuilds a region's various criminal justice institutions, they are expected to hit the highway.

Our marching orders were clear: assist in the peaceful transition of constitutional power to the Bosnian and Croatian governments; monitor and inspect law enforcement activities and facilities, including associated judicial organizations and proceedings; assess threats to public order, and advise government authorities on restructuring effective civilian law enforcement agencies. We were also charged with gathering intelligence, and reporting threats to life in general and to NATO units in particular.

No problem.

Well, not exactly. We had to find families willing to rent rooms to us. In return we paid nearly $150 a month for full room and board, which was a fortune in these former Soviet bloc countries, and a win/win for everyone on both sides.

My initial assignment saw six of us entering Sarajevo after riding for two torturous days in a UN van. Along the way we passed through towns blackened by fire, areas littered with land mines, and blown-up bridges that once spanned major rivers. To complicate matters, we had to reach a mile-long pontoon bridge before nightfall if we hoped to reach the other side, since NATO troops would secure the bridge until dawn.

Sarajevo itself was a hodgepodge of untouched districts bordered by areas that had been leveled by artillery. The patchwork lent a sense of fable too, since so many European buildings, shops and homes can be centuries old. It was as if I'd been plopped into the middle of a WWII movie set, complete with French villagers drinking coffee at outdoor tables, amid the rubble of the bombed buildings. They weren't French and it wasn't the 1940s, of course. These were modern-day Europeans, with only the rubble to lend it the '40s aura.

Despite the destruction, almost everybody greeted us warmly despite the traditional powder blue UN berets we had to wear, because our American flags all but popped out from our sleeves. Talk about opening doors to a population isolated not only from the United States for so many decades, but also from the rest of Europe. This made us so mystical that it became easy to establish their trust.

Our official duties would also have us do something while on-duty that is quite common among European cops, but unheard of in America—we were to enjoy a beer or two while eating our meals at various cafes. I quickly embraced this concept, for what better way to assimilate with a culture than by joining their ways?

I felt very self-conscious the first few times our group did this. Then again, it didn't take long before we routinely signaled waiters and told them, "*Molem, vas dua piva,*" or, "Please bring us two beers."

One evening while my patrol partner and I were in the Muslim section of Sarajevo, we stepped inside a centuries-old restaurant for dinner. We'd no sooner taken seats at a cloth-draped table when two soldiers in unfamiliar uniforms appeared in the doorway. They were carrying assault rifles at the ready, and as they took positions against the wall on either side of the door, both of us uttered that immortal line, "This is it."

"This" turned out to be a British VIP protection detail, and the soldiers were there to ensure the safety of the man who strolled in seconds later. It was John Major, Britain's prime minister at the time, and he and two others in his party took a table near ours. I could all but feel his gaze as it fell upon the American flag patch on my shoulder, and after a slight frown he looked away. So did we, 'cause hey...our food had arrived and we were hungry.

Yeah, it was just another day of life in the trenches.

THE NEXT DAY I was at the CIVPOL headquarters when a new batch of Americans arrived. An older man among them caught my attention with his impeccable uniform and the alertness that lit his eyes. I stepped over to welcome him, and as we shook hands I checked his nametag. "Mazur, huh? I knew a Mazur. Larry Mazur. We worked on a tiny little island in the Pacific. I doubt you've ever heard of it."

"Kwajalein," he said at once. "Larry's my son."

Small world.

Larry Mazur, Sr. turned out to be a retired LAPD captain, and we discovered several things in common. Among these were our attitudes toward police work. "I believe in being firm, but fair," he told me that first day. I wanted to hug him.

However, mention of Kwajalein also resurrected my shameful treatment of Ragnar "Opie" Opiniano, the firefighter friend I dressed down prior to leaving. I was as wrong as anyone could be, and though I'd written him several times to explain my actions and to ask forgiveness, I never heard back. I didn't blame him.

However, my father would have blistered my butt if I'd done something like that as a child. Then there's Toby, who taught me that karma demands resolution of whatever wrongs we commit. Even so, on a deeper level I didn't need to be told. I had done wrong, I knew it, and if I didn't have what it took to make amends, then that made me a sad son of a bitch. That's why I made a journey to Kwaj three weeks later.

* * * *

I told my UN boss that I had to take a sabbatical. He wasn't pleased, but I had unfinished business to take care of and that was that. A few trans-oceanic phone calls followed until I wangled a way to get onto Kwajalein.

Days later I stepped off the C-141 Starlifter and onto the tarmac at Kwaj, uncertain of my reception and prepared for rejection. I had to be here though, and fortified by a gut instinct for what I must do, I checked in at the Entry/Exit office and then marched on.

ASTONISHMENT IS A subjective adjective, yet I can find no other way to describe the look on Opie's face when I walked into the fire station to greet him. By coincidence, his wife and their young son were also there.

Opie's jaw dropped. "Rick. I, um...what're you doing here?" Watching me carefully, he waited for an answer.

I offered to shake hands. He accepted at once. I saw it as a good sign. "I came here to apologize to you, and to do it in person."

His face clouded. He stepped away from his wife and son, and as I followed him outside he said, "I hope you don't think we'll ever be friends again."

"My only hope is that you'll hear me out. Afterward? Then you can tell me to go to hell and I'll never bother you again."

Lines erupted across his forehead as he mulled it over. Finally he said, "Come back tomorrow at noon."

"Thank you, Ope." I had used his more personal nickname as a way to nail down the first plank in the bridge I needed to build. "I'll be here."

The next day I showed up promptly at twelve. Opie was an assistant fire chief now, and engulfed in paperwork when I appeared in his office doorway.

"Let's take this off-campus," he said, and marched outside. I followed him to a shaded picnic table. The sky was its usual deep blue, green palms swayed overhead, and the salt-tinged air never smelled so sweet. It was a Partly Bali Day, all right.

I began talking. "I wrote several times to apologize. When I didn't hear back I figured you were too angry, and probably wanted to forget that you'd ever met me." When he nodded, it meant that at least I had sized things up correctly. I pressed on. "Here's the thing—"

"...So that's it," I finished. I had dumped on him; described the effect my father's death had on me; explained the concepts that Toby taught me; put things in perspective; told him how sorry I was for what I had done, adding that I had never been that person before, while reassuring him that thanks to the grief therapy, I would never be that person again.

Opie stared at some unseen thing for a long, long time. Then he looked me in the eye. "Rick, I understand. But you didn't hurt just me. Your words and actions also crushed my wife."

"Then please ask her to let me apologize in person."

He pressed his lips together, looked away, and finally faced me. "I'll ask. I can't promise she'll agree. I'll ask, though. Now if you don't mind, I need to get back to work."

Opie called the next day. "Be at our house at twelve noon. She'll be waiting for you."

"Thank you so much." Hanging up, I felt encouraged by the fact that they were inviting me into their home.

I showed up exactly on time and was about to knock when the door opened. We were on a military base after all, and anyone who has lived or worked on a base knows that twelve noon literally means just that, and not one minute earlier or later. She invited me in. I kicked off my flip-flops and placed them on the floor next to the door so that they faced out. It's a matter of etiquette in Asian countries, a way to show that you won't overstay your welcome. Sure, we were on a U.S. base. But we were also in Micronesia, so the custom held. I saw her nod approvingly.

As she led me into the kitchen, their son looked up at me with large curious eyes. When she pointedly did not offer a chair and stared at me with folded arms instead, I began talking.

I repeated almost verbatim what I told Opie the day before. When I finished, she smiled and offered a soft drink, adding, "We can take it to the living room."

"Wait," I said, and after closing my eyes, I recited seventeen-year-old Johnny Gunther's Unbelievers Prayer:

Almighty God
forgive me for my agnosticism;
For I shall try to keep it gentle, not cynical,
nor a bad influence.

And O!
if Thou art truly in the heavens,
accept my gratitude
for all Thy gifts
and I shall try
to fight the good fight. Amen.

Next, I reminded myself of a definition of spirituality that I embraced, the one about how spirituality is the relationship we have with ourselves, with others, and with the universe.

Lauren Statum and me at a 1987 wedding near Ocean City, MD.

Peering through a natural rock formation at Joshua Tree National Monument (now a national park) after leaving the state police for the State of California, 1988.

My "brother from another mother," Michael DuFour, and me on Roi-Namur Island, 1990.

Michael DuFour inside the WWII-era underground hospital on Roi-Namur.

Contemplating the opening of a WWII Japanese tunnel complex at Truk (aka, Chuuk) Lagoon in 1990.

Gripping a machine gun on a sunken Japanese ship in Truk Lagoon.

Taking a rest following the deep-dive above.

Top: Riding my horse, Magic, into the Irish pub in the summer of 1993.

Bottom: Magic remaining steadfast while I smile as the flashbulbs start popping.

Nathan in Pearl Harbor, shortly after we became the best of friends in 1994.

During my time as a Civilian Police officer while assigned to the Sarajevo area in the waning days of the War in Bosnia, 1996.

With Belgian soldiers in Sector East, while keeping the peace after the war in the former Yoguslavia, 1997.

A DOOR LEFT OPEN

RICHARD CRAIG ANDERSON

PART THREE

Albedo*

*Albedo: reflective power; luminescence.

257

A DOOR LEFT OPEN

CHAPTER TWENTY-ONE

Gliding over
Greenland Glaciers

T HAT'S WHAT I was doing, all right. Gliding over beautiful glaciers, after the KLM 747 captain swooped low enough to provide stunning views of blue ice and snowy peaks. There were other
images as well—not below us, but to the sides, because we were on
an eastbound flight heading toward Amsterdam, and it was winter,
so darkness draped the left side of the 747 while sunshine streamed
through the windows on the right side. What a trip, and make no
mistake about it—I was in between two worlds—the old one, and a
brave new one.

Yeah, I was tripping all right. Once Opie and his wife forgave me,
I knew deep down that by doing this penance I had finally broken
the old patterns. I felt...free.

It was all there; my chance meeting with Larry Mazur in war-
torn Sarajevo, only to discover that I knew his son from Kwajalein;
that it was a father and son connection that sent me on a journey
to Kwaj in the first place—a micro-dot on maps, and yet one that
my dad had been to. And finally, I sensed without fully understanding the reasons why I had to apologize to Opie in person, since

that's what my father would have done. Two fathers, two sons, at opposite ends of the planet, and yet with fewer than six degrees of separation connecting them.

Call it what you will—karma, fate, or destiny. What matters is that I had come full circle, and was now ready to climb back into the saddle.

FOLLOWING MY RETURN to CIVPOL, the headquarters staff assigned me to northeast Croatia. Designated "Sector East," it remained divided from the rest of Croatia because it's where the Bosnian War started, this after Serbian troops and tanks demolished the ancient city of Vukovar before plowing on.

More specifically, I would live in Darda village but work at the Batina outpost while reporting to higher authorities in the larger city of Beli Monastir (White Monastery). However, if I thought reaching Sarajevo had been grueling, getting into Sector East was exhausting. The trip required an initial stop in Osijek, a large city within Croatia's troubled northern frontier. From Osijek my new colleagues and I climbed into white UN pickup trucks and crossed the River Darva. But it wasn't until we reached the other side of the river that things turned interesting.

First, we had to enter the Zone of Separation—the ZOS—which meant driving along a barren narrow road made treacherous by winter snow and ice, in a region that had no snowplows. That's just for starters, because the road traversed an area saturated by up to five *million* land mines. Yeah, don't slide off *that* road and expect Triple A to send a wrecker.

Once past the minefields, we encountered a permanent roadblock manned by Pakistani troops that were doing their part for the UN effort. A tank partially blocked the road, and the fact that it was manned and that its cannon was pointed directly at us confirmed what I'd already begun to suspect: that we weren't in Kansas anymore—or Croatia, for that matter.

A soldier with an AK-47 slung over his shoulder inspected our identification cards and scrutinized our faces before allowing us to pass through. Following another short drive, we reached Darda, home to our new CIVPOL outpost. Later that day I dropped my bags in an upstairs bedroom of the home where I would live. The houses on either side had been destroyed by artillery, and the family of four—father, mother and two teenage sons—could definitely use the hundred and fifty bucks that I would pay for room and board. As an all-around bonus, they could practice their English while teaching me Serbo-Croatian.

OUR CIVPOL DUTIES in this region included monitoring a checkpoint in Batina, where the Danube River sets the boundary between Croatia and Serbia, and where Belgian troops had established a forward base. We also conducted patrols and talked to locals.

Because the region boasted several vineyards, and because growers stored their finished products inside the many caves that dot the hills, we made a point of crawling through them on a random and unannounced basis. Only, we weren't looking for grapes. We were searching for illegal POW holding cells, since the belligerent factions had not, shall we say, fully embraced the terms of the Dayton Accords, and diehards were still holding captive soldiers within makeshift prisons.

Not only did the Dayton Accords not carry as much weight as the politicians hoped they would, the hostilities were still ongoing. Serbs hated Croats, who hated Bosnians, who in turn loathed Croats and Serbs. In a sidebar that might be an *I Love Lucy* skit if not for the misery involved, one thing did unite the three ethnic groups: their mutual hatred of the Romani, aka gypsies. So of course the Romani became our new best friends.

Winning them over wasn't easy. They'd endured discrimination for so long that they had long-since closed ranks for their mutual protection. Fortunately, the U.S. flags on our shoulders thawed suspicions and opened minds.

Our happy-go-lucky attitudes also drew their interest, and before long I would walk along a certain street until a straight-faced Romani drew close enough to mutter while in passing the details of Serb nationalist plans to attack one of the NATO units.

The first time this happened, I sent the info to CIVPOL headquarters at once. A few days later the regional commander told me that the information had been pristine, and that NATO troops had taken the Serbs into custody.

One of the locals eventually befriended me and three other Americans. Boris opened his soul to us, and in time he invited us to a social event at his home. I can only say that you haven't lived until you've attended a Romani party. Their parties are right out of the movie *Titanic*, in the scene where DiCaprio and Winslet leave the stuffy first class dining room for the fun that could be found among the steerage passengers.

When we arrived for Boris's party, he swung the door wide open. I saw a fat man in a corner playing an accordion, and ten or so couples performing a line dance. There were also tables heaped with food and drink, not to mention a deluge of hospitality.

However, the first order of business upon entering any Eastern European home is to drink a toast even if it's early morning. The head of each household takes pride in their home-brewed *Rakia*, and we accepted the tiny shot glasses that Boris presented. After he filled them, we tossed the liquor down.

Rakia is strong stuff. What the hell am I saying? The damn stuff will melt the enamel from your teeth! Well, if not literally then at least figuratively. It's why you toss the drink down and shake your head like a dog that's smelled something disgusting, and then rear back in surprise because hey—this stuff is downright tasty. When you put your glass down upright, the host automatically refills it so you can toss back another dram of the high-octane drink. A guest must put the shot glass on the table upside down to politely indicate that they've had enough. At least for now.

And in the spirit of drinking spirits, it wasn't until we entered the home that the party really began. Boris guided us to the food table first, where we heaped our plates with meat and potatoes and who-knows-what-else. Next, he led us to a table where he introduced the seated guests. Only one of them spoke any English at all, most of it broken. Meanwhile, my feeble attempts at Serbo-Croatian met with polite smiles that concealed their apparent bafflement at what I was trying to get across.

In the meantime the music picked up, the men and women who were dancing matched the new beat, their energies reached greater heights inside a heated room that spoke of sweat and smiles—along with a sequestered people determined to live life on their own terms.

I missed another transition in the party though, the one during which the weapons appeared.

The first weapon was a long knife that a husband drew from a concealed sheath after one of my colleagues made a pass at his wife. I knew enough about the Romani to realize that in keeping to tradition, the husband was about to cut our American cousin's balls off...and he *was* gonna cut 'em off, and he was gonna do it *now*. He stood and came for our idiot friend. But we got to numb nuts first and rushed him out the door and into our UN vehicle. One of our guys drove him home at once, because this wasn't Kansas, and our friend's balls almost ended up on a platter...and for real, 'cause the Romani don't friggin' bluff.

At least the idiot's balls would've been next to the other plates of pork.

The party continued with more food, more drinks. But it wasn't until after a few more drinks that the "bigger toys for bigger boys" doctrine kicked in. It began when Boris went upstairs and came back down with a Soviet AK-47, which he began firing across the room full of people and through a small window.

My friends and I wondered if that would be the end of it. But Boris trooped back upstairs only to re-emerge with a hand grenade. We froze. He smiled. He pulled the pin. He squeezed the Soviet-style grenade to trigger it. All at once dirty-gray smoke streamed from the fuse. We all ducked while Boris made like Joe D., and threw the damned thing across the room and through the same small window.

WANG! Not *Bang*, but *Wang!*

The chickens were still squawking outside the window while everyone shrugged and got back to eating, drinking and dancing. Then Boris produced an RPG—a rocket propelled grenade. It was definitely time to beat feet—no question about it—and we burst through the door. Except for one problem: our UN truck had a diesel engine, and diesels are difficult to start in sub-zero temperatures. The driver must turn the key and wait until a heating element warms the engine. And until it reaches a target temperature, the engine simply will not start.

We waited breathlessly until the pre-heat light went out and the diesel rattled to life. It started just as Boris fired the RPG. And believe me, that bad-boy rocket took off with a bang, and the rocket's red glare streamed past us. But we weren't waiting around for *that* bomb to burst in air. No, sir. We made like bandits and got the hell outta there.

Then again, ya just gotta love parties that are not only balls to the wall, but a real blast. Yeah, no question about it.

IF SARAJEVO STRUCK me as something out of a war movie, there were other movie moments. In November of 1996, the UN asked a New Zealand two-star general to prepare a Croatian special forces unit for a clandestine mission. The men were to slip across the Danube River at night. Their goal: kidnap bellicose Serbian belligerents whose attitudes threatened the stability of an already fragile peace. However, the general wanted the assistance of Americans who were not only experienced in night tactics, but also able to teach others.

My boss knew that I had provided security for the super-secret facilities on Kwaj, and that I'd been an instructor, so he sent me to the general, who turned out to be as likable as he was direct in his manner. In addition, after he spotted the captain's bars on my uniform collar and learned that I'd traveled extensively throughout Kiwi Land, he treated me as a colleague rather than a subordinate. Once he gathered the troops, he brought me and some others to a former prison in the city of Erdut. It wasn't far from Vukovar but it wasn't close to anything either, which I suppose was the point.

The prison complex sat in the middle of a huge open expanse, a fortress right out of the movies, with ancient guard towers manned by soldiers equipped with modern machine guns. But the machine guns didn't point in. They pointed out, a tactic designed to protect the personnel inside, which would include us. So as we approached the prison from an access road, I couldn't help but visualize Clint Eastwood seated in a director's chair amid lights, cameras, and ready for action.

An administration building, a dining hall, and a clutch of dormitories sat idle within the walls. Unlike western prisons, Eastern European institutions are a study in humane treatment. Inmates live in furnished studio apartments, they wear civilian clothing, and there are no gangs or fights or fear of being raped.

In place of inmates, we found three dozen young Croatian soldiers. They were mostly tall and slender, and none appeared to be older than twenty. Their eagerness to learn was self-evident the moment they fell into a line to personally greet us. After the howdy-do's, and with an interpreter in tow, we split off into groups of twelve and filed into makeshift classrooms.

The lessons we would teach had nothing to do with reading, writing and arithmetic, though. Our topics were all about staying alive, and we taught by lecture and by demonstration such things as, how a man wielding a knife from thirty feet away can charge and close that distance long before a cop could even hope to draw his or her weapon.

In order to express one lesson, we placed gym mats on floors, selected the two largest soldiers, and gave them rubber "red guns" that are incapable of firing bullets. Then I asked the gathered students if they had seen the Rodney King video. Every hand shot up.

"Ahh, the wonders of CNN," I said, and started the lecture. "Critics claim the police didn't have to use their batons on Rodney. They contend that with so many cops on the scene, all they had to do was jump on him and wrestle him into submission." I waited for the translator to convey this before continuing. "But there's a reason why cops don't jump on struggling men, especially struggling men who've already been hit not once, but twice with tasers."

I pointed a finger at the two soldiers. "We're going to conduct an exercise in which I'm a criminal. Your job it to arrest me. Only, I'm not going to let you. In fact, I plan on killing both of you." I paused to let our translator pass along my challenge. "Bear in mind that I am unarmed. Even so, you may do whatever you think appropriate to take me into custody. That includes punching me." I spoke the next six words slowly. "Even though I am not armed." I waited, then continued. "Furthermore, I'm not going to let you arrest me. No. I *am* going to kill you." I paused for effect, then asked, "Any questions?" When they shook their heads, I nodded. "Fine. Game on."

They rushed me. I went wildcat. The instant they tried to hit me, I ducked and grabbed the first one, knowing that the other would not be able to resist jumping into the fray. I waited until he did. Then I began twisting and squirming. They were huffing and puffing so much within mere seconds, that I was able to pull a red gun from one of their holsters and point its business end at each of their heads while saying, "Bang, and...bang."

The soldiers nodded. They had learned to never underestimate someone just because they are smaller, older, or unarmed—and they would never again ask, "Why didn't those cops just jump ole' Rodney's ass and wrassle that sucker into submission?"

I DON'T KNOW if the soldiers were ever deployed on clandestine midnight raids. Our group simply did our best to teach these new kids a few old tricks before we moved on to other duties—duties that included gaining intel by proactive rather than reactive means.

To accomplish this, two or three of us would don civilian clothes and transit the ZOS with an interpreter in tow in order to reach Osijek. Why Osijek? Because an ultra-nationalist Croatian bar sat alongside the serene Drava River.

Upon entering the holdover Second World War establishment one particularly warm and sunny afternoon, we found a gloomy main room featuring a huge oil painting of a Croat soldier giving a Nazi salute. The painting was the norm in these bars, Croatia having sided with Germany during the war—a war that still raged on in the customers' minds.

A group of five men at the bar had been talking in raised voices, but they clammed up and stared pointedly at us when we sat at a nearby table—only to resume their discussion after a waiter took our order. While our interpreter cocked her head to listen, the waiter returned with our beers. We had taken just a sip when the largest of the men approached our table and loomed over us.

"What are you doing here?" he demanded in a basso profundo voice.

Without taking my eyes away from his, I told the interpreter, "Tell him word-for-word that I said it's none of his fucking business what we're doing, and that he should fuck off."

After she told him, he maintained the stare-down a little longer. Then he shrugged and joined the others. Hell, they already knew who we were. And they clearly didn't give a damn. But the men respected the strength of my response, and they continued to openly plan an ambush against a group of Serb nationalists in Sector East, as if we didn't exist.

If there's one thing I learned over there, it's that Balkan people don't brag, they don't care who might hear them planning violent attacks, and they don't talk trash. They meant to carry out the attack, and we were determined to throw a wrench in their plans.

We hung around for another hour before taking our leave and recrossing the ZOS to brief our commanders. The following day we drove into Serbia and enjoyed a few beers inside one of their Chetnik tough-guy bars, while listening to some hombres planning an ambush of their own against Croats. And so it goes.

OUR ACTIONS WERE not without consequence. Following one of these intel trips, an informant told me that a group of Serb nationalists were out to assassinate some American CIVPOLs. "They figure it'll make for good news on CNN," he added. Bearing in mind that these men don't talk to hear themselves talk, and knowing that their favorite tactic is to employ snipers to pick off targets, I went to the one man who could give me the *word*—my landlord.

I'd already guessed that his family carried a lot of weight in the region, so I told him what I had heard. He nodded at once and said, "This is true. They will kill some Americans. But not you. No, you are safe so long as you live under my roof." He swept a hand in a wide arc. "All people in this region know who you are. They know where you live. They will never harm you." Then he turned grim and pointed down the street where another American lived. "But Mr. George? He better not step out of the home he is in, or they will kill him."

It was just that simple. At any rate, obviously no harm ever came to me. However, one evening soon after this incident, while walking along a dark and forbidding village street where locals gather fallen acorns for food, an image from *The Deer Hunter* leaped to mind. I'm talking about the scene where De Niro walks Saigon's back streets in search of Christopher Walken. When I first saw the film I felt overwhelmed by the implied dangers that De Niro's character faced, and I asked myself then, *What would I do in a similar situation?* Now here I was after all, surrounded by Serbs who might not recognize me in the dark as one of the "untouchables," and it hit me that I'd come full circle in a life that now imitated art.

CHAPTER TWENTY-TWO

Imbibing Beer in Bruges

A RT AND BEER are my two greatest memories of Bruges, Belgium. Bruges, the "Venice of Northern Europe," is as much a work of art in its own right, as was the Chimay Blue I'd been sampling. No, wait. I wasn't just sampling the Chimay. I was imbibing it, and at nine percent alcohol by volume, the copper-brown ale had a light creamy head and a slightly bitter taste. "Ahh," I said after downing a bit more.

It was a warm and bright April afternoon, the CIVPOL gig had ended, and I'd flown to Bruges to relax for a few days before returning to the States. A Trappist monastery in nearby Hainaut brews the Chimay beers, and I felt duty-bound to sample all three varieties. So while a friend and I sat and sipped and ate a light lunch, I watched the unhurried pace of men, women and children stepping along cobblestone streets bordered by canals and multi-colored flowers. They were everywhere, those flowers, and the flora were such a contrast to the post-war zone I had been living in.

Life was fresh and sharp here, though. Passersby had ready smiles, everyone was at ease, and I couldn't help but reflect upon the death and destruction that prevailed in the Balkans. And while taking in the scenery and enjoying the cold refreshments, I considered a

269

tidbit that the New Zealand general offered before I left. He had stopped by the airport to see me off, and before I boarded he said, "Rick? You love to travel. You're also a pilot, and you have spent a lifetime protecting others from harm." He paused. "There's a job that would suit you, one that involves a cadre of counter-terrorist operatives. They're known as air marshals."

"Sky marshals," I said at once. "They were a big deal in the sixties, back when 'Take this plane to Havana' became a regular thing. But didn't the sky marshals ride off into the sunset?"

"Not *sky* marshals," he corrected. "*Air* marshals. A new breed. From what I gather, most of them are former SEALs, Delta Force types, and retired state police troopers."

"Is that so?" I arched a *Star Trek's* Mr. Spock-like eyebrow. "Hmm. Interesting."

* * * *

"I would love to hire you, Mr. Anderson. Unfortunately, I can't." Bob LaChance leaned back in his office chair and watched my face while I formulated a reply.

After leaving Bruges, I had flown to Sunny Sandy Eggo where I landed a job as a city code inspector. Having never owned property, I knew zip about side and displaced front yards, so I entered a fascinating learning curve that encompassed the minutiae of running a city. Better still, the salary was great, I truly enjoyed the job, and I made new friends.

I also made daily checks of the 'net for air marshal openings, only to turn away in disappointment when nothing popped-up. Then one evening after ten long months, the job announcement materialized as if in a dream: *The Federal Aviation Administration is Seeking Applicants for the Position of Federal Air Marshal.*

I filled out the fifteen-page application that night, mailed it the next day, and figured on another ten-month wait. But to my pleasant surprise a letter arrived twelve days later, inviting me to come to the air marshal facility for testing and evaluation.

Their facility was inside the FAA's 5,000 acre William J. Hughes Technical Center near Atlantic City. A high fence topped with concertina surrounded the center, and armed security officers were maintaining a vigilant patrol when I arrived.

The Federal Air Marshal Division Headquarters was sequestered within the Center's most isolated area. Cyber locks, alarms and further fencing doubly secured its various facilities, and this explained why other FAA employees referred to air marshals as "those high speed operators behind the fence, *behind* the fence." Telling myself that such a high level of efficiency was a good sign, I made plans to be there no matter what.

"WE WANT YOU," Mr. LaChance continued as he leaned forward. "But you're up against military veterans. They get preference. That's the law." He paused and looked past me. "There is a back door, however. The 'Outstanding Scholar Program.' If you earn a bachelor's degree with a 3.5 GPA, we'll hire you in a New York nanosecond."

"Say no more," I told him.

* * * *

"Mr. LaChance, I now have a bachelor's with a 3.5 GPA."

His voice over the long distance lines—when long distance meant something—showed no surprise. "*Good. Consider yourself hired. Fax your transcripts to us while we await the official ones. I'll have my secretary call and tell you when to report for duty.*"

I loved that fact that he said "duty" instead of "work," since it meant that the position carried with it a sacred obligation: that of a task that was not to be confused with counting beads or inspecting grapefruits.

It's why I compressed two years worth of college into one year; it's why I aimed for the stars to get a GPA that would open a new door for me; it's why I didn't care that it meant taking a forty percernt cut in salary to go with the Feds. And it's why I fairly leaped to answer the phone when the secretary called the next day, as promised.

THE NEXT DAY I gave my employer two-week's notice, adding, "This new job requires a top secret clearance, so an investigator will drop by to talk with you." My supervisor nodded, the investigator made a melodramatic appearance, and everyone at work gave me a great going-away party. Then at the ripe old age of forty-four, I loaded my car and drove to New Jersey. Four days later, on February 10, 2000, I reported for duty with the FAA's Federal Air Marshal Service—FAMS for short.

After a weeklong orientation, two other new-hires and I reported to the Federal Law Enforcement Training Center (FLETC) in Georgia to attend the prestigious Criminal Investigator Training Course. The course is identical to the one new FBI agents are subjected to, and the program includes imposing academics, firearm qualifications and physical training. At the end of the first week my classmates chose me to be their class president by acclamation, even though I hadn't put in for the job, and this sure as hell didn't hurt my standing within the FAMS.

Three months later I walked onstage as the Honor Graduate. I had the highest GPA, and at the age of forty-five I'd earned 487 points out of a possible 500 to achieve the best physical fitness score. Finally, as class president I gave a farewell speech that emphasized community, commitment, and conscience.

From there, my two colleagues and I flew to the United Airlines headquarters in Chicago, where we spent a week crawling through every airliner in existence until we knew them inside in and inside out. We also joined flight attendant trainees for practical training in opening airliner doors and deploying emergency escape chutes, then flew to FAM headquarters for a month of even more intensive training.

But this final level of training carried a caveat: although the FAM Division had invested about fifty grand on each of us just to attend FLETC, and despite the additional costs of our hotel rooms and meals in Chicago, the bosses made it clear that we still had to pass the notorious TPC, or Tactical Pistol Course. In order to ramp-up the psychological factor, the Division held the big test on the final day of training. We had three chances to shoot a minimum score. Anyone who failed would be fired on the spot, as in, you're outta here. They didn't transfer you to another agency, they wouldn't help you find other employment, they just...fired you. End of message, see ya later, and don't let the door catch you in the ass on your way out.

Talk about motivation.

But it made sense, because FAMs carry .357 magnum pistols while flying all over the world. If terrorists did attempt a takeover, we couldn't afford a missed shot—or worse, missing a bad guy and hitting a passenger. I suppose it justified the FAM motto: "We don't miss."

To live up to the motto, FAMs spend an enormous amount of time on the range. While an average cop only shoots fifty to perhaps up to five hundred annual practice rounds, a FAM fires at least twenty *thousand* practice rounds per year.

I'm happy to report that on a seasonally mild day in May, all three of us passed the TPC on the first go-around. This accomplishment was due in no small terms to the quality of our instruction. With that rite of passage behind us, we joined the ranks of the top one percent of the world's "shooters." This elite standing naturally reminded me of my state police medevac days, when I was among the top twenty-five echelon of paramedics on the planet. Now I was one of the only thirty-three federal air marshals in existence before and during 9/11.

* * * *

Prior to the 9/11 attacks, the FAM Division fielded three teams of eight that were organized and run like SEAL teams. We played hard but trained hard, and nobody pulled punches during close-quarter combat training. This resulted in bruises, split lips, broken fingers and busted toes, but nobody cared. The cadre also routinely "ran" the FBI combat stress course at Ft. Dix, cross-trained with elite units from around the world on a regular basis, and worked with Delta Force, Israel's Shin-Bet, and Germany's GS-G9.

Each of us constantly honed our skills with handguns by cutting the TPC's times in half, running in effect a "Super TPC." We also trained with our MP-5 submachine guns, and they were even equipped with special briefcases that could let us fire the weapon by aiming the case and pressing a concealed button. Yeah, it was right out of 007, and anyone who thinks that it isn't cool to carry something like that aboard an airliner is either a liar, or in denial of their friggin' inner child. Finally, we were the only federal agents that were equipped with fighting knives and trained to attack with them—and that is big-time.

Operationally, the teams deployed for three weeks at a time on mission profiles that might see us circumnavigating the entire planet. Worldwide or not, our journeys always began in the operations center with the team huddled around a STU-III encrypted telephone for a top-secret briefing.

The ops center commander had to activate the phone with a crypto-key. Next, he called CIA Headquarters. Once he established a link and activated the speaker, we went around the room announcing our names. Only then would the CIA person make a formal announcement: "Okay, ladies and gentlemen. We're going Top Secret *now—*"

Our destinations were driven in part by intel, but random flights also kept terrorists—aka *tangos*—guessing. Once the ops specialists selected our routes, the CIA briefed us on the countries we would visit. Following the briefing, team members left the Ops Center to prepare their specialized equipment.

Since I was one of two medics on our team, this meant checking my trauma bag. All medics were prepared to treat everything from massive gunshot wounds to dental problems. We carried I.V. solutions, intubation devices, surgical instruments, suturing kits—even a medical stapling gun for closing massive lacerations if there was no time to perform a knit one, purl two suturing job. I also had a small O.B.

kit in my bag, just in case. And "just in case" is why we carried so much stuff, since a shootout 35,000 feet over the Pacific could occur while the aircraft was still hours away from the nearest safe airport.

We also stocked the bags with meds to treat diarrhea—or what we jokingly referred to as New Delhi Belly—along with pain and allergy solutions, and tape—mostly for when one of our own twisted an ankle after falling from camels that we'd rent while in Cairo. After all, "if one wants to see the pyramids, it's simply bad form for one to arrive by taxi, not when one can make like Lawrence of Arabia and saunter up to the ancient monoliths." Medics also carried plenty of condoms for those "just in case" instances when our single guys forgot to stock up, because let's not be disingenuous—there were plenty of opportunities for guys to pair off with gals.

In fact, because few secrets exist among men and women holding top-secret clearances, everyone knew each other's tastes. I remember landing in Tokyo on a mission. As the team deplaned, we split up and pretended not to know one another, which helps maintain our covert identities by spreading us out within the lines of the other travelers who are going through immigration.

In Tokyo's Narita International Airport, rope barriers herd travelers in a serpentine manner toward the waiting agents. On this particular flight, a young and single team member was far ahead of me—and he was a guy who loved the ladies, and was loved by them in return.

When his segment of the line eventually snaked around until we were approaching from opposite directions with only the rope between us, I spotted four gorgeous Asian girls shuffling along behind him. They were in their twenties, and experience suggested that they understood at least some English. So when my buddy drew abreast of me, I pointed excitedly at him and said, "Wait! Aren't you...yes! You are! Hey, I love your films. Are you, um, like um, here to do another movie?"

He caught on at once. "Aw, shucks. I was hoping nobody would recognize me."

Then as the girls leaned closer to examine this celebrity, I thrust paper and pen at him. "Would you mind?"

As laughter filled his eyes, he hammed it up with a shy smile. "Of course." He scribbled something and handed it back. Naturally, I read it: *You probably molest sheep.*

Once we met on the other side of immigration, he grinned and opened a hand to reveal phone numbers from all four girls. We high-fived each other—hey, we're guys—and the next morning I saw two of those girls looking down the hallway and sharing secret smiles as they left his hotel room and scurried away. But as a guy I also had to know—so I lingered out of sight until, sure enough, a third girl hurried out of the room.

* * * *

After returning from that mission, I found a court summons commanding me to appear for a trial in Ocean City. The Delaware burglar I arrested after impounding his boat trailer had gotten into trouble again. This time he did his dirty deed within Ocean City's jurisdiction, and the state's attorney wanted me to testify about this character's—ahem—character.

It's a routine matter in law enforcement, and I crossed the mouth of the Delaware Bay aboard the Cape May, NJ-to-Lewes, DE ferry to reach Ocean City. I arrived at the courthouse only to come face-to-face with an old acquaintance. He even had on the parka I'd bought for him. He had something else, too—an infant in his arms and a toddler at his side, along with a young woman who was using a handkerchief to clean a smudge from the boy's face.

His face lit up. "Officer Anderson! How're you doing? Hey, meet my kids!" The proud papa stepped closer and flashed a shy smile while flicking his eyes at the boy. "This is Nick, and here's my daughter." He hefted the beautiful little girl up in his arms. "Her name is 'Hope.'"

"Hope. I remember." I beamed at him. He nodded, and he clearly wanted me to touch her, so I ran the backs of my knuckles along her cheek until she cooed. "She's gorgeous," I told both parents. Then I pulled him close and said loudly enough for his wife to hear, "You're a good man, and I'm proud to know you."

He swiped at his eyes and said, "Thanks." Then he shrugged helplessly and explained that he had gotten into trouble again, but hoped to gain the judge's sympathy by showing what a good daddy he could be. "What can I say? I kinda sorta took some stuff that wasn't mine."

It happens that way sometimes. Recidivism is a societal disease. All we can do is try our best while hoping against the worst. I wished him and his girlfriend well, but didn't hang around after I finished testifying to learn his fate. Sometimes it's better that way.

* * * *

"We're like Kentucky Fried Chicken," I began. "We might not do a ton of things. But what we do, we do very well."

Earlier, a Miami airport security specialist had spirited our team aboard a Boeing 777 flight to Rio well before passengers would begin boarding. Following my opening line, I spent another minute talking to the flight crew. "We're a counter-terrorist unit of the FAA. We are not inspectors. Our job is to safeguard the flight crew, the passengers, and the aircraft ..."

We provided in-depth briefings to flight crews because FAA rules mandated that legally armed personnel must identify themselves to the crew—and we were usually armed to the max. The briefings were also crucial, because prior to 9/11 most U.S. flight crews didn't know we existed. Hell, even I didn't know there were FAMs until a New Zealand general clued me in.

Post-briefing we searched the aircraft for IEDs—improvised explosive devices—and reviewed our team strategies. After finding nothing suspicious, we broke into two-man cells and deployed throughout the aircraft. Once the passengers began boarding, we covertly examined faces and checked hands for clenched fists and other signs of aggressive personalities. Then when the airliner took off, we settled in for the eight-hour flight to Rio. The passengers dozed. We did not. Remaining awake and alert came with the job. None of us complained.

WE OVERNIGHTED IN Rio, returned to Miami, and caught a flight to Ecuador's capital city of Quito. The destinations didn't really matter. We had the cheapest places to eat already dialed in, knew where to buy the best jewelry, tailored suits, and electronics, and of course there were always gifts to bring home. And no matter what corner of the world we were in, the team got together to see the sights, meet the locals, and party with the flight crews. The local language could be German or Mandarin or Tahitian, but a smile combined with an effort to speak at least one simple phrase of their patois opened doors that might otherwise remain closed to tourists. What a way to earn a living, by seeing the world on the government's dime while packing heat. Yet none of us ever forgot that we were there to stop tangos from hijacking American-flagged aircraft.

CHAPTER TWENTY-THREE

Atlas Shrugs

T HE TENTH OF September, 2001 began normally enough. Our team gathered around the STU-III phone for a top-secret briefing of our next mission, and listened as Langley's spook informed us that Palestinians were threatening international flights going into Israel. And so it was that when the Ops Center assigned our team to fly that night on a Continental redeye from Newark to Tel Aviv, we got more "locked and cocked" than usual.

Our ex-Green Beret team leader had flown Huey gunships in Vietnam. He and Scott would sit in first class to protect the Boeing 777's cockpit. Butch, a retired Massachusetts State Police lieutenant and I had business class seats.

Our team had made this flight so often that the flight crew knew us by name. Even so, we stuck to the ritual of secret handshakes and briefings, we watched the passengers board, and we settled back when the flight took off as scheduled at 10:40 pm, on a departure heading that took us directly over the World Trade Center—albeit at a very high altitude. I clearly recall glancing down from my window and thinking how serene the city looked.

THE BRIGHT LIGHT made me blink when I opened my window

shade. All of the shades had been drawn so passengers could sleep, while the flight crew and our team remained awake and on the alert. Eleven hours had elapsed since we took off from Newark, and those hours brought the sun well to the west of Tel Aviv so that it was still late-morning in New York City. But the date on world calendars applied to both places. It was September 11, 2001.

The flight attendants took to the aisles to collect lunch wrappings, cups, and other trash. There were no spent brass casings to gather from the aftermath of a firefight, nor dead terrorists sprawled in aisles to add to their tidying-up chores.

While thinking that not having a gunfight was a good thing, as we drew closer to Israel I began to note the aircraft's shallow descent. Then I began squinting, not against the sun's glare, but out of concern as I wondered why the pilot wasn't executing the usual steep descent into Ben Gurion Airport. Arriving airliners fly at high altitudes until directly over the airport. Then they begin a series of steep, spiraling descents designed to keep them away from the ocean, where tangos on small boats can fire shoulder-launched missiles at aircraft crammed with Jewish passengers. Maybe our pilot felt relaxed enough to set aside the business-as-usual. After all, it had been such a quiet trip.

Continental Flight 90 touched down precisely on schedule at 4:40 p.m., leaving me anxious to get up and stretch even as we rolled along a long taxiway. However, SOP specified that we remain seated until the passengers were gone, so I felt restless and I wasn't paying attention when the purser welcomed everyone to Tel Aviv, and then told the passengers they could now use their cell phones. A flurry of activity followed as people reached for their electronic connections to the rest of the world.

I'D JUST TURNED my head to the left when a passenger seated nearby brought a phone to his ear. He was offering a smattering of greetings in Hebrew and English when all at once he stiffened. His eyes widened. He gripped the phone. His knuckles blanched. When he spoke, his voice trembled. "*Both* Towers? Collapsed?" A pause, then, "The Pentagon, *too*? My God!"

My pulse shot to one-twenty. I glanced around. Other callers' eyes were rolling wildly as they too spoke with shocked voices.

A woman abruptly stood up. "Four planes? Hijacked?" She listened briefly, then gasped. "And they flew them *into* the Towers? Both towers?"

My instant thought: *That's it. Anything's possible now.*

When I sensed Butch watching my changing facial expressions with interest from the other side of the cabin, I jabbed a finger at him and pointed at his POD—his Position of Dominance. His eyebrows arched but he sprang from his seat at once and stood with his back against the bulkhead separating Business Class from First, his hand clearly near his weapon as he prepared to draw it—just in case.

Getting up, I hurried into First and tapped Scott's shoulder. He jumped a little, startled to see me looming over him.

"Soft PODs," I said in a clipped voice. "*Now.*"

Scott tilted his head and squinted at me. But then he took his place near the front of the cabin as I headed to our team leader.

He turned his head and regarded me with mild amusement, as if asking, "Okay, who farted back in business?"

I jutted my jaw at the short corridor that leads to the cockpit. "Soft PODs."

He looked as if he'd bitten into a lemon. Then he opened his mouth to say something.

"Listen up," I began. "The Pentagon and the World Trade Towers have just been attacked. Both Towers are down."

He sniffed, as if offended by an odor. "Rick, this is no time for games."

"Soft PODs. Do it *now.*" I turned on my heel while muttering, "God damn it. I'd never friggin' play that kinda game." Looking over my shoulder, I saw him take his position with one hand reaching inside his jacket to be at the ready.

I hurried back to my POD and stood in place. Several passengers stared at me. A few nodded slightly—they'd done the math and figured out who Butch and I were, since air marshals have always been on El Al flights. In the meantime I kept a poker face while thinking, *Those poor people in the Towers.*

Our 777 arrived at its designated parking area in short order. The passengers somehow knew to remain seated and silent, even when the grizzled, hard-bitten captain bolted from the cockpit, his face flushed red. I wondered if he was about to suffer a stroke.

I heard him tell our team leader, "I didn't get word of the attack until we landed, or I'd have told you earlier."

The TL stared at me, and nodded slowly.

Now the captain asked in an ominous tone, "What kind of ammunition do you guys carry?"

"SIG .357 magnum." After a second the TL added, "Hollow point."

The captain nodded. "If you guys run into any more of the bastards? Kill 'em."

THERE ARE NO jetways at Tel Aviv's airport. It's why I could hear a low growl when we descended a portable stairway to the tarmac. I looked up in time to see a trio of F-15E Strike Eagle fighters with Israeli markings streak past the airport perimeter. From another direction, a Cobra gunship skittered overhead.

Butch grunted. "I see Israel's ready for war."

"Maybe," Scott began, and bit off each of the next words in anger. "But. So. Are. We."

Once clear of immigration and customs, we hailed taxicabs for the trip to the David InterContinental hotel, got checked in, and raced to our rooms to turn on televisions. I remember clenching my jaw while watching footage of the second plane hitting the South Tower, and muttering angrily at the billowing clouds of black smoke obscuring the Pentagon.

I made two phone calls. The first was to my mother, who expressed anger—but not at the attacks. I had interrupted her bridge game, she said, and was in a hurry to get back to playing games. "No prob," I replied. "I won't keep you any longer."

Then I called Nathan. It had been awhile since I last saw the tall Brazilian, and his relief at hearing my voice was palpable.

"I called FAM headquarters," he began. "The girl who answered remembered me. Only, she wouldn't tell me where you are. Only that you're safe."

WE WERE SAFE, but stranded. The United States had closed its borders to international flights. We didn't like it—we wanted to be back home flying missions—but it just wasn't gonna happen. Not at first. Then on our fourth day in Israel, FAM headquarters told us the U. S. Air Force might fly us home on one of their aircraft.

In the meantime the Israelis were treating us like gold. Whether we were on a street or in a hotel corridor, the locals picked up on our accents and offered their condolences. And in every place we went to eat, managers always appeared to say, "Everything is on the house. That includes all drinks. Do not try to pay. Your money is no good here."

The generosity and the gestures struck each of us to our hearts, although we weren't surprised; the Israelis were simply showing their gratitude for the decades of America's support.

* * * *

After five days we returned to an America that had gone to war. That included all FAMs, and we were prepared to lead the charge.

Things changed quickly. The FAA's Federal Air Marshal *Division* became the Homeland Security's FAM *Service*. The number of air marshals rocketed from thirty-three, to thousands upon thousands (exact numbers are classified). Field offices sprang up across the nation. The bosses promoted most of us. I got jumped two pay grades to GS-14—a mid-management level equivalent to a military lieutenant colonel, or a civilian assistant police chief.

I transferred to the new Miami Field Office, where I took charge of one of several teams, and the number of FAMs on each team staggered imaginations. Regardless of the numbers, we trained and worked as hard as before—and in a world of men and women putting it all on the line on a daily basis, we played hard.

I TOOK OVER the FAM Liaison unit at Miami International Airport in 2007. Five air marshals worked directly for me, and in addition to augmenting the Miami-Dade plainclothes officers, we formed a deep relationship with El Al's station chief, since armed terrorists had previously attacked El Al operations at other airports.

We vowed that no attack would go down on our watch, so I called a meeting with El Al's chief and the Miami-Dade police major in charge of airport security. Over the course of several hours the three of us outlined a threefold plan.

Since there are always at least twenty air marshals awaiting flights in Miami's terminal at any given time, I had them report to me whenever El Al's ticket counter was in operation. They would pose as passengers and discreetly position themselves in concentric circles radiating from the ticketing area outward—including the sidewalks outside. Uniformed police officers carried assault rifles and submachine guns, and were posted in plain view at the ticketing area and other strategic locations. Finally, our liaison unit met El Al's air marshals far from the concourse to take them through secure passageways so they could board their flight unseen.

Our operation became a success story. Federal Security Officers from major airports came to study our methods. Israel's chief of security for North, Central and South America paid a visit, only to boast that he would have no problem spotting my people. "Watch as I pick out all of your operatives."

"You won't spot them," I fired back. "In fact, let's take a walk and see."

He smiled and stepped jauntily alongside me as we ambled throughout the operational area. "Him," he said at once, flicking his eyes at a forty-ish man seated nearby with an open book on his lap. "And him," he chirped while tilting his head at a young man clad in a T-shirt and jeans. "Also, her...and this man here." At the end of our little tour, he turned to me with a smug expression and said, "I got them all, did I not?"

"You got none of them," I replied. "Now follow me." I led him to each of the twenty-two air marshals that had been there all along—including two flip-flop shod, love-bead adorned, dreadlock wearing guys who looked for all the world like surfer dudes—and each FAM subtly nodded at the security chief. His jaw dropped.

Everyone from the El Al ticket agents to the Miami-Dade police officers and the FAMs were also taught that if they saw a suitcase or a bag left unattended for more than thirty seconds, then they were to repeatedly shout, "Bomb, bomb, bomb, bomb..."

Here is what happened each time: the Israeli citizens in the crowd instantly dropped their bags, picked up their children, and quickly walked away. The American passengers? Without fail, they dropped their kids to the floor, grabbed their bags, and ran like headless chickens. And so it goes. But nobody ever successfully planted a bomb.

Did any of our efforts ever payoff? While making a routine sweep of the El Al area's outermost portion one day, a member of our multi-agency team spotted two men taking videos. While that's not unusual under normal circumstance, in this case they were focusing on the ticket counter—plus the heavily armed uniformed officers. The team member summoned one of my air marshals, and together they took the men into custody.

They turned out to be tangos. The FBI entered the case. The suspects had indeed been plotting an attack on El Al—but not at Miami, because they saw that it would never succeed. Surprisingly, the media never mentioned the incident. None of us could figure out why, either. It's not as if our people made the arrest in secret; they hadn't. In any event, El Al stopped its Miami operation a few months later for financial reasons. However, while they were up and running, no attacks ever took place. Not on our watch.

DESPITE A HEAVY work schedule that had me putting in at least sixty hours a week, I made time to earn a Master of Arts in history. I also returned to creative writing, beginning with *Rivers of Belief,* a hardboiled mystery that asks, "How far will a man go to protect the people he loves?" Published in 2008, it did well—especially in India, where it flew off bookstore shelves, the publisher reasoning that the title might've inspired sales. I don't know about that, but it was nice to stick my head into an airport bookstore while changing flights, and see my book on its shelves.

In 2013, I wrote *Cobra Clearance,* the first in a series of thrillers that introduces a recurring protagonist named Levi Hart. Yep, the Levi Hart (now Levi Bailey) from National City. *Follow Apollo* came next, and both titles earned literary award nominations. In the third thriller, *Mark Air,* Levi and his team pursue a domestic terrorist. But they must also face a growing threat against law enforcement officers throughout the country—criminals now target police officers' family members in reprisal. Even hardcore criminals considered this taboo at one time. No longer. *Mark Air* has done well, and was nominated for a book of the year award. In the end it didn't make the list of finalists, but to paraphrase Marlon Brando, "It was a contender."

CHAPTER TWENTY-FOUR

Transcendence

I 'M RETIRED NOW, and I start each day by walking my Rhodesian Ridgeback through the neighborhood. Ridgebacks were bred to hunt lions, and in keeping with that legacy we named him Kobi, an African name that means "big hearted." We added a last name, Rindurr, which translates as "walks like a lion." Yeah, he has a big heart, he walks like a lion, all the neighbors know him, and he loves all of them. In addition to our walks, I hit the gym three days a week, swim laps or go cycling in between, and write every day.

The latter activity is important to me, since dreaming of becoming an author is what sent me from a richly-rewarding job in Maryland to near-destitution in San Diego. But that dream took me to Kwajalein, to Bosnia, and ultimately to the air marshals—not to mention the lifelong friends I made along the way. Back in Ocean City, fresh blood and new direction eased the few negative people out of the police department, so that the many professional men and women who have been there all along shine even brighter.

Do I regret any of my choices? Here's what Fellini once said: "Regrets are a waste of time. They are the past crippling you in the present—"

Then there's Abraham Maslow's theory of self-actualization,

which amounts to internal motives that drive us to realize our full potentials.

And so I have no regrets. How could I, considering all the great people I met along the way—not to mention living every dream I've ever had. And while they might not have been the most glorious dreams—some might say that wanting to be a firefighter, or hoping to live on a Pacific island are on the lame side—who cares? They were *my* dreams.

My father also had few regrets, and if a person's value can be measured by the number and the quality of the people who attend their funerals, then he died a wealthy man.

Unfortunately, my mother remained crippled by the twists and turns of her life. Even so, she kept trying. One morning not too long ago, she had her hair done and then went to lunch with some friends. Midway through the dessert, she suffered a massive stroke. My sister Janice rushed to her side at the hospital, and Janice was holding my mother's hand when she died. Although everyone who knew her agrees that she had never been truly happy, she did have a good heart, and her friends packed the church for her memorial service.

Thank God she at least had that.

AT LEAST I'VE had something of value, too. I've had happiness. I also have a son from a long-ago relationship. Phil recently retired from the U.S. Air Force as a lieutenant colonel, and now divides his time between family and flying for FedEx. We talk often and see one another when we can, although he lives in Seattle and I'm in South Florida. But we still manage to bust each other's balls, so how good is that?

I also have a relationship with Nathan. We got back together in the wake of 9/11, and we're alive and well and busting on each other. As for Joyce Emge, the long-ago love of my life? We're best friends again, and yeah...she also takes delight in bustin' my chops.

I wouldn't have it any other way.

Thanks to the internet I see plenty of other old stalwarts online.

They include LeRoy Wilkison and Buzz Griner. Then there's Don Gibson. He retired as a battalion chief, and we run into each other now and then at reunions and graveside ceremonies. Nelson Pyle went on to become a deputy chief of my old department, and after retiring he became the chief of a county fire department in North Carolina.

Russ Hewitt finished a stellar police career as a lieutenant, and now does background investigations. Tim Doegen and his wife, Babs, are living the rich life of retirees, and my old friend Scott Collins recently pulled the pin.

I still keep in touch with Ragnar "Opie" Opiniano, along with many others—although a couple of my Kwajalein friends have since died. Many of those I knew in my youth are also gone—"Uncle Calvin" Sears and Clyde Willis, the surrogate fathers from my first days in the fire service, along with many others are long gone. So I make it a point to get together with the ones who are still around while they are still around.

Levi moved to another part of California, where he lives fewer than ten minutes from my brother Bob. But this oddity of life's throw of the dice provides me with the option of a two-fer, by letting me drop by to see Levi and his family before sliding down the road to visit Bob and his wife, Emma.

I see my oldest brother Jim and his wife, Jackie, often, and we also talk by phone. The same goes for my sister Janice, countless nephews and nieces, and the great derivatives thereof. As for my younger brother Tom, he and his wife travel often to distant lands.

Lauren and I also remain in close touch. We trade photos, brag about grandkids, and discuss the finer points of riding horses—she breeds show horses. Meanwhile, her husband the judge conducts trials.

Then there's Michael DuFour, my brother-from-another-mother. When he retired from the Washington State Patrol not too long ago, I flew to Seattle for the party. We joshed and joked of course—although earlier, he had turned solemn after seeing me suffering from vertigo. It turns out that a middle-ear problem now prevents me from equalizing during landings, and the pain is so bad that by final approach I wanna put a gun to my head. The only remedy is to put valves in my eardrums, but then I wouldn't be able to swim or scuba dive. Now I only fly in emergencies.

What an irony. I once owned an airplane, I served with the aviation division, and danged if I didn't fly all over the world as an air marshal. But what if I had never taken advantage of those opportunities to dream and fly and travel when I was able to? What then? Nah, I have no regrets.

I suppose it all comes back to that day not too long ago when firefighter Steve Preslipsky praised me for having the courage to leave the comfort of one job, and take on others without any guarantees of at least breaking even. All I can say is, "Thank you for seeing me, Steve. And thank you LeRoy and Buzz and Calvin, along with Nelson Janz and Nelson Pyle and all the others who shaped me during my volunteer firefighter days, and even kicked my butt for me whenever I got too cocky. Thank you—all of you—for imparting your wisdom while also defining what it means to have heaping measures of *joie de vivre*. Thank you, all of you, for those gifts."

In part, my friends' encouragement gave me the courage to visit forty-eight states and live in six of them. I have traveled to more than fifty-five countries, lived in Europe and on two Pacific islands. During my life, I've also climbed mountains, dove deep beneath the seas, trekked across desert sands while perched atop a camel, and flown airplanes at dawn and dusk while being damned sure to appreciate the sun's rising and setting rays.

And in traveling throughout the world; in visiting and sometimes living in villages and farms and towns where winds blow and rain falls and the sun shines; where wheat and honeysuckle and salt air make your nostrils dilate, and where chickens and cows and pigeons make their presence known throughout; where kids cry and laugh and persevere despite famine, pestilence and armed conflict—in all those places I've learned a few things, and they are these: be sure to learn a few phrases of the local language, always bear in mind that a ready smile and long-term patience are the real keys to getting your needs met, and pack light. One other thing: no matter what village or country or region you find yourself in, basic human needs are always the same: people cherish their children. They hope, they pray, and they don't want to feel lonely.

It was loneliness that initially sent me on a quest, and in time I discovered that people were at my side all along. Or as the saying goes, many of us go a very long distance out of our way to correctly return by a shorter distance.

If this is true then maybe I've done it right after all, and in the process I reinvented myself many times over. I have also come face-to-face with absolute terror, and experienced bursts of pure ecstasy. Success or mistakes, bruises or rapture—in the final analysis it's been a helluva ride...and it ain't over yet.

With Kobi, our beloved Rhodesian Ridgeback.

Epilogue

L IVING A ROUGH & tumble life has taken a toll on me. Injuries from firefighting and law enforcement, combined with being thrown from horses or hurt while practicing close quarter combat, have left me with more than a few aches and pains. I've also broken several fingers and toes, not to mention my neck after I stupidly arched it while bench-pressing.

In all I've endured nine surgeries, and the four titanium rods that now hold parts of me together set off airport metal detectors. Arthritis antagonizes my neck, shoulders, hands and feet. My hearing is no longer acute—although I do have 20/10 vision—and my physician unilaterally authorized a handicapped parking placard. In other words, I've joined the ranks of "the gray hairs and the no-hairs." But who cares? After all, I managed to survive all the stupid things I did while growing up, things that could've left me dead. Better yet, I still smile and laugh, and I do those things a lot these days.

However, when some misaligned vertebrae formed an alliance with a stenosis or two in 2017, they attacked my lower back with vengeance. I could only walk while stooped-over, and only for short distances. Surgeons sliced my belly open to more safely reach those vertebrae for an anterior lumbar intra-body fusion. They bolted a titanium clamp to my spine, and the procedure relieved some of the pressure.

Unfortunately, the forces of good and evil remained locked in battle, and within a month the slightest movement left me writhing on floors or sidewalks while screaming in pain. I could neither get in or out of bed by myself, nor bathe nor get dressed without assistance.

Friends invariably said, "Rick, your skin's turned gray, you've aged five years in five months, and you're in a walker. Nathan says you're only a step away from being in a wheelchair for life. Gosh, you must feel devastated."

"You'd think," I always began, "but I'm not. Because I did those things that mattered to me while I could. Now imagine how pissed I'd be at myself if I hadn't taken advantages of life's opportunities?"

The surgeons performed a second surgery. They went in from the back this time. I spent four hours on the table and acquired three more rods, along with some other hardware to resolve the problems. The next few days were marked by bouts of projectile vomiting and the inability to even roll onto my side. Thank god for the nurses who rushed to my bedside whenever I hit the buzzer. By discharge day I'd lost ten pounds, and gained a new walker. Meanwhile, Kobi glued himself to me, refusing to leave my side and demanding to sleep next to me in bed.

I'M FINE NOW. I avoided that wheelchair, although images from my youth of kids stricken by muscular dystrophy flashed through my mind. Naturally I recalled raising money for research into the disease, so how can I ignore the bittersweet irony of turning to friends for financial aid after catastrophic medical bills ravaged my once-substantial savings.

Thanks to them and to a few anonymous donors, I'm literally back on my feet after doing the hard rehab that ultimately let me chuck the walker into a corner. Now I walk and cycle, swim and work out at the gym, and hook up with friends for a laugh or two.

But one day following the second surgery, when I was still shuffling along in that walker, I walked to where the Intracoastal Waterway forms a large basin just a block from my home. Green palm fronds were rustling in the breeze under a cobalt-blue sky, and dolphins were fishing and frolicking only yards from where I stood. However, I'd overdone it, and while turning for home I nearly collapsed. What a sight I must have been—a gray-haired man in a gray shirt gripping his burnished-gray walker for support.

I was still catching my breath in order to get my butt in gear when an eight-year-old boy materialized at my side. My jaw almost dropped because he so closely resembled Matthew, that brave lad I came face-to-face with at that horrific auto accident so many years ago. Then I wondered, maybe it *is* him, reborn along the lines of Buddhist beliefs in reincarnation.

The boy's mother was standing nearby, and he glanced at her. When she nodded, he took my elbow in his hand and said, "It's okay, Mister. You're not alone, and I'm not going to leave you."

I whispered, "Oh my god," and jammed a hand against my eyes as if to shield them from a brilliant light. When I opened them, I felt the boy's reassuring hand on my elbow as he walked me home;

With a walker in 2018 following my second round of surgery—just before the young boy appeared as if by magic at my side to offer assistance. (Unk photographer)

I heard distant sirens and air horns coming at me from distant memories; saw my father handing out cigarettes to German laborers. There were images of places seen; of going barefoot in Bali and gliding over Greenland's glaciers. And those images dazzled me.

Perhaps one day I'll set foot on that green land of ice, and by looking beneath the ice I might find the souls of Pat and Georgie, of my mom and dad, and of all the others I've met along the way. But especially of the Matthews of this world, and the innocence they represent.

I am haunted by memories of his bravery.

And yet as the late afternoon light fades, here he is after all in the spirit of this young boy. His mother follows a short distance away, and I want to tell him, "I see that your mommy came back after all."

I don't say this, of course. But as we walk I tell myself, *The boy's right. I'm not alone. Not anymore. And who knows? Maybe he'll take me to yet another open door.*

Acknowledgments

I WANT TO thank the following people for graciously permitting me to mention their names and exploits. They include: Levi Bailey, Kenny Bohn, Scott Collins, Tim Doegen, Michael DuFour, Joyce Emge, Don Gibson, Pat Garvey, John Griner, Keith Hammack, Ed Hanna, Russ Hewitt, Nelson Janz, Quenton Josey, Phil Lynch, Mike Marsiglia, Lauren Statum-Martz, Larry Mazur, Ragnar Opiniano, Frank Pleyo, Steve Preslipsky, Nelson Pyle, Jack Reckner, John Riggin, Joe Rolles, Joe Rumenap, Mike Schultheis, George Weaver III, Ph.D., and LeRoy Wilkison. Jimmy and Jackie, Janice and Dave, Bob and Emma, and Tom and Becky have also given of themselves for this memoir.

Of course I also want to thank my long-time editor, Jean Jenkins. Jeannie, I couldn't have done any of this without your insight, your assistance, but most of all your friendship.

Finally, I'm blessed by the relationships I have with my family, my friends, and the one I had with Kobi, our beloved and too-recently deceased Rhodesian Ridgeback.

hellgatepress.com

Made in the USA
Middletown, DE
07 September 2020

18879779R10172